Political Reform in
Post-Mao China

Political Reform in Post-Mao China

Democracy and
Bureaucracy in a Leninist State

Barrett L. McCormick

UNIVERSITY OF CALIFORNIA PRESS
Berkeley • *Los Angeles* • *Oxford*

University of California Press
Berkeley and Los Angeles, California

University of California Press, Ltd.
Oxford, England

© 1990 by
The Regents of the University of California

Library of Congress Cataloging-in-Publication Data

McCormick, Barrett L.
    Political reform in post-Mao China : democracy and bureaucracy in
a Leninist state / Barrett L. McCormick.
        p.   cm.
    Includes bibliographical references.
    ISBN 0-520-06765-7 (alk. paper)
    1. China—Politics and government—1976–   2. China—Economic
policy—1976–   3. Communist state.   I. Title.
JQ1502.M34   1990
951.05'7—dc20   89–20440
                                                                    CIP

Printed in the United States of America
1   2   3   4   5   6   7   8   9

The paper used in this publication meets the minimum requirements of American
National Standard for Information Sciences—Permanence of Paper for Printed Library
Materials, ANSI Z39.48–1984

for democracy

Contents

Preface

To explore the prospects for reform in China, I have developed in this book a theory of Leninist states. Theories of the state are by now prevalent in the study of comparative politics. Their chief attraction is that they allow for the autonomy of politics. Politics is not just a reflection of economics, is not subject to the dictates of economic modernization, is not just class struggle, and is not just a set of cultural values enacted in a public sphere. Politics, political leaders, and political institutions are connected to these spheres and more, but they also respond to their own imperatives.

It is doubly attractive to apply theories of the state to the most autonomous type of state, a Leninist state. By "autonomous" I mean that Leninist states tend to respond to their own needs and are relatively able to avoid being constrained by social demands. In their first decades, the Chinese and Soviet Leninist states were able to mount cataclysmic revolutions from above and were often dominated by individual leaders' cults of personality. More recently, individual leaders have been more constrained by state institutions, but Leninist state institutions have maintained the autonomy of the state and are also relatively able to escape social constraints.

Part of the work of this book has been broadly comparative, to analyze what makes Leninist states different from other kinds of states. It is ironic that most of the literature on the autonomy of states has been written about liberal-capitalist states, which in comparative terms are surrounded by a dense and active civil society and hence are among the most constrained states. In contrast, the comprehensive vertical hierarchies of Leninist state institutions constrain and confine society, leaving state leaders and state institutions relatively free to respond to their own agendas.

I have also analyzed what constitutes a Leninist state and have developed an argument about the nature of Leninist rulership that helps to explain the autonomy of Leninist institutions. In this I have drawn most of my inspiration from Max Weber's ideal types and, in particular, his concept of patrimonial rulership. I argue that the structure of Chinese units makes people personally dependent on their leadership and inhibits the autonomy of society. At the same time, patrimonial state bureaucracy dilutes official purposes and resists reforms imposed from above. In discussing Leninist rulership, I have tried to make frequent references to the Soviet Union and Eastern Europe to make this book as comparative as possible.

I have also endeavored to build an argument that would make sense to Chinese intellectuals. To accomplish this, I have tried to comprehend Chinese understandings and incorporate them into my argument. I have searched for kindred understandings, particularly from Eastern Europeans. I have tried to cast these arguments in the terms and traditions of Western social science and have therefore used a language that is not readily comprehensible. Nonetheless, I still hope that the basic argument, stripped of its jargon, will make sense to Chinese, although most would reject major points.

The tension in this analysis comes from two sources. First, while Leninist states may dominate society, they have never completely absorbed or eliminated society. Instead, decades of violence and coercion, limited economic achievements, and the widespread use of official position for private gain have alienated society from the Chinese, East European, and Russian states. In ordinary times the state may be able to suppress and mask these tensions, but in moments of crisis like those described in chapter 1 or the crisis of the spring of 1989, they give stark testimony to the depth of conflict between the state and society. While the existence of a deep conflict between state and society is a fundamental premise of my argument, I have analyzed only how society is shaped and limited by Leninist rulership. There is certainly more to Chinese society than can be seen through an analysis of the Chinese state, but it is beyond the scope of this work to provide an autonomous explanation of Chinese society.

The second source of tension in my analysis comes from the attempt of reformers to restructure the Chinese state. After Mao died, many leaders saw the need for radical reforms to bridge the gap between state and society. They saw that other forms of rulership might provide the state with more security and make the state more effective. They attempted to make the state more inclusive and more rational-legal. They did not attempt to create a Western-style democracy, but they did seek to maintain the leading role of the Party. This effort brought reformers into conflict with Leninist state institutions. Patrimonial networks have been able to passively resist and dilute the reformers' intentions. Moreover, as long as the reformers are committed to maintaining Party leadership, their own authority depends on the same hierarchies that generate this resistance. Consequently, political reforms in post-Mao China have failed to live up to the reformers' hopes or expectations.

Despite the reformers' intention to maintain the Party's leading role, there is still an important element of democratization in these reforms. First, despite the limits to reforms, reformers created a more open, more transparent, more lawful, and more humane government. This counts as an important step toward democracy. Nor is Western-style democracy the only conceivable form of democracy. Second, society has gained more autonomy, and in the more open atmosphere many intellectuals have pushed past the reformers' limited aims to discuss still more far-reaching reforms.

The brutal violence used against the people of Beijing and other Chinese cities in June 1989 demonstrated that the conflict between state and society has not yet been resolved. The reforms have so far failed to provide an institutional mechanism that can effectively mediate between state and society. Instead, when faced with broadly supported demands for more democracy, state power holders responded with a hail of gunfire and a wave of arrests.

The future is difficult to foresee. A decade of reform has left the Party in worse political shape than it was at the end of the Cultural Revolution. The leadership is isolated and discredited. Substantial sectors of society are now likely to reject not just this leadership and its policies but the Party and socialism as well. There will be tremendous pressure, not just to maintain the pace of economic reforms, but also to return to open and inclusive political reforms. At the same time, many in the Party leadership will accurately perceive that the gap between state and society will be harder to bridge now than it would have been before and that a return to openness will expose the Party to greater risks than it did before. Neither repression nor reform is likely to solve the Party's difficulties.

One of the most important conclusions to this analysis is that Leninist states are open only to a limited range of transformations. Reformers have found it very difficult to remold existing institutions to meet the demands of restructured economies or more autonomous societies. The alternatives may not be as stark as the contrast between the formal end of party leadership in Hungary and the repression in China, but reformers have yet to effect a stable compromise between recalcitrant institutions and alienated societies. What can or could have been accomplished in China and other reforming Leninist states will remain an open question that scholars can ponder for years to come.

I have many people to thank for their help in the making of this book. I encountered Guenther Roth early in my career, and he helped me to get started on Weber as well as social science and then later provided critical advice and support. Once in Madison, I became the student of Edward Friedman, and his brilliant mind and acute perception of Chinese perspectives have provided inspiration ever since. My ideas about the role of the state in China were developed by my contact with Maurice Meisner. Others on the faculty in Madison who were particularly stimulating include Booth Fowler, Murray Edelman, and Melvin Croan. Chen Gwang-tsai and Clara Sun of the Chinese Languages and Literature Department in Madison helped me to begin communicating with Chinese people. Some of my fellow students in Madison deserve special mention, including Steve McDougal, Steve Schier, and Isabel Souza. The next stage of this project found me at Nanjing University. Professor Hu Fuming was very kind to me, although he would repudiate most of my book, as were and as would several Chinese classmates. Many of the foreigners then at Nanjing University helped me to sift through an intensely rich experience, but I want to thank in particular Katie Lynch, Maryruth Coleman, Jenny Louie, Kam Louie, and Elizabeth Perry. Elizabeth Perry continued to provide advice and useful criticism during the next stage of the work, which was at the University of Washington. At that time Kent Guy was also very helpful, as were Dan Chirot and Jack Dahl. During this time, I received encouragement from Tsou Tang and help from Mike Lampton, who perhaps unintentionally, but nonetheless painstakingly, taught me much about writing. Andrew Nathan offered useful criticism of chapter 4. Connie Squires Meany and Jean Oi organized panels where my thoughts could be refined and offered their own excellent suggestions. During the final stage of making this book, I have found a supportive environment at Marquette. I want to thank the Bradley Institute for its support for one summer. Jack Johannes and Jim Rhodes both deserve special mention. Rich Friman has helped me in more ways than he knows and has my respect and gratitude. I also want to thank my students at Marquette, who have helped me to understand China. I thank the anonymous readers for the University of California Press for their helpful criticisms. Last but not least, I thank Amy Klatzkin and Gladys Castor for their excellent editing.

My family has kept me on track through thick and thin. My parents, Ralph and Mary Lou McCormick, have encouraged and inspired me. Connie Compton, though far away, has helped me along. Spencer McCormick gives me joy. Leslie Spencer-Herrera gave more than I could ask for at every stage of this book and is as glad as I am to see it finished.

Introduction

Since the death of Mao the leadership of the Chinese Communist Party has embarked on a series of ambitious reforms. In December 1978 the historic Third Plenum of the Eleventh Party Central Committee declared that the main focus of the Party's work should shift from class struggle to the Four Modernizations. Subsequent economic reforms have given more power to managers in state enterprises, facilitated the development of collective and private enterprises, expanded the use of markets, shifted from planning outputs toward indicative planning, and promoted profits and bonuses as the primary incentives for factories and workers. Economic reforms have been the most extensive and successful in rural China. The once hailed communes have been dismantled, and land has been contracted to individual families. Some families have been encouraged to specialize in producing commodities. Markets have been reestablished, even for sensitive commodities like grain, and all peasants have been encouraged to work hard and "get rich." The result has been a few record harvests and historic increases in rural incomes. Reforms to the urban economy have been more incremental and more difficult to implement and have had more mixed results, but they are nonetheless very significant. Steps have been taken toward establishing markets for credit and labor and toward making firms responsible for their own profits and losses. Particularly in coastal areas, China's economy is now significantly more open to the world economy. While inflation is currently a pressing problem, prices of many goods are no longer established by the state.

To facilitate economic reform and to some extent as an end in itself, the Party has also initiated a series of political reforms. Chinese politics is now more open and inclusive. Many of those condemned as counterrevolutionaries in previous political campaigns have been exonerated. After being excoriated in the Cultural Revolution, intellectuals and technical experts have been officially declared members of the working class. The range of permissible public debate is much broader, and culture is more lively, even if the Party has attacked "bourgeois liberalization" and "spiritual pollution." The Party has reestablished and strengthened representative institutions such as the people's congresses and has promulgated many new laws. The Party has also moved to improve state and Party administrative capacity through a series of administrative reforms and by decreasing the age and increasing the educational standing of personnel.

All of this might indicate that the nature of the Chinese state is being fundamentally transformed. The reforms seem to suggest the strengthening of horizontal relationships at lower levels vis-à-vis the "leading role" of the Party. Considerable evidence can be marshaled to support this interpretation. The Party's new constitution indicates that the Party is to operate within legal limits. It states: "The Party must conduct its activities within the limits permitted by the [state] Constitution and the laws of the state."[1] The promotion and use of contracts in areas as diverse as agriculture and public security is evidence of the new strength of horizontal relationships. The wider range of opinion, new institutions like the people's congresses, and greater freedom for mass organizations such as unions to pursue the interests of their constituency all indicate a revitalized civil society.

Leading scholars have summarized these developments as the transformation of a totalitarian system into an authoritarian one. Michel Oksenberg and Richard Bush state: "In 1972, totalitarian revolutionaries ruled the nation; by 1982 China's rulers had become authoritarian reformers."[2] Harry Harding labels the new system a "consultative authoritarian regime."[3] Tang Tsou makes a careful theoretical argument, defining "totalitarian" in terms of a continuum, with greater "totalitarian-ness" indicating the "extension of state functions" into

---

1. "Constitution of the Communist Party of China," 10.
2. Oksenberg and Bush, "China's Political Evolution: 1972–82," 1–19.
3. Harding, "Political Development in Post-Mao China," 13–37.

civil society. He argues persuasively that for most of the twentieth century the role of the Chinese state grew and that the current "retreat of politics" reverses that trend.[4]

This terminology succeeds in calling attention to very real changes that have occurred within China; but to define the limits of change or to compare China with other states, we need to think very carefully about the institutional structure of China's Leninist state. The scholars cited above agree that there has been only limited change in China's institutions. Oksenberg and Bush write that "the major instruments of totalitarian rule have been weakened but not eliminated."[5] Harding writes that "much of the basic structure of late Maoist China remains intact."[6] Tang Tsou states that the limits to change are defined by "the four fundamental principles," of which "the most basic" is the leadership of the Party.[7] Besides the Party there are still secret police, a comprehensive network of neighborhood and village organizations, and a system of files to keep watch on all citizens; and the state still owns the major means of production and communication. I agree with Chalmers Johnson, who argues that China is *not* just "a large, developing country that happens to be ruled by a Communist party." Instead, these institutions are part of a Leninist state that is not at all the same as other kinds of states.[8]

The reforms can be viewed as a Leninist revival as well as liberalization or relaxation. The reforms may somewhat decrease the autonomy of China's Leninist state, but they are nonetheless intended to increase its capacity to rule. Before drawing conclusions about the direction of change in China, it is important to consider the past. The Cultural Revolution and the overall direction of Mao's politics were not only a catastrophe for society but also a serious threat to the state. Mao created an extremely autonomous state that could arbitrarily intervene in any sphere of social life. Wang Xizhe, a leader of China's unofficial democrats, argues that Mao initiated the Cultural Revolution "precisely because he was not satisfied that the party/state set up after the model of Stalinism was authoritarian enough."[9] Au-

4. Tang Tsou, "Back from the Brink of Revolutionary-'Feudal' Totalitarianism," in *The Cultural Revolution and Post-Mao Reforms*, ed. Tang Tsou (Chicago: University of Chicago Press, 1986), 144–88.

5. Oksenberg and Bush, "China's Political Evolution."

6. Harding, *China's Second Revolution*, 4.

7. Tang Tsou, "Back from the Brink."

8. Johnson, "What's Wrong With Chinese Political Studies?"

9. Wang Xizhe, *Mao Zedong and The Cultural Revolution*, 25.

tonomy was purchased at a high price, however. The essentially charismatic nature of Mao's politics and the legitimation of attacks on
institutions and procedures meant that there were few hard or fast
rules for leaders or followers. Campaigns, interventions, arrests, and
purges could create a climate of fear and conformity, but without
rules and institutions central authority could be maintained only
through more campaigns, interventions, arrests, and purges. Even
then each successive campaign further undermined the state's administrative capacity. The power of modern states is rooted in part in
their monopoly of the legitimate means of violence—which campaigns tended to grant to any self-proclaimed revolutionary. It is
rooted also in the development of a rational-legal state bureaucracy
that will consistently conduct administration according to rules and
routines established by political authorities. Campaigns debilitated
rules and routines, increasing the ability of cadres at all levels to respond to their personal agendas and diminishing supervision from
above or below. Consequently, the state gained the ability to intervene
anywhere and anytime, but central authorities lost the ability to guide
the use of that power.

Viewed in these terms, the campaign to strengthen laws and institutions can be seen as an attempt by the Party center to increase its
administrative capacity. Two of the most consistent themes of the
post-Mao Chinese press have been exposés of corrupt cadres and
Party organizations and criticisms of lower levels for failing to implement the Party center's policies. These criticisms suggest that the Cultural Revolution's attack on institutional authority left in its wake
pervasive networks of informal and personal authority, which are
very difficult for central authorities to penetrate or control. Initiatives
from the Party center, such as the Party's new constitution, new Party
rules, the reestablishment of a hierarchy of discipline and inspection
committees, and the recent campaign for Party rectification, can be
viewed as means of combatting the general diffusion of authority.
Even reforms such as promoting the use of technical experts in enterprises can be seen as means of binding organizations to their formal
purposes and limiting the ability of lower-level cadres to use them for
private purposes.

While reform may reduce the Party's autonomy, the Party has no
intention of abandoning its "leading role." Party spokesmen have em-
phatically rejected any intention of creating a Western-style democracy and continue to insist that the Party has a special capacity to

lead society in a transition to socialism and therefore deserves exclusive privileges. Even though the Party has retreated from the extremes of the Cultural Revolution, it still devotes tremendous energy to defining ideology and encouraging the study of its current line. It continues to occupy an exclusive organizational sphere. The reform program has strengthened the Party's grass-roots organization in urban neighborhoods, and the neighborhood committees still form the foundation of an extensive surveillance system. While the central leadership now utilizes institutions such as the people's congresses and regularly "consults" with non-Party personages on political events, there can be no doubt that it maintains a close monopoly on policy formation. The mass organizations have greater freedom to voice the demands of their constituents, but there is little evidence of genuinely autonomous interest groups. Harro Von Senger writes:

> The Party does not want to relinquish, but merely refine and rationalize its leadership position. The main force is to be engaged, as it were, to steer the ship. But for the ship's maintenance and operation auxiliary forces are employed. . . . Thus the democratization and legalization of life in the P.R.C. remain within the broad limits which in the last resort are set by the political leadership of the CCP.[10]

The Party's leading role makes China's Leninist state different from other authoritarian states. A wide range of states can be considered "authoritarian," including the former regime of Augusto Pinochet in Chile, South Korea's developmental capitalism, Mexico's once successful corporatism, and personal rulership in Africa. While there are similarities among these states, their different institutional structures and different relationships between state and society indicate fundamentally different prospects. Leninist states penetrate civil society and the economy more thoroughly. This gives the state a tremendous ability to co-opt and promote collaboration. Civil society in a Leninist state has considerably less autonomy than in other kinds of states and is less able to organize significant pressure for change. To justify their leading role, Leninist parties must maintain at least the pretense of charismatic legitimacy, which places limits on ideological reform. This undercuts the prospects for promoting the rule of law and the development of rational-legal organization. In turn, the inability of society to communicate with the state through legal chan-

10. Von Senger, "Recent Developments in the Relations Between State and Party Norms in the People's Republic of China."

nels promotes the use of informal, particularistic, and corrupt channels. Reforms from above, although intended to address these problems, tend to reinforce the structures that create them. Despite "relaxation" or "liberalization," Chinese institutions remain distinctively Leninist and will continue to influence the course of reform.

I will examine this theoretical argument in detail for the rest of this introduction. Chapter 1 will examine the nature of the relationship between state and society in China by looking at two instances of open conflict between state and society: the attempt to establish a "commune" in Shanghai in 1967 and the abortive demonstration against the so-called Gang of Four in Nanjing in 1976. This will illustrate that while Leninist states are generally able to limit the expression of social interests, such limitation is not the same as creating a mass of atomized individuals. To the contrary, the Cultural Revolution's violent attack on existing social norms intensified the isolation of the state from society and the general weakening of the state. Chapter 2 will examine how interests are expressed within the confines of Leninist organization. I will argue that when Leninist states attempt to build comprehensive organization to transform society and also strictly limit the ability of that organization to respond to day-to-day problems, individuals inevitably seek personal and informal solutions, thereby creating patronage networks that balance the state's formal organization. In chapter 3 I will show how the creation of criminal codes and the strengthening of legal procedures in criminal matters are primarily intended to strengthen the state's ability to control social order and have resulted in only the limited ability of individuals to assert rights against the state. In chapter 4 I will show how, despite various "democratizing" reforms, the revived people's congresses still serve the Party center's definition of democracy and are consequently co-opted into the existing political pattern of contrasting patrimonial and rational-legal organization. In chapter 5, using the recent round of Party rectification as an example, I will discuss how existing institutions make it difficult to reform the Party, which is itself the main obstacle to reform.

THE LENINIST STATE

The argument of this book is based on two central ideas. First, Leninist states are relatively autonomous of society. In the words of Leszek Kolakowski, Leninist states begin with "the progressive destruction of civil society and the absorption of all forms of social life by the state."[11] The state's penetration of society—the Party's presence in all formal organizations, its control of mass media, its commanding presence in the economy—becomes the main factor limiting change. Second, to examine the nature of this limit, I will use Max Weber's three ideal types of rulership: rational-legal rulership, traditional or patrimonial rulership, and charismatic rulership. The relationship of a Leninist state to society establishes a basic pattern of authority. Leninist states claim charismatic legitimacy and attempt to build rational-legal institutions from the top down. In practice, the Party's comprehensive penetration of society results in extensive patron-client networks, or patrimonial rulership, which undermine the state's ideological legitimacy and economic efficiency. As long as the Party seeks to maintain its leading role, attempts to remedy this problem will feature more charismatic political campaigns and further attempts to build rational-legal authority from the top down. Charismatic movements have not provided a basis for solving day-to-day problems and have had tragic social costs. Further attempts to build rational-legal authority from the top down have had only limited success and have had the unintended result of strengthening patrimonial networks. Leninist states change but tend to remain within the broad patterns of Leninist politics.

What characterizes a Leninist state? First, state organization thoroughly penetrates society. Usually one of the first steps in establishing a Leninist state is to extend political organization from a single center outward to include all political parties, unions, professional associations, firms, and service organizations. This organization is so comprehensive that it reaches all neighborhoods and villages. In turn, the autonomy of civil society is severely restricted. Second, the state has a hegemonic role in the economy. In some Leninist states this is accomplished through state ownership of nearly all significant economic organizations and through command-style economic planning. Even those Leninist states that have adopted "market socialism" have retained a degree of economic authority far surpassing that in other authoritarian states. This results in political domination of economics. In particular, social stratification is based more on political status than economic class. Third, Leninist states use their extensive organi-

---

11. Kolakowski, *Main Currents of Marxism* 3:7. In this passage Kolakowski is discussing the Soviet Union in the 1920s.

zation to supervise public speech. They propagate a relatively formal ideology that seeks to justify the Party's leading role in society. This requires claiming that the Party has unique charismatic virtues, such as a "scientific" understanding of the future, the ability to bring about a utopia eventually, the lack of any selfish interest, and the ability to represent all "progressive classes," or good people. They may tolerate more or less dissent, but they always maintain boundaries. In addition, Leninist states practice extensive supervision of personnel matters. Higher levels supervise promotions and appointments at lower levels in political, social, and economic organization. Finally, Leninist states maintain an extensive system of secret police coupled with an extensive system of files or dossiers on individual citizens.[12]

There are two fundamental assertions underlying the use of "the state" as a basic unit of analysis. First, politics is or can be a relatively autonomous sphere of human activity. This is not particularly controversial from the vantage of mainstream American political science, and contemporary Western Marxism has followed arguments advanced by Lenin, Gramsci, Mao, and Poulantzas among many others and rejected strict economic determinism.[13] Second, the state can be a relatively autonomous actor. This argument is more controversial, whether examined from a pluralist perspective that views the output of government as determined largely by the input of autonomous interest groups or from a Marxist perspective that reduces the state to an intermediary between ruling and ruled classes.[14] In contrast to these positions, the last two decades have produced a substantial lit-

---

12. Edward Friedman's "Three Leninist Paths Within a Socialist Conundrum," 11–45, was helpful to me in formulating the central characteristics of a Leninist state, but Professor Friedman bears no responsibility for the way I use that term.

13. Vajda, The State and Socialism, esp. 10 and passim, deserves to be read for this argument.

14. In pursuing the latter case, it is important to note that even Marxists such as Poulantzas who grant politics and the state a relative autonomy ultimately link the state to the (indirect) control of the ruling class, whose power is based on economic might, as is indicated by the phrase "the capitalist state." See, for example, Nicos Poulantzas, Political Power and Social Classes. Alvin Gouldner states: "The tension between Marx's historical materialism, which plainly assigns a derivative role to the state, and the relative autonomy of the state in society—evident to Marx as a political journalist—was never resolved systematically at the level of theory. It remains a troublesome difficulty leading generations of Marxists to attempt to salvage the theory with countless, ingenious but ad hoc glosses" (The Two Marxisms [New York: Oxford University Press, 1980], 304). The contemporary Marxist literature on the state is by now very large, but is ably summarized in Carnoy, The State and Political Theory, and for those with the ability to penetrate jargon, in Bob Jessop's The Capitalist State.

erature arguing that the state needs to be considered an independent variable.[15]

The argument to follow is not that all states should be seen as independent actors, but that certain kinds of states have far more autonomy than others. In capitalism the economy or the market tends to dominate politics and the state. Marx was right to lament that under capitalism all things, men as labor power included, are degraded to the status of commodities. However, Leninist states are more similar to precapitalist formations, such as European feudalism or China's Confucian empire, in having developed political organization that subordinates market pressures. This is not to say that Leninist states can avoid economic pressures any more than the American economy can avoid political "interference." The essential point is only that in Leninist systems the state is the most important unit of analysis.

Liberal-capitalist states, of all modern states, have the least freedom of action vis-à-vis their own societies. Ironically, the bulk of the literature on the autonomy of states, especially Marxist literature, focuses on liberal-capitalist states. Stephen Krasner provides an approach to the relative autonomy of liberal-capitalist states when he discusses strong and weak states. He argues that weak states, like the United States, are "completely permeated by pressure groups," whereas a strong state, such as France or Japan, "in comparison with the United States has more power over its society." He continues: "The United States has a strong society but a weak state."[16] This distinction seems an attempt to incorporate the insights of a pluralist perspective within the bounds of state-centered analysis—that is, Krasner must concede that pluralists, such as Robert Dahl, have identified an important aspect of liberal-capitalist political systems when they point to a multiplicity of relatively autonomous interest groups.[17]

---

15. See, for example: Barnet, *Roots of War*; Schurmann, *The Logic of World Power*; Krasner, *Defending the National Interest*; Stepan, *The State and Society: Peru in Comparative Perspective*; Skocpol, *States and Social Revolution*; Vajda, *The State and Socialism*; Nordlinger, *On the Autonomy of the Democratic State*.

16. Krasner, *Defending the National Interest*, 55–61. Chalmers Johnson makes much the same distinction in his discussion of "plan-rational" and "market-rational" systems (*MITI and the Japanese Economic Miracle*, 17–34). This brings to light a contradiction in terminology—what appears a "strong" state in terms of its relationship with its own society may be a "weak" state in international terms and vice versa. Consequently, Immanuel Wallerstein uses "strong" and "weak" to refer to different states than Krasner does. See Wallerstein, *The Modern World System* (New York: Academic Press, 1974).

17. Dahl, *Pluralist Democracy in the United States*.

Some Marxists tacitly concede the limited autonomy of the capitalist state even as they attempt to establish its autonomy. Antonio Gramsci's discussion of "hegemony"—which attempts to explain why crises of the severity that led to revolution in Russia in 1917 had not led to the overthrow of capitalism in the West—concludes that civil society in the Western capitalist states is particularly strong and permeated with bourgeois values and ideology.[18] Contemporary Marxists such as Poulantzas and Althusser are making the same point when they emphasize the importance of "ideological state apparatuses," such as religion, private schools, families, political parties, and trade unions, in maintaining the stability of capitalist states.[19] However, as Ralph Miliband notes, they lose sight of important distinctions between liberal-capitalist states and other states when they include these "ideological apparatuses" within the bounds of the state.[20] Whether these "ideological apparatuses" are inside or outside the formal boundaries of state organization marks a very important distinction between liberal-capitalist states and other states. Just as Krasner is grappling with phenomena noted by Dahl, Marxists like Gramsci, Althusser, and Poulantzas are grappling with Almond and Verba's "civic culture" or even the self-perpetuating social traditions described by conservatives such as Michael Oakeshott and Edmund Burke.[21] The central point is that, even granted a "relative autonomy," liberal-capitalist states are restrained by a vigorous society.

In contrast to liberal-capitalist states, bureaucratic-authoritarian states have a greater ability to structure or restructure society. In part, bureaucratic-authoritarian states are a response to the problems of late development and speak to the failure of any class to attain a "hegemonic" role, a difficult task in the straitened circumstances of periphery of the world market.[22] In the absence of a hegemonic ruling

18. Gramsci, *Prison Notebooks*, 235 and passim. It is important to note that what appears to Krasner as weakness is strength to Gramsci.

19. Poulantzas, *Political Power*, and Althusser, "Ideology and Ideological State Apparatuses."

20. Miliband, "The Capitalist State: Reply to Nicos Poulantzas." It should be noted that the boundary of the state shifts several times through the corpus of Gramsci's work, as is noted by Anderson in "The Antinomies of Antonio Gramsci."

21. Almond and Verba, *The Civic Culture*; Burke, *Reflections on the Revolution in France*; Oakeshott, "Rationalism in Politics." Louis Hartz is defining the character of these traditions in *The Liberal Tradition in America*.

22. Thus the intellectual precursors of this argument include Marx's discussion of "Caesarism," as in the "Eighteenth Brumaire of Louis Napoleon," and Gramsci's discussion of the role of the Piedmont in Italian national unification (*Prison Notebooks*, 44–122).

class, bureaucratic-authoritarian states take a direct role in creating the conditions for capital accumulation and in structuring civil society to maintain domestic order. As opposed to Krasner's example of the strong French (liberal-capitalist) state whose "administrative elite has been able to choose those interest groups that it has preferred to deal with,"[23] bureaucratic-authoritarian states build "corporatist" political structures[24] to "statize" political organizations of the popular sector.[25] Through strategies ranging from co-optation to repression, state-sponsored corporatist structures attempt to shape or limit political demands from below. This constitutes a rather different political environment from liberal-capitalist states, but one in which civil society still has an important role. While bureaucratic-authoritarian states penetrate society to a far higher degree than prior "clientelistic states," owing in large part to the increased efficiency of new "bureaucratic" structures of authority,[26] there are still limits to its administrative capacity. Fernando Cardoso writes:

> Latin American authoritarianism is still "underdeveloped": it may kill and torture, but it does not exercise complete control of everyday life. The state is sufficiently strong to concentrate its attention and repressive apparatus against so-called subversive groups, but it is not as efficient when it comes to controlling the universities, for example, or even the bureaucracy itself.[27]

In addition, bureaucratic-authoritarian states remain open to input from significant sectors of civil society—especially bourgeois sectors—through what Guillermo O'Donnell calls the "privatization" of state agencies, that is, the interpenetration of private bourgeois organizations and the state.[28] Nora Hamilton argues that the Mexican

23. Krasner, *Defending the National Interest*, 58.
24. Philippe Schmitter states: "Corporatism can be defined as a system of interest representation in which the constituents are organized into a limited number of singular compulsory, noncompetitive, hierarchically ordered and functionally differentiated categories, recognized or licensed (if not created) by the state and granted a deliberate representational monopoly within their respective categories in exchange for observing certain controls on their selection of leaders and articulation of demands and supports. See "Still the Century of Corporatism?"
25. Guillermo O'Donnell, "Tensions in the Bureaucratic Authoritarian State," and "Corporatism and the Question of the State."
26. That is to say that the new bureaucratic structures are more efficient and reach a broader segment of the population. See O'Donnell, "Corporatism and the Question of the State," 68–69. Jackson and Rosberg find "clientelistic states" or personal rulership the norm in Africa, in "Personal Rule: Theory and Practice in Africa."
27. Cardoso, "The Characterization of Authoritarian Regimes."
28. O'Donnell, "Corporatism and the Question of the State," 74–77.

state, despite its birth in a revolutionary movement that activated the working class and peasantry and despite the attempts of leaders such as Cárdenas to incorporate those classes into the political process, is constrained by "the economic power of private capital" and "the socio-economic structure in which it functions."[29] Private property, however ill distributed, is a political right as well as a form of organization and potential political power, and bureaucratic-authoritarian states suffer defeats at the hands of private capital.[30]

Finally, the limits of the bureaucratic-authoritarian state's impact on society are demonstrated by the relative lack of change through their tenure. In the recent round of "re-democratization" in Latin America, in many countries the same forces that contested power before the emergence of the bureaucratic-authoritarian state have returned since it departed.[31]

Leninist states have still more autonomy vis-à-vis society. O'Donnell observes that the leaders of bureaucratic-authoritarian states often use "surgery" as a metaphor for their rule, that is, they intend to remove the infected parts of the body politic.[32] "Surgery" has high enough social costs, but Leninist states promise far more—a total transformation of society. The "transition to socialism," according to Rudolf Bahro, has involved "a desperate attempt to adapt the whole of living society into the crystalline structure of the state."[33] Unlike bureaucratic-authoritarian states, the Leninist revolution from above "liquidated the bourgeoisie as a class" and dispossessed elites at all levels of society. While this process redistributed wealth, it also generated violent political campaigns with many innocent victims.[34] On the wings of these violent campaigns, all significant economic interests were "statized," and party cadres assumed leading roles in all social and political organizations. Unlike bureaucratic-authoritarian states, Leninist states have not tolerated semi-independent institutions

29. Hamilton, *The Limits of State Autonomy: Post-Revolutionary Mexico*, 31.

30. This brings to mind Hannah Arendt's arguments linking "shallowness" in public affairs with the lack of "the four walls of one's private property," although she refers to a home rather than to productive assets. *On the Human Condition*, 71 and 22–78 passim.

31. Karen L. Remmer, "Redemocratization and the Impact of Authoritarian Rule in Latin America." The fact that bureaucratic-authoritarian states are dismantled, though often used for political apology, remains an important observation.

32. O'Donnell, "Tensions in the Bureaucratic-Authoritarian State," 294.

33. Bahro, *The Alternative in Eastern Europe*, 38.

34. For example, Stalin's campaign to dispossess the Kulaks made many victims of middle peasants as well. See Medvedev, *Let History Judge*, 97–101.

such as autonomous universities. Not even the bureaucracy itself has been immune from state-sponsored violence—Stalin's purges and Mao's various campaigns have extracted millions of victims from the state apparatus. Leninist authoritarianism is not "underdeveloped"—it reaches into every corner of society.

Leninist states must change. The violent transformation of society cannot last forever. Even Brezhnev's form of Leninism, which eliminated large-scale terror yet sought to maintain the state's thorough domination of society and the economy, has proven economically and administratively inefficient. Consequently, Leninists are under pressure to promote limited social and economic autonomy. Nonetheless, reformers are constrained to work within existing institutions and especially to respect the Party's leading role. It has proven very difficult to regain social support or promote stable economic growth within this constraint.

There are two controversies in the literature on Leninist states that deserve brief comment. The first of these is whether or not there is a "ruling class" in Leninist states, and the second is whether or not Leninist states are "pluralist." There are good reasons to label the elite in a Leninist state a ruling class. For example, while the ideology of Leninist states links the ruling parties in an organic unity with the working class or with the whole people,[35] many observers have noted that as the "vanguard party" assumed the historical role that Marx had assigned the working class, its "unity" with that class became increasingly abstract and formal.[36] Empirical studies document substantial inequality in "really existing socialism."[37] The Party's leading role in society generates and justifies a wide range of privileges for Party members. Leninist states' economic monopoly also creates the potential for systematic exploitation. For example, both Stalin and Mao imposed terms of trade highly unfavorable to the peasants.[38] Wlodzimierz Brus argues:

35. Gregory Grossman aptly labels this image the "solidary society" in "The Solidary Society."

36. For example, Benjamin Schwartz argues that "it becomes patently clear that the proletarian consciousness and proletarian virtue could become entirely divorced from their presumed class moorings and be lodged in the political organization itself" (*Communism and China*, 16).

37. See, for example, Walter Connor, *Socialism, Politics, and Equality;* Donald Hodges, *The Bureaucratization of Socialism;* and Maria Hirszowicz, *The Bureaucratic Leviathan.*

38. Alvin Gouldner argues that this is the central feature of Stalinism and calls it "internal colonialism" ("Stalinism: A Study of Internal Colonialism"). Revising prior judgments on China, economist Nicolas Lardy writes: "Although much of the data

In certain situations the relations of dominance and subordination based on public ownership can be far more relentless than those which are based on private ownership . . . since (1) the state, gathering in one center disposition over all—or almost all—the places and conditions of work, has in its hand an instrument of *economic coercion* the scale of which cannot be equalled by individual capitalists and corporations; (2) the state can directly link economic coercion with *political coercion*.[39]

Consequently, many distinguished social critics have argued that the elite constitutes a ruling class,[40] and if the question is considered solely in terms of the amount or degree of inequality or exploitation, it is hard not to find merit in their argument.

These arguments use the term "class" out of context.[41] Marx defines class in terms of economic relationships, but economic relationships are not the source of Leninist stratification. Attempts to use Marx's usual scheme to explain Leninist states encounter difficulties, therefore. For example, Jacek Kuron and Karol Modzelewski argue that the Party's claim not to control the means of production can be justified only with a "formalistic, legal notion of ownership," that such a conception of a ruling class is fundamentally alien to Marxism, and that in practice the "central political bureaucracy" collectively controls production and therefore qualifies as a ruling class.[42] Their argument is based on an attempt to demonstrate that the relationships between state, class, and economy in a Leninist system are essentially the same as in a capitalist system, with the simple substitution of collective ownership for private ownership. But this "collective" is not just a large joint stock company, but the state. The rela-

---

required for a more definitive analysis is lacking, enough evidence exists to postulate that the state transferred significant resources out of the agricultural sector over a sustained period" (*Agriculture in China's Modern Economic Development*, 127).

39. Wlodzimierz Brus, *Socialist Ownership and Political Systems* (Boston: Routledge & Kegan Paul, 1975), 17–18.

40. These include Milovan Djilas, *The New Class;* Jacek Kuron and Karol Modzelewski, *Open Letter to Party Members;* George Konrad and Ivan Szelenyi, *The Intellectuals on the Road to Class Power;* Chen Erjian, *Crossroads Socialism;* Michael Voslensky, *Nomenklatura;* Donald Hodges, *Bureaucratization of Socialism;* Alec Nove, "The Class Nature of the Soviet Union Revisited," *Soviet Studies* 35, no. 3 (July 1983): 298–312.

41. To his credit, Nove states: "Another [conclusion] is that our terminology (including the word 'class') needs to be adapted to new phenomena, that Soviet-type societies do not fit our inherited labels" ("Class Nature," 309–10).

42. Kuron and Modzelewski, *Open Letter*, 18–29. Kuron and Modzelewski's "Letter" was one of the last serious attempts by Polish intellectuals to understand Poland in Marxist terms, which indicates the difficulty of explaining Leninist regimes of the twentieth century with terminology from nineteenth-century political theory.

tionship between the "central political elite" (or *nomenklatura*, to use Michael Voslensky's term) and the state is rather different from the relationship between the bourgeoisie and the capitalist state. In Marx's understanding of capitalism the bourgeoisie was the dynamic factor, and the state was largely derivative. In Leninist systems the state is the center of gravity, and the "ruling class" is derivative. The *nomenklatura*'s values do not autonomously reproduce themselves throughout society, and the *nomenklatura* has virtually no existence outside of the state and is consequently dependent on the state.[43] Gyorgy Markus writes:

> The ruling group is constituted in a way that is in principle different from a class. The members of the apparatus are not constrained to act in a definite way by the position they occupy in the structure of social reproduction; they have to follow consciously the rules and objectives pre-set by the apparatus—otherwise they would be sanctioned. . . . The difference here from the class of capitalists . . . emerges through the fact that in this . . . case membership in an organization is the pre-condition of, and therefore logically prior to, any structural position of power the individual may occupy.[44]

The second controversy is whether or not there is "pluralism" in Leninist systems. Like the term "ruling class," "pluralism" carries meanings derived from its association with political systems manifestly different from Leninist systems. Pluralism was originally intended to describe liberal-capitalist states, and not just any liberal-capitalist state, but particularly weak states in which civil society has a high degree of autonomy. Pluralist states provide relatively less leadership or structure, and politics tends to consist of bargaining between the various groups.

The strong point of applying this model of politics to Leninist states is the argument that societies in Leninist states are more complex than is admitted by either the totalitarian model or prereform Leninist ideology. According to the totalitarian model, socialist society

43. Ferenc Feher, Agnes Heller, and Gyorgy Markus, *Dictatorship Over Needs*, 116–17.

44. It could well be argued not only that Leninist states lack a ruling class, but that society under a Leninist state is stratified by state-assigned status and not class. Markus writes: "This [Eastern Europe] is in truth already a classless society . . . because everybody is in fact a member of the apparatus of power, only occupying different functional positions within it" (Feher, Heller, and Markus, *Dictatorship Over Needs*, 123). Jean-François Billeter points out that until the current reforms, Chinese were stratified according to class labels, which did not correspond to existing classes but were actually state-assigned statuses. See Billeter, "The System of 'Class Status.' "

was nothing more than a mass of atomized individuals. This is clearly not true. Individuals in Leninist states are woven into a dense network of formal and informal social and political relationships. Moreover, there are conflicts of interest within what Leninist state ideology calls the "working class." In the next chapter I will present strong evidence of the existence of groups and their awareness of their common interests.

Those who apply pluralist arguments to Leninist states must recognize that the institutional and ideological hallmarks of pluralism do not exist in Leninist states.[45] Groups have limited opportunities in Leninist states to organize autonomous organization, to articulate interests, or to bargain. Sophisticated "pluralistic" arguments try to circumvent this problem by arguing that group interests are aggregated and articulated through other, possibly informal, channels, and despite the attempt by leaders to maintain the image of unanimity, there is covert or tacit bargaining. For example, Victor Falkenheim argues that interest representation in China usually occurs through informal, one-on-one contacts, usually between superiors and subordinates.[46] Alternatively, Jerry Hough argues that while central authorities ban the formal organization of interest groups or factions in the USSR, informal groupings are more important than formal organization, and that the diffusion of power in practice is more important than the constitution. He concludes that the USSR qualifies as "institutional pluralism."[47] Both of these arguments are essentially factually correct: individuals in Leninist states do pursue their interests through informal particularistic channels, and there is competition between informal groups within Leninist state bureaucracy.

Institutions are important, however, and implicit informal pluralism is not the same thing as real pluralism.[48] The means by which interests are aggregated and articulated and the institutional context within which policies are adopted all have a significant impact on what kinds of policies are advocated and implemented. For an analogy, in liberal-capitalist states it makes a difference whether interest-

45. One reasonable alternative is to note that groups exist and have interests, but to reject the broader implications of the pluralist argument. Peter Ferdinand takes this approach in "Interest Groups and Chinese Politics."

46. See Falkenheim, "Political Participation in China" and "Citizen and Group Politics in China."

47. Hough and Fainsod, *How the Soviet Union Is Governed*, esp. 518–55.

48. Two of the most persuasive critics of the pluralist approach to Leninist politics are Andrew Janos, "Group Politics in Communist Society," and Archie Brown, "Political Power and the Soviet State."

group structures are pluralist or corporatist. Corporatist structures are more able than pluralist structures to implement incomes and industrial policies. Similarly, a single worker seeking a favor from his boss is likely to raise issues different from those of a union bargaining on behalf of all the workers in a plant. A bureaucrat will have a different relationship with his superiors and subordinates than the leadership of a lobbying group has with its clients and policy makers, and each will seek different goals. The root of this argument is, again, that states are not just neutral transmission belts for economic or group interests, that their structures and institutions have an influence on policy output. To analyze how Leninist states structure political outcomes, I now turn to a discussion of Leninist rulership.

LENINIST RULERSHIP

Most previous analysis of China has implicitly contrasted two of Max Weber's three ideal types of rulership, rational-legal rulership and charismatic rulership, and neglected the third, patrimonial rulership.[49] For example, Richard Lowenthal contrasts "rational" economic goals with "ideological" utopian goals.[50] Some have praised "rational" bureaucratic goals: Barry Richman found this aspect of Chinese government responsible for economic progress until 1966 but condemned Mao's revolutionary endeavors as a "new religion."[51] Others find bureaucracy repressive and revolution rational, but have accepted essentially the same two alternatives.[52] The focus on these two categories is understandable, for at one time the Chinese state also exclusively propounded a "two line theory." But in post-Mao China an overwhelming amount of evidence and, as I will argue in chapter 2, theoretical discussion suggests that Weber's third category,

49. The term "rulership" was suggested to me by Guenther Roth. It is preferable to possible alternatives, such as "modes of domination," "modes of legitimacy," or "authority," because it clearly conveys Weber's intention to discuss both ideas and administration. I thank Professor Roth for his help in this, but he bears no responsibility for my use of the term.

50. Lowenthal, "Development vs. Utopia in Communist Policy."

51. Richman, *Industrial Society in Communist China,* esp. 47, 913. Richman's line of analysis foreshadows much of what is said about post-Mao China.

52. Steven Andors, for example, writes: "The choice, however, was not, as opponents of the new system argued, between the order and regularity of one side and the chaos of the other. Rather it was between two different methods of management" (*China's Industrial Revolution,* 77).

patrimonial rulership, is equally relevant.[53] Putting rational-legal and charismatic authority in the context of patrimonial rulership will lead to an understanding of the limits of reform and rulership in Leninist states.

Weber defines charismatic rulership as rulership based on the belief that the ruler is "endowed with supernatural, superhuman, or at least specifically exceptional powers or qualities."[54] In its pure form charisma is revolutionary, as it justifies abandoning or overthrowing prior beliefs and institutions. Members of a charismatic movement are chosen because they possess charisma or charismatic virtue, not for any technical competence. Charismatic movements are not bound by ordinary economic considerations, and charismatic administration is usually ad hoc. The central challenge for charismatic movements is the transformation from a revolutionary force to everyday administration.

Western studies of China explicitly or implicitly recognize the importance of charisma in the revolution and in the dramatic mass movements like the Great Leap Forward and the Cultural Revolution. Victory in revolution confirmed both the Party's institutional charisma and the personal charisma of its leader, Mao Zedong. Mao and his associates subsequently drew on Mao's personal charisma to attempt to impose strict standards of "revolutionary virtue" on the whole of society. Mao's personal authority, his artful manipulation of the symbols of the revolution, and the mobilization of various sectors of society produced mass movements that effectively overcame the attempt by other leaders to strengthen rational-legal institutions. The costs were enormous: estimates on the number of deaths resulting from the Great Leap Forward alone range from ten to thirty million.[55]

Less attention has been afforded to another equally important role of charisma in China's Leninist state. The "revolutionary virtue" of

53. Until recently very few scholars have taken this category seriously. Andrew Nathan, "A Factional Model for CCP Politics," was an excellent beginning, and Andrew Walder, Communist Neo-Traditionalism, uses these categories to excellent effect. Jean Oi has discussed similar phenomena in a rural context in "Communism and Clientelism: Rural Politics in China."

54. Weber, Economy and Society, 241; for his discussion of charismatic rulership, see pp. 241–54, 266–70, 1111–57.

55. Estimates of the number of deaths caused by the Great Leap Forward can be found in Judith Bannister and Samuel H. Preston, "Mortality in China," and Ansley J. Coale, "Population Trends, Population Policy, and Population Studies in China."

the Cultural Revolution recognized no other authority and therefore proved destructive even to Party and state institutions. Because of this, and because of society's bitter experience, post-Mao reformers have had to suppress "revolutionary virtue." Nonetheless, they still must claim a less dramatic form of charisma on behalf of the Party to legitimate its exclusive privileged role in Chinese politics. The Party can no longer claim that Mao is "the greatest genius in ten thousand years," but it must claim that "without the Party, there would be no new China." The Party center argues that rational-legal strategies are most appropriate for this stage in history, but it claims that it knows this and can take the appropriate action because of its special charismatic nature. Moreover, the Party's chosen policies are usually defined in charismatic terms: the Four Modernizations are treated as a heroic quest or a "new long march."[56] However, as is discussed in chapter 5, exactly what virtues the Party claims, how to gain social recognition of these virtues, and how to coordinate charismatic and rational-legal rulership remain unsolved problems.

As Franz Schurmann noted nearly twenty years ago, the leaders of the Party have also attempted to build rational-legal organization, or bureaucracy.[57] According to Weber, the most important characteristics of rational-legal rulership are (1) continuous rule-bound conduct of official business, usually involving a systematic appeals procedure; (2) hierarchical organization, that is, each lower office is under the control and supervision of a higher office; (3) organization according to specified spheres of competence, that is, a system of formal job descriptions allocating formal authority and responsibility to each position; (4) employment of specialized, technically competent staff; (5) separation of official and personal property; (6) the recording of administrative acts, decisions, and rules. Finally, Weber associates bureaucratic organization closely with economic efficiency, arguing that the ability to bring technical competency to bear on the productive process and the ability to build a stable organization that can extract profits over a long period of time are crucial components of capitalism.[58]

56. Kenneth Jowitt argues, in "Soviet Neo-Traditionalism," that "storming" is a charismatic approach to the economy in the USSR.
57. Schurmann, *Ideology and Organization in Communist China.*
58. For Max Weber's discussion of rational-legal rulership, see Weber, *Economy and Society,* 217–25, 956–1005.

The Party's present attention to laws and organization is an attempt to strengthen rational-legal rulership. Some Western observers have interpreted this as Western-style modernization, but there is an important difference. Whereas in the West legal systems developed in the context of a vigorous civil society, and rational-legal organization developed in the context of a market economy, in China both developments have occurred under the leadership of the state. Both in the 1950s and at present, the building of rational-legal rulership has been, in large part if not exclusively, a means of strengthening central leadership. This may be preferable to either the attempt to revive failed charismatic mass movements or de facto patrimonial rulership. However, law imposed from above is not nearly as attractive to society as contract law in a market setting and will not result in a similar rationalization of social relations. Instead, many individuals are likely to seek and gain particularistic exemptions, and the overall effectiveness of rational-legal rulership from above is likely to be limited.

The Party's appeals to both charismatic and rational-legal rulership can best be understood in the context of pervasive patrimonial rulership.[59] Guenther Roth distinguishes two kinds of patrimonialism, one based on tradition and one based on "loyalties that do not require any belief in the ruler's unique personal qualification, but are inextricably linked to material incentives and rewards."[60] In other words, patrimonialism is a system of rulership built on networks of patron-client relationships.[61] Weber does not isolate patrimonialism from other forms of rulership. In particular, he argues that rational-legal rulership, which is bound by rules and bureaucratic organization, and patrimonial rulership are *not* mutually exclusive. In Andrew Nathan's words: "The hierarchy and established communications and authority flow of the existing organization provides a kind of trellis upon which the complex faction is able to extend its own informal, personal loyalties and relations."[62]

59. For Max Weber's discussion of patrimonialism, see *Economy and Society*, 1006–1110.

60. Roth, "Personal Rulership, Patrimonialism, and Empire Building."

61. Patron-client relationships are usually defined as distinctly personal relationships that involve direct exchanges between participants, which are usually mutually profitable but unequal. For a bibliography of literature on patron-client relations, see S. N. Eisenstadt and Louis Roniger, "Patron-Client Relations as a Model of Structuring Social Exchange."

62. Nathan, "A Factional Model," 44.

The strength of formal organization in Leninist states makes extensive patrimonialism inevitable.[63] In post-Mao China an unending stream of media "exposés," denunciations from the central leadership, and trenchant literary commentaries leave no doubt that "webs" of personal relationships often displace the formal Party hierarchy and that individual Party members often allow private gain to dilute the Party's larger purposes. In part, this is a remnant of China's traditional society. It may also be consciously fostered as an attempt to build legitimacy, but the frailty of this kind of legitimacy makes this a strategy of last resort.[64] Patrimonialism is also a result of the structure of the state. The comprehensive hierarchical organization of Leninist states enables the Party to control access to social mobility, including education, employment, and promotion. Because Chinese organization limits lateral movement—that is, peasants cannot easily move to a city or even to a more prosperous district, and workers cannot easily look for a job with another factory—most people find themselves dependent on individual supervisors; this inevitably creates opportunities for leaders to use their official rulership for personal advantage.[65] In addition, rigid planning and supply systems mean that surpluses and scarcities abound, with informal interpersonal ties being a primary equilibrating mechanism. While these patrimonial results of Leninist institutions are inadvertent in the sense

63. For evidence of patrimonial politics in the USSR, see Konstantin Simis, *USSR: The Corrupt Society,* and Wayne Di Franceisco and Zvi Gitelman, "Soviet Political Culture." Di Franceisco and Gitelman argue that a substantial majority of Soviet citizens find bribery and "personalized relationships" the most effective means of effecting political outcomes and relate this to the structure of Leninist systems. For Poland, see Andrew Smolar, "The Rich and the Powerful." For an excellent discussion of Romania with broad theoretical implications, see Jowitt, "An Organizational Approach." For a discussion of Bulgaria that contains rich examples of patrimonial politics, see Georgi Markov, *The Truth That Killed.*

64. Many people have pointed out that patron-client relationships can be a means of building legitimacy. However, the type of patronage in China and other Leninist states destroys legitimacy. Leninist states institutionalize systems of privilege for ranking cadres, such as restricted shops, special distribution of scarce consumer goods, etc. In Poland, as other bases of legitimacy deteriorated, Gierek made ample use of this kind of patronage to recruit loyal followers. (See Smolar, "Rich and Powerful.") However, this official Leninist patronage, as well as unofficial corruption, is available primarily to those who already have power and position. For example, the child of a ranking cadre is far more likely to have strings to pull to obtain favorable employment and housing than is an ordinary person. Faced with fundamental inequalities of power and privilege, it is only natural for ordinary people to question the nature of the system and the motives of leaders. The net result is a deep and widespread cynicism. Edward Friedman is very good at capturing typical Chinese reaction. See Friedman, "Three Leninist Paths Within a Socialist Conundrum."

65. Walder, "Communist Neo-Traditionalism."

that they were not intended by original theorists or founders, they are so pervasive that they must be considered an integral aspect of Leninist rulership.

It is now possible to describe the pattern of rulership in Leninist states. In general, the central leadership of Leninist states has the autonomy to establish goals and policies. Potential interest groups cannot form autonomous organizations to articulate universalistic political demands, and consequently their influence on policy formation is restricted. This does not mean, however, that power is effectively centralized or that society is without any means of responding to state initiatives. Individuals and particularistic interests often request and gain exemptions from the implementation of the center's chosen policies.[66] Over time this results in extensive networks of patron-client ties that blunt the leadership's ability to implement policies. The leadership may respond with top-to-bottom efforts to strengthen rational-legal rulership, but inasmuch as this reinforces the organizational monopoly that led to patrimonialism in the first place, it will tend to be self-defeating. Alternatively, the leadership may turn to charismatic revivals, but inasmuch as charisma provides no basis for day-to-day administration, neither will it provide a long-term solution. In Kenneth Jowitt's terms, Soviet-style systems are "neo-traditional," endlessly generating rational-legal reforms that are inevitably overcome by a patrimonial environment.[67]

A critical reader will observe that the two central ideas in this book—the autonomy of Leninist states and the importance of patrimonial rulership—are in some ways contradictory. In particular, with the decline of terror and the routinization of patrimonial rulership, clients at all levels develop fixed expectations and, in some ways, are established as entrenched interests. Conversely, high-level leaders often find that their policies are effectively sabotaged by the passive resistance of their own bureaucracy, which in turn forms a check on their autonomy.

The apparent loss of autonomy occasioned by institutionalized patrimonialism is in part relative and in part a shift in power from individual leaders to the state as an institution. First, the very high degree of autonomy exercised by Stalin during the purges or by Mao during the Cultural Revolution is inherently unstable and cannot be sus-

---

66. James Scott argues that similar dynamics lead to political corruption in authoritarian Thailand. See *Comparative Political Corruption*, 162.

67. Jowitt, "Soviet Neo-Traditionalism."

tained. Purges, land reforms, and violent campaigns cannot follow each other in endless succession. Even after this period has passed, *most* of the time state power holders in Leninist states have more autonomy than leaders in other kinds of states. Second, the routinization of patrimonial rulership means that central leaders do lose some autonomy, but it does not include the rise of an active and autonomous civil society that can challenge central leaders through institutional channels. The key relationships are vertical relationships. Society remains segmented along vertical lines, and within each vertical segment most relationships are inherently unequal. Third, and most important, the institutionalization of a patronage system makes state institutions more impervious to change, whether directed by leaders or demanded by society. As the coming chapters on strengthening socialist law, electing deputies to people's congresses, and Party rectification will demonstrate, Leninist state institutions have been able to passively resist and transform critical reforms.

CONCLUSION

It is often said that liberals have a better theory of institutions than Marxists, but scholars who study contemporary Chinese politics seldom ask why. A. J. Polan traces this problem to Lenin's *State and Revolution*.[68] He argues that the lack of democracy in contemporary socialist states is not a result of neglecting the "libertarian" arguments of *State and Revolution*, but to the contrary, it is a direct result of Lenin's concept of democracy. Polan charges Lenin with two fundamental mistakes: misunderstanding the problem of modern bureaucracy and proposing an inadequate alternative to parliamentary democracy.

Lenin fundamentally misunderstood the nature of modern bureaucracy. Lenin believed that modernization simplified administrative procedures and resulted in less specialization. He wrote: "Accounting and control . . . have been *simplified* by capitalism to the utmost, till they have become the extraordinarily simple operations of watching, recording and issuing receipts, within the reach of anybody who can read and write and knows the first four rules of arithmetic."[69] Moreover, as Polan points out, Lenin ascribed the propensity of bureau-

68. Polan, *Lenin and the End of Politics.*
69. Lenin, *State and Revolution*, 83–84 (Lenin's emphasis).

cracies to displace political leadership to the material greed of individual bureaucrats. This led Lenin to believe that bureaucratic domination could be checked by limiting the wages of functionaries and subjecting them to recall at any time. While the former remedy is largely irrelevant, the latter is more likely to make bureaucrats dependent on politicians and to result in a more corrupt and inefficient bureaucracy.

In contrast, Weber understood that the strength of modern bureaucracy lay in its ability to coordinate the expertise of a range of specialists, and that the threat of bureaucratic domination originated in this same expertise. Weber's solution to the problem of bureaucracy, which he admitted was only a partial solution to an insoluble problem, was a strong system of parliamentary inquiry, particularly one in which parliamentary committees would have the ability to establish their own expertise.[70]

Lenin also failed to grasp the potential for parliamentary democracy. He stated that socialism involves the "conversion of representative institutions from mere 'talking shops' into working bodies."[71] Polan points out that Lenin not only criticized the ineffectual parliaments of the early twentieth century, but rejected the division of executive and legislative branches of government. Lenin wrote: "Representative institutions remain, but parliamentarism as a special system, as a division of labour between the legislative and the executive functions, as a privileged position for the deputies, *no longer exists.*"[72] Polan points out that according to Lenin, "The elected deputies are to be civil servants, ministers and representatives of their constituents at one and the same time. They have to make the laws, carry them out *and* criticize them. . . . Further, of course, and the implications here are major, there is no conceptual space for a parliamentary *opposition.*"[73]

In Lenin's argument this is possible, first, because administration is simple work that any educated elected representative can do, and second, because Lenin has at his disposal a "true" politics that demonstrates the essential unity of the working class such that any

---

70. See Weber, "Parliament and Government in a Reconstructed Germany," in Weber, *Economy and Society,* 1381–1462. For a comparison of Lenin and Weber that reaches a conclusion in striking contrast to Polan's, see Erik Olin Wright, "To Control or to Smash Bureaucracy."

71. Lenin, *State and Revolution,* 40.

72. Ibid., 41 (Lenin's emphasis); see Polan, *Lenin,* 79–82.

73. Polan, *Lenin,* 82–83 (Polan's emphasis).

opposition is an expression of an enemy counterrevolutionary class that does not have the right to be heard. This is in turn based on the reduction of politics to economics. According to Lenin, since all workers have the same role in the economy, they have the same economic interests, and therefore they have identical political interests and can be served by one political center and one political truth.

Polan concludes that because Lenin has neither an understanding of what bureaucracy is (or how to control it) nor an understanding of parliamentary democracy, states like China and the Soviet Union, which were set up with Leninist goals in mind, end up with neither a rational bureaucracy nor a democratic parliament. Instead of a rational-legal bureaucracy, politics and administration are fused in an inefficient, often corrupt, and poorly supervised bureaucracy that bears too much similarity to the czarist or Confucian bureaucracies that the revolutions were waged to eliminate. Instead of a parliament where elected representatives meet to bargain over the allocation of resources, Leninist parliamentarians meet to reaffirm the wisdom of slogans that leaders ritualistically proclaim to be derived from the eternal truths of Marxism-Leninism.

Lenin's arguments have not withstood the test of time. In China major tenets of Lenin's argument have been rejected even by the leaders of China's Leninist Party. There is widespread recognition that efficient administration requires highly trained experts who must be protected from political interference. The leadership has also proclaimed the importance of separating the Party from government, again in order to separate politics from administration. Reformers also agree that common membership in the working class still leaves room for conflict and contradictions "among the people." Moreover, reformers are committed to a more open parliamentary system, with real inquiries and real debates.

However, neither dissatisfaction with the status quo nor a theoretical critique of Lenin gives reformers, leaders though they may be, the ability to make a decisive break with the Leninist tradition. Lenin's *State and Revolution* may have been mistaken, but the institutions created by Leninist political parties are very real. They structure the thought and activity of all the citizens of Leninist states. They have created a social and political logic that must change, but that finds change very difficult.

CHAPTER ONE

The Shanghai Commune and the Nanjing Incident

Two significant incidents took place, one in Shanghai at the beginning of the Cultural Revolution and one in Nanjing at the end. The following discussion of these events will make three main points, all of which are about the autonomy of China's Leninist state. First, both of these incidents demonstrate that even when China's Leninist state was in its most ideological and violent phase, society still had an autonomous, albeit limited and fragile, existence. In Shanghai and Nanjing special circumstances enabled previously suppressed social groups to form ad hoc organizations and to articulate long-standing grievances. Leninist states may be able to suppress civil society temporarily, but they are not able to absorb or eliminate civil society. To the contrary, these events suggest that the most important conflict in Leninist states is between the state and society. Second, both of these incidents demonstrate how autonomous Leninist states can be. State power holders in Shanghai had the capacity to overwhelm their social opposition, and in Nanjing they literally mobilized the whole of society to support the official agenda and crush the autonomous opposition. Third, these incidents demonstrated the need for reforms. The Cultural Revolution was the culmination of a coercive and violent revolution imposed from above. Before state power was consolidated, China's Leninist leaders sought to reshape Chinese society and readily applied coercive force to this goal. While society was substantially transformed, the revolution from above also created a widening gulf between state and society. In the long run, this left the state isolated and vulnerable. Reforms are a necessary attempt to establish a more stable and harmonious relationship between state and society.

Theda Skocpol argues that social revolutions in general produce stronger states. Revolutions won by Leninist parties and armies have resulted in especially strong and autonomous states.[1] Though the duration and sequence of events was different, in both China and Russia Leninist parties organized armies and fought civil wars to establish and consolidate a new state. Desperate measures were adopted to win the war. In Russia the Bolsheviks seized grain at gunpoint, causing famines and arousing the peasants' lasting enmity, and sacrificed their only base of support, the urban working class, to the enemies' guns. Local governments established by the Red Army were too frequently imposed from above, not controlled from below. The outcome was a well-armed hierarchical state all too accustomed to adopting violent measures to deal with its own citizens.[2] In China, some theories argue, the need to cultivate peasant support during the lengthy period of civil and international war and the peasant origins of many cadres gave rise to the Yan'an Spirit and linked the Party to the peasantry. The experience of Cambodia's Khmer Rouge and Peru's Sendero Luminoso indicates, however, that even Leninist party-armies that are extremely violent and repressive toward the peasants whom they are theoretically liberating can prosper and win victories.[3] As Raya Dunayevskaya points out, there is an enormous difference between strikes and demonstrations organized by urban workers and Mao's military Marxism.[4] Although the CCP did build a large rural organization, it did not establish institutions whereby peasants could effectively voice political demands, let alone veto policy initiatives or choose national leaders. In both these revolutions, victory was won not by a class but by an armed political party.

In both China and Russia the Party's victory in revolutionary war proved a prelude to a violent revolution from above. Leninist states

1. Skocpol, *States and Social Revolution*. In a recent article, Skocpol argues that what Leninist states are really best at is mobilizing populations to fight wars. See "Social Revolutions and Mass Military Mobilization."

2. I have learned much from Mary McAuley, but she bears no responsibility for what I say here. See her *Politics and the Soviet Union*.

3. Ben Kiernan reports that little is known about the Khmer Rouge prior to their seizure of power, but his descriptions of their base areas makes them seem more like concentration camps. See *How Pol Pot Came to Power*.

4. Dunayevskaya, *Marxism and Freedom*, 299–316.

are able to impose especially violent and thorough revolutions from above. In other types of states, revolutions from above have been limited. Ellen Kay Trimberger argues that authoritarian states in Turkey, Japan, and Peru were checked by the remaining power of elites and the fear of unleashing a peasant uprising.[5] In Russia and China the old elites lost their property, and millions of people lost their lives. Land reform, a particular stumbling block for other revolutions from above, was transformed into gruesome oppression.[6] In the Soviet Union collectivization led to the deaths of fourteen and a half million peasants.[7] In China collectivization led to the Great Leap Forward and a famine in which ten to thirty million people died.[8] These catastrophes paved the way for assaults on other sectors of society. Anton Antonov-Ovseyenko estimates that at the height of the purges, one Soviet citizen in twenty was in prison or in the camps, whereas in Uruguay, the worst of Latin America's bureaucratic-authoritarian regimes, only one in four hundred was imprisoned.[9] In China, instead of repudiating the Great Leap Forward, Mao instigated the Cultural Revolution.

The Leninist revolution from above was made possible by what Ezra Vogel calls "the political conquest of society."[10] It was guided by an ideology that was imposed on society. Concepts like "class struggle" legitimated the designation of portions of society as enemies and absolved the revolutionaries from any moral obligations to them.[11] Franz Schurmann points out that the ideas would not have

5. Trimberger, *Revolution from Above*. Nora Hamilton makes a similar argument on the limits of state autonomy in Mexico after the Mexican revolution in *The Limits of State Autonomy: Post-Revolutionary Mexico*.

6. For a comparison of Soviet and Chinese policy toward peasants, see Thomas P. Bernstein, "Stalinism, Famine, and Chinese Peasants." See also Alvin Gouldner, "Stalinism: A Study of Internal Colonialism."

7. Robert Conquest, *The Harvest of Sorrow: Soviet Collectivization and the Terror-Famine*, 301.

8. See, for example, Judith Bannister and Samuel H. Preston, "Mortality in China," and Roderick MacFarquhar, *The Origins of the Cultural Revolution*, vol. 2, *The Great Leap Forward 1958–1960*, esp. 326–36.

9. Antonov-Ovseyenko, *The Time of Stalin: Portrait of a Tyranny*, 210–13.

10. Vogel, *Canton Under Communism: Programs and Politics in a Provincial Capital, 1949–1968*, passim and esp. 350–54.

11. Hu Ping, a candidate for People's Deputy to a local people's congress, commented on the irony of a state able to determine arbitrarily the boundaries of society: "Imagine: If a government pledges its allegiance to its people and yet it also has the right to call its supporters the 'people' and its detractors 'non-people,' isn't it a logic of sheer self-contradiction? If this logic were allowed to stand, there would be no government in the world not enjoying the whole hearted support of its people!" See Hu Ping, "On Freedom of Speech."

had the same impact without the organization to implement them.[12] Victory in revolution meant that Party organization could be extended throughout society. The Party established control of the major means of production, control of mass media, representation in neighborhoods and villages, a pervasive network of secret police, and so forth.

This conquest proved a hollow victory. Leninist states removed many of the institutions through which an autonomous civil society formulates and articulates ideas, including a critical media, independent political parties, and autonomous universities. The absence of these institutions clouds any understanding of society's perception of the state. Some observers, including many Americans who visited China in the years prior to Mao's death, took the state's representation of society at face value and assumed that society was happily integrated with the state. Others, such as Hannah Arendt, argued that society is "atomized" and unable to resist.[13] Both these extremes underestimate the potential for conflict between Leninist states and society—just as many Americans were surprised by the Tiananmen demonstrations of 1976, Hannah Arendt was hard pressed to explain the Hungarian insurrection.[14] The incidents described in this chapter demonstrate the depth of conflict between state and society in China and how many other Leninist states have been periodically shaken by these kinds of convulsions.

In practice, the violent and coercive politics of China's Leninist state alienated society and isolated the state. Antonio Gramsci likened the process of revolution from above "to colonial wars or to old wars of conquest, in which the victorious army occupies, or proposes to occupy, permanently all or part of the conquered territory."[15] Even though an occupying power, or the state, may possess physical mastery, the struggle must also be waged in the realm of ideas. From Gramsci's perspective, as long as the relationship between state and society is essentially coercive, the state "dominates" society. Only when the state's new ideas permeate society and become common

12. Schurmann, *Ideology and Organization in Communist China.*
13. Arendt, *The Origins of Totalitarianism.*
14. See the epilogue to *The Origins of Totalitarianism.*
15. Gramsci, *Prison Notebooks,* 229. In Gramsci's study of Italian history he argued that the Italian bourgeoisie was too weak to unify Italy or to lead a bourgeois revolution as a class and thus had to depend on the leadership of the state. He labeled this process "passive revolution" or "progressive Caesarism" and likened this to a "war of position," which referred to the trench warfare of World War I (108).

sense has the revolution really been won. This is what Gramsci calls hegemony.[16] A dominant state is both weaker and stronger than a hegemonic state. A hegemonic state may appear weak inasmuch as it is limited by society, but precisely because it is not isolated from society and is surrounded by a supportive civil society, it may be very resilient. For example, even in the face of grave threats such as the Depression, the American state was unshaken.[17] In contrast, the Chinese state was not limited by society in the short term but has had to surmount several serious crises to survive.

In sum, Leninist states are very powerful but are nonetheless incapable of achieving the goals of their founders. In its original guise, China's Leninist state was capable of instituting dramatic social change but was not capable of building hegemony. Eventually, the frailty of a state based on domination would become clear even to state power holders, and they would be forced to institute reforms in search of a new relationship between state and society.

THE CULTURAL REVOLUTION

The Shanghai Commune and the Nanjing Incident occurred in the context of the Cultural Revolution. In general, the Cultural Revolution, like Stalin's purges, can be seen as part of the Leninist revolution from above. There were important differences between Stalin and Mao, but their purposes were not so very different. Both sought to concentrate power and to "purify" organization. In both cases, Party members and the Party as an institution suffered. Neither established democratic institutions. The secret police were the beneficiaries of the purges, whereas the Cultural Revolution allowed for the creation of grass-roots organization through which civil society was temporarily able to express opposition to central authorities. This had important consequences and revealed much about the relationship between the Chinese state and Chinese society. Nonetheless, the mass organizations were soon dismantled, and the Cultural Revolution culminated with state leaders who, like Stalin, glorified the use of state power to impose a ruthless dictatorship.

16. Gramsci uses these terms in conjunction with class struggle and, like other Marxists, views an autonomous state as an anomalous and temporary situation. Hence, for him, "new ideas," though introduced by a party or embodied in a state, are ultimately the ideas of a rising class. I argue that the Chinese state is not identified with any class, which may be one of the reasons it has difficulty in building hegemony.
17. See Gramsci, 229–39.

There is a large literature that argues that Mao was critical of Stalin and Leninist states, and that the Cultural Revolution was his attempt to promote a truly socialist and democratic alternative.[18] I will make three counterarguments: first, the Cultural Revolution began with an attempt to impose more rigid ideological discipline; second, the Cultural Revolution was premised on the cult of Mao, which stifled real democracy; and third, the Cultural Revolution involved mass participation, but this was manipulation, not democracy.

By many accounts the Cultural Revolution began with the publication of Yao Wenyuan's criticism of Wu Han's play "Hai Rui Dismissed From Office." Arguments that the Cultural Revolution was an attack on the autonomy of the state argue that Yao's article was an attack on the bureaucracy on behalf of the "revolutionary" masses. Yao criticized the play for attacking Mao, arguing that Hai Rui, who had been wrongly dismissed by an emperor after speaking out on behalf of ordinary people, was a metaphor for Peng Dehuai, who had been dismissed by Mao for criticizing the Great Leap Forward. Thus Wu and his associates in the Party were charged with attacking Mao and the revolution. Yao did not mention that because Peng's warning was not heeded, tens of millions of people died. Nor did he mention that the play was first performed in 1959, before Peng had been criticized and while Mao was also praising Hai Rui.[19] Yao and Mao argued that despite the famine, anyone who criticized the Great Leap or anyone who wished to provoke even an allegorical discussion of Mao's mistakes was an "enemy of the people." Yao and Mao sought a politics of fear and conformity, not democracy.[20]

18. According to this interpretation, sometime between 1962 and 1964 Mao determined that various leading Party figures were implementing opportunistic economic policies that would lead to the restoration of capitalism and therefore represented a capitalist class inside the Communist Party that was threatening to take control. Given this analysis, Mao allegedly expected that a period of revolutionary conflict would create a new proletarian culture, and he therefore encouraged various social groups to attack the institutions of the old order to root out capitalist influences. Works taking this line are very numerous, but two outstanding examples are Charles Bettelheim, "The Great Leap Backward," and Bill Brugger, *China: Radicalism to Revisionism 1962–79*.

19. See Roderick MacFarquhar, *The Origins of the Cultural Revolution, vol. 2, The Great Leap Forward 1958–60*, 207–12. MacFarquhar suggests that Mao himself may have asked Wu to write the play.

20. By the time he published his article criticizing Wu Han, Yao Wenyuan already had over a decade's experience in criticizing and censoring intellectuals. Yao had first been published criticizing Hu Feng in 1955. He took an active role in the Anti-Rightist Campaign of 1957, criticizing Ding Ling among others. In the early 1960s some intellectuals again began to push the limits of Party censorship, and Yao Wenyuan again

Mao encouraged a cult of personality, which eliminated any chance of democratic politics. According to the cult, Mao was not an ordinary human being. His portrait was prominently displayed in all homes and public places, and people were expected to stand before it and "receive instructions in the morning and make a report in the evening." People wore badges displaying Mao's image,[21] said grace in his name before meals,[22] and danced ritual dances in his name.[23] In art and prose he was often equated with the sun. Beijing Radio gave him the following tribute:

> All rivers flow into the seas and every Red heart turns toward the sun. O Chairman Mao, Chairman Mao, the mountains are tall, but not as tall as the blue sky. Rivers are deep, but not as deep as the ocean. Lamps are bright, but not as bright as the sun and moon. Your kindness is taller than the sky, deeper than the ocean, and brighter than the sun and moon. It is possible to count the stars in the highest heavens, but it is impossible to count your contributions to mankind.[24]

Political discussion devolved to memorizing and repeating isolated phrases from Mao's *Selected Works*. Severe sanctions awaited those who violated the norms of the cult. The post-Mao press, post-Mao literature, and many Chinese people have related incidents where individuals were incarcerated for several years or even executed for

---

joined the attack on the side of stricter controls (interview with Shanghai cadre, 1980). Ba Jin described how many intellectuals feared people like Yao: "I am a little afraid of those who, holding a hoop in one hand and a club in the other, go everywhere looking for men with mistakes. . . . If somebody lets them hear some new songs or see some new writings to which they are not accustomed, they will become furious with him and bring the club down right on his head" (cited in Lynn T. White III, "Leadership in Shanghai, 1955–69," 334; see also 335–36).

21. In Liu Xinwu's short story "Awake, My Brother," a young man pins his Mao badge through the skin of his chest in a futile attempt to demonstrate his dedication to Mao despite his suspect class background. Interviews in Nanjing suggest this was not just a literary device. Liu's story appears in *The Wounded* (Hong Kong: Joint Publishers, 1979), 179–203.

22. A Nanjing cadre told of an episode where, traveling to another province where the grace was said before a different meal than was the custom in his province, he began to eat as others began to intone a "Mao-grace" and only narrowly escaped serious trouble.

23. According to one account, even stewardesses on airplanes danced "Mao-dances" for the benefit of the passengers. See George Urban (ed.), *The "Miracles" of Chairman Mao*, 137.

24. Broadcast 6 December 1967. The Chinese press attributed surprising powers to those who correctly studied and applied "Mao Zedong Thought." His "Thought" enabled deaf-mutes to speak and blind people to see, and brought back the dead (Urban, *The "Miracles" of Chairman Mao*, 13, 20, 29).

seemingly trivial mistakes.[25] The cult of Mao can hardly be considered an attack on the autonomy of the state. Politics was reduced to competitive flattery and fawning, and any opportunity for critical debate was obliterated.

Finally, many people have argued that mass participation in the Cultural Revolution indicates a form of democracy. But as Svetozar Stojanovic points out, participation is not equivalent to democracy:

> A great number of people have been very impressed by the participation of the people, especially the youth, in political actions, campaigns, and clashes in China. But the critical mind can distinguish political participation from political freedom. The manipulation of mass dissatisfaction on the part of an untouchable charismarch [Mao] has nothing in common with democracy.[26]

One of the standard political strategies of the Cultural Revolution was for ranking leaders to covertly encourage social groups to attack rival leaders. Unfortunately, the social groups formed in these struggles made few lasting gains and were forcefully suppressed when they no longer served the interests of individual leaders. Red Guard Dai Hsiao-ai shares Stojanovic's conclusions:

> In my opinion, all of the factionalism, fighting, the shifting alliances, and the different positions arose because the instructions from Chairman Mao just didn't work. . . . His statements were so general that everybody, even those who opposed him, could find something to justify his own position. . . . Naturally it occurred to me that vagueness was a tactic deliberately employed to see how different people would react. I didn't really believe that this was true, but because I had a suspicion it might be, I began to like him even less. It meant that he was playing god and actually causing people to die so that he could maintain his power.[27]

25. Chen Jo-hsi's short story "Chairman Mao Is a Rotten Egg" relates the story of a family whose future is nearly ruined by a child who shouts "Chairman Mao is a rotten egg!" even though the child is too young to understand the meaning of the consequences of this act. (See Chen Jo-hsi, *The Execution of Mayor Yin* [Bloomington: Indiana University Press, 1978], 37–66). Students in Nanjing told of an old woman who went to labor reform for accidentally having wrapped fish in newspaper bearing Mao's picture instead of having sent the picture to the Red Guards for ceremonial disposal.

26. Stojanovic, *In Search of Democracy in Socialism*, 75.

27. From Gordon A. Bennett and Ronald Montaperto, *Red Guard*, 212–13. Lin Biao makes the same point: "Today he [Mao] uses this force to attack that force; tomorrow he uses that force to attack this force. Today he uses sweet words and honeyed talk to those whom he entices, and tomorrow he puts them to death for some fabricated crimes. Those who are his guests today will be his prisoners tomorrow. Looking

In sum, Mao's critique of the state was not a rejection of the use of centralized political power in the construction of socialism. Like Rousseau, Mao believed that freedom is the recognition of necessity, not an absence of constraint, and that enlightenment requires a guiding force.[28] Contrary to liberalism, Mao did not believe that there was a contradiction between centralized political power and democracy, as long as political power was leading society toward the "necessary" future.[29] The Cultural Revolution was an effort to purge the corrupted and to promote the virtuous, but not to diffuse political power. While mass participation in the Cultural Revolution may have contributed to the emergence of independent and autonomous democrats in post-Mao China, this was hardly what Mao intended.[30]

THE SHANGHAI COMMUNE

In January 1967 Zhang Chunqiao closed a violent period in Shanghai's Cultural Revolution with an unsuccessful attempt to establish a commune. In these events, first, long-standing social interests previously suppressed by the state took advantage of a conflict among the leadership to organize and articulate their interests, and second, Cultural Revolution leaders ruthlessly reimposed the state's domination. Events in Shanghai in the autumn of 1966 and the January Storm of 1967 were replete with revolutionary imagery: mass organizations were established and proclaimed popular and unpopular political demands, demonstrated, organized massive strikes, and struggled violently against each other and the forces of order. At first examination, the Shanghai Commune appeared to be an attack on an autonomous

---

back at the history of the past few decades, [do you see] any one whom he had supported initially who has not finally been handed a political death sentence?" From Michael Y. M. Kau, *The Lin Piao Affair*, 89.

28. Benjamin Schwartz has described similarities between Mao and Rousseau. See "The Reign of Virtue: Some Broad Perspectives on Leader and Party in the Cultural Revolution."

29. Mao stated: "Within the ranks of our people, democracy stands in relation to centralism and freedom to discipline. They are two conflicting aspects of a single entity, contradictory as well as united, and we should not one-sidedly emphasize one to the detriment of the other. Within the ranks of the people, we cannot do without freedom, nor can we do without democracy, nor can we do without centralism" (*The Political Thought of Mao Tse-Tung*, ed. Stuart Schram, 307).

30. For a strong comparison of Mao and Stalin that deserves a wide readership, see Wang Xizhe, *Mao Zedong and The Cultural Revolution*.

and exploitative bureaucracy and an analogue to the Paris Commune, which Marx and Lenin argued was a step toward the "withering away" of the state.[31]

The Shanghai Commune was not devised to limit the arbitrary use of state power. First, Zhang Chunqiao, the commune's leader, was far more closely associated with the state center in Beijing than with social forces in Shanghai. The commune was conceived and abandoned at the discretion of leaders of the state, not least Mao, and not as a result of the desires of the mass organizations or their members. Second, while various social groups were mobilized by Mao's associates during the course of the struggle, pressed their own political demands, and even "revealed the latent hatred of the masses against those who were governing them,"[32] despite their apparent victory, Zhang and his associates used the state's coercive apparatus to silence voices and suppress their organizations. In sum, events in Shanghai revealed that within the structures of China's Leninist state, society still had its own opinions and, given the chance, was eager to fight for change, but that the state would remain dominant in the end.

From the outset of the Cultural Revolution, Zhang Chunqiao's power was derived primarily from his relationships with Mao and Mao's close associates. Both Zhang and his main rival in Shanghai, the incumbent mayor, Cao Diqiu, had been in the administration of the former mayor, Ke Qingshi. Ke was an associate of Mao's, a member of the Political Bureau, first secretary of the Party's East China Bureau, and mayor of Shanghai. When he died unexpectedly in 1965, his regional posts were divided between Cao and Zhen Peixian, and neither succeeded Ke to the Political Bureau.[33] Through his support for Ke's and Mao's attacks on intellectuals, Zhang Chunqiao received a series of promotions leading to full membership in the Municipal Party Committee and leadership of the Shanghai Party's propaganda department.[34] In these positions, Zhang was nominally Cao's subordinate, but he soon rose past Cao. His work to create "proletarian" culture in Shanghai attracted the attention of Jiang Qing (Mao's wife), and Zhang's direct connection with the highest levels in the

31. See, for example, Jean Daubier, *A History of the Chinese Revolution*, 115–34; Jean Esmein, *The Chinese Cultural Revolution*, 179–90; and Victor Nee, "Revolution and Bureaucracy: Shanghai in the Cultural Revolution."
32. Maurice Meisner, *Mao's China*, 318.
33. Lynn T. White III, "Leadership in Shanghai, 1955–69," 346.
34. Andrew Walder, *Chang Ch'un-Chiao and Shanghai's January Revolution*, 7–8. This is by far the best available study of the events in Shanghai.

Party were confirmed when his subordinate Yao Wenyuan published his essay criticizing Wu Han on behalf of Mao. On May 16, 1966, the Central Committee issued a circular that purged Peng Zhen, mayor of Beijing and in charge of the Cultural Revolution (claiming he was the "black hand" behind Wu Han and other writers "not loyal to Chairman Mao") and established a new Cultural Revolution Group directly under the Standing Committee of the Party's Political Bureau. Zhang and Yao were named members.[35] For the remainder of Cao's ill-fated administration, Zhang was not Cao's subordinate but a representative of the Party center. Cao's eventual defeat at Zhang's hands was more a purge from above than a revolution from below.

While attacks on provincial-level leaders like Cao made the Cultural Revolution seem like an attack on the state, they succeeded primarily because the attackers had better connections with Mao than the attacked. Leaders like Cao were victims of the violent and dishonest politics engineered by Mao and his allies. Cao initially conformed to the policies that Mao suggested and thereby unleashed forces that eventually deposed him. For example, in August 1966 he stated: "We must rebel against all those in power who take the capitalist road. We must knock down all the reactionary authorities of the bourgeoisie. . . . We must oppose all those who repress revolutionary acts."[36]

Cao's first serious crisis arose when two of his subordinates were attacked. If he defended them he would seem guilty by association, but it would be equally dangerous not to defend his own administration. Ironically, one of these first victims was Yang Xiguang, acting head of the propaganda department since Zhang Chunqiao's promotion to Beijing.[37] One can only speculate that had Zhang not moved to higher ground, he too might have been caught in the current. The contrast between Zhang and Cao suggests that as China's politics grew increasingly brutal, survival depended more on being in the right position and knowing the right people than on commitment to any ideals.

35. Chi Hsin, *The Case of the Gang of Four,* 6–7. "May 16" became a Cultural Revolution symbol.

36. Walder, *Shanghai's January Revolution,* 18. Walder states that from the very beginning of Cao's term as mayor, he endorsed Ke Qingshi's policies and "went to the core of what was later to become known as the Maoist line . . . stress[ing] that class struggle did not end with the Socialist Education Movement and that continued ideological revolutionization was a necessity," arguing that such transformation would improve production, but that this was not the primary goal (10).

37. Neale Hunter, *Shanghai Journal,* 31–37.

Zhang's attack on Cao gave previously suppressed social groups an opportunity to organize. Contract workers or temporary workers, whose organizations had a major role in Cao's downfall, are an excellent example. Contract workers were relatively underprivileged in comparison with regular workers. Regular workers not only were virtually guaranteed lifetime employment, but also received various fringe benefits from their unions, including medical services, access to credit, pensions, and some special disbursements of food, clothing, consumer goods, and even cash for special purposes, such as a child's tuition.[38] Contract workers were hired for a limited period of time or a specific job, lacked security, were paid less, and enjoyed few fringe benefits. The system had redeeming features inasmuch as many contract workers were hired from the countryside or suburban communes and gained higher wages and access to the city. In addition, the localities that contracted out their services gained income and perhaps technology.[39] Moreover, their temporary status provided a flexible alternative to permanent employees. Nevertheless, contract work was a disappointing second choice for urban youths. Consequently, while contract labor decreased the inequality between the city and the countryside, it also created an urban underclass that eagerly seized a chance to protest.

Mobilized contract workers were a far greater threat to Cao than to Zhang, if only because of their different careers. Owing to Cao's tenure in the city's economic departments and his support for state policies to increase the use of contract workers, he was a natural target for the contract workers, who would rather have become permanent workers.[40] In the early 1960s he stated: "Factories and enterprises must employ few workers who are permanent. More workers should be temporary."[41] Zhang Chunqiao's work in propaganda and

38. In addition, unions controlled access to technical schools crucial to advancement to better jobs, and activism in the union was a stepping-stone to either Party or factory administration. Before the Cultural Revolution, unions even managed resorts and arranged group tours. See Joyce Kalgren, "Social Welfare and China's Industrial Workers," and Paul Harper, "Trade Union Cultivation of Workers."

39. Contract labor also had the advantage of being cheaper and more flexible for factory managers. See Current Scene 5 (15 Mar. 1968); and Lynn T. White III, "Workers' Politics in Shanghai." For a discussion of contemporary rural contract workers, see Marc Blecher, "Peasant Labour for Urban Industry: Temporary Contract Labour, Urban-Rural Balance, and Class Relations in a Chinese County."

40. Between the end of the Great Leap and 1964, state policy called for expanded use of contract workers. See Current Scene 5 (15 Mar. 1968), and Lynn T. White III, "Workers' Politics in Shanghai."

41. White, "Workers' Politics," 111.

culture had not required him to take a stand on these issues. More-over, as mayor of Shanghai, Cao would be hurt by disorder or violence, whereas the same would create opportunities for Zhang.

Zhang and his allies encouraged the contract workers and others to press their demands. They supported the formation of Revolutionary Rebel Workers General Headquarters, a mass organization that included a large contingent of contract workers.[42] In the summer and early fall of 1966, Zhang was evidently involved in preparing Beijing Red Guards to enter factories and mobilize workers.[43] A million Red Guards from other localities flooded Shanghai later that fall—producing a serious strain on public services—and began to circulate through factories.[44] On November 8, 1966, a group of workers demanded that Cao recognize the new organization. Official policy, evidently endorsed by Mao, still called for workers to remain at work.[45] Cao was in a no-win situation. He could stick with policies publicly endorsed by Mao and be charged with suppressing the Cultural Revolution, or he could attempt to anticipate the next wave of the Cultural Revolution and help to turn loose another storm that would surely batter his own administration. He chose to follow official policy and refused to offer recognition or the requested subsidy. In protest, a large contingent from Workers General Headquarters commandeered a train and departed for Beijing. Cao sidetracked the train at a suburban station, where the workers remained. On November 12 Zhang Chunqiao arrived, and as an official emissary of the Cultural Revolution Group, granted Workers General Headquarters recognition in exchange for their return to Shanghai.[46] One group of

42. The high proportion of contract workers in Workers General Headquarters was confirmed in an interview with a former leading member of Workers General Headquarters.

43. Walder, *Shanghai's January Revolution*, 28.

44. Ibid., 46, and Hunter, *Shanghai Journal*, 136–37.

45. Point Fourteen of the "Sixteen Points" published in August with Mao's endorsement promoted the slogan "Grasp Revolution and Promote Production" and declared that the Cultural Revolution would enable "work in all fields to be done with greater, faster, better, and more economical results." For a translation of the "Sixteen Points" see *Selections From Chinese Mainland Press* 3761. On September 15 Zhou Enlai and Lin Biao "flatly ordered the Red Guards not to trespass in the factories or on the fields" (Walder, *Shanghai's January Revolution*, 27). On November 10, 1966, *Renmin Ribao* stated that "in industrial and mining enterprises, business units and people's communes, production decidedly cannot be stopped" (*Selections From Chinese Mainland Press* 3825:2).

46. Zhang Chunqiao's concessions violated not just the Party's public policy but also direct instructions from the Cultural Revolution Group. Cao received a telegram from Chen Boda, Mao's secretary and a member of the Cultural Revolution Group,

workers was still not satisfied and, led by Geng Jinzhang, who later
became a prominent rival of the Shanghai Commune, set off on an
unsuccessful effort to reach Beijing. Cao and the municipal Party
committee not only lost considerable prestige but were left to cope
with the turbulent consequences while Zhang returned once again to
Beijing.

Cao and the municipal Party committee created a larger mass organization, but soon learned that depth of social support mattered
less than the support of Mao and the military. The new mass organization, the Scarlet Guards, was linked to the city trade unions;[47] soon
it grew to be the city's largest mass organization.[48] However, the
ensuing violent conflict between the Scarlet Guards and Workers
General Headquarters rebounded to Cao's disadvantage.[49]

From afar, Mao and his allies continued to incite the contract
workers to press greater demands more forcefully until at last Cao
resigned. On December 26 an editorial in *Renmin Ribao* ordered back
pay for contract workers who had been laid off and approved of limited disruption of production.[50] Zhang Chunqiao's ally Jiang Qing
met with a delegation of contract workers in Beijing and called for
abolition of the contract labor system.[51] The following day Workers
General Headquarters presented Cao with a list of demands incorpo-
rating this new policy, which he promptly signed, only to face a list of

---

stating that he should stand firm and not give in to demands from Workers General
Headquarters (Hunter, 139–42; Walder, 31). When Cao protested Zhang's concessions, Chen reversed himself and refused to countermand Zhang.

47. Edward Rice, *Mao's Way*, 292.

48. Hunter, *Shanghai Journal*, 167.

49. In a typical incident, Nie Yuanzi, who had been praised by Mao for writing the
first "big-character poster" at Beijing University, arrived in Shanghai on November 25
and decried the crimes of the municipal Party committee. In the meantime, the Central
Committee had instructed lower levels to offer all student groups access to publishing
facilities. A group of Red Guards, the Red Revolutionaries, who had used the presses of
one of Shanghai's largest papers, *Liberation Daily*, to publish eight issues of their tab-
loid, now demanded that *Liberation Daily* produce 650,000 copies of Nie's accusations
and distribute them with the regular paper. When they were denied this request, they
occupied the *Liberation Daily* building, halting publication. Public sentiment seems to
have run against the occupation. Hunter reports that while there were never more than
five or six thousand people occupying the building, more than a million people demonstrated outside the building against the occupation (*Shanghai Journal*, 152–68). Despite this expression of public sentiment, Cao gave into the Red Revolutionaries'
demands. However, his decision was opposed by the *Liberation Daily* staff and the
Scarlet Guards and was not implemented.

50. *Selections From Chinese Mainland Press* 3825:1.

51. *Current Scene* 5 (15 Mar. 1968) and David and Nancy Milton, *The Wind Will
Not Subside*, 186–90.

counter demands from the Scarlet Guards. A wave of strikes known as the January Storm followed, and large amounts of money were disbursed to groups of workers from enterprise treasuries. In the face of a complete collapse of order, Cao was forced to resign. In the first week of January 1967, Zhang again arrived from Beijing to take direct charge of affairs in Shanghai.

The defeat of Cao proved to be a victory only for state power holders like Zhang and a few hangers-on and not for social groups like the contract workers. In a series of proclamations that received national attention, Zhang repeated Cao's message of some months before and ordered workers to return to production.[52] Ignoring Jiang Qing's role in legitimating contract workers' requests for back pay, Zhang argued that the monetary disbursements had been "sugar-coated bullets of the bourgeoisie" inspired by Cao, ordered workers to return any money they had received, and demanded that they cease to concern themselves with monetary issues.[53] Zhang also blocked attacks on grass-roots cadres much desired by Red Guards and others who resented the lower-level cadres' intrusions into their daily lives.[54] Zhang used force to make these policies stick. Detachments from the People's Liberation Army were dispatched to guard banks and other buildings, took over the radio station and the airfield, and broke strikes.[55]

While these measures restored some order and production, they cost Zhang his social support and created a formidable opposition. Neale Hunter, an eyewitness, reported: "Many Red Guards, especially those who belonged to the massive and famous Shanghai organizations, were bitterly disappointed at the way things turned out. They plainly felt that Zhang Chunqiao and his forces were interlopers and did not have the allegiance of the Shanghai people."[56]

The leaders of mass organizations that supported Zhang soon found themselves short of followers. For example, Wang Hongwen

52. See, for example, "Urgent Notice," in *Selections From China Mainland Press* 3867:4.
53. Point Two of the Urgent Notice stated: "Questions concerning wage adjustments, back pay and other material benefits detract from the Cultural Revolution and are to be dealt with later" (see Victor Nee, "Revolution and Bureaucracy," 235). The day after Jiang Qing had called for an end to the contract labor system, Zhou Enlai had declared that with China's limited economic resources, it was impossible to eliminate the contract labor system (*Current Scene* 5). Jiang Qing subsequently refused to meet with delegations of contract workers. On February 17 the Central Committee ordered all contract workers' organizations disbanded (Walder, 57).
54. Hunter, 248–49; also *China News Analysis* 653:2, and 654:4.
55. Walder, *Shanghai's January Revolution,* 57.
56. Hunter, 228.

used his position in Workers General Headquarters as a stepping-stone toward national political prominence, but by the end of January Workers General Headquarters was a "mere shell," devoid of popular support.[57] Other Red Guard and workers' organizations broke with Zhang. On January 27 hostile Red Guards interrogated Zhang and Yao Wenyuan for over six hours. In late January Geng Jinzhang, a leader of a former division of the Workers General Headquarters, the Workers Second Regiment, went on the offensive in an attempt to shut down what was left of Workers General Headquarters.[58] Hunter reported that they "were able to defy Zhang Chunqiao precisely because they had put down the deepest roots among the people."[59]

Despite this opposition, Zhang's connections with Mao and the support of the military enabled him to press on. On February 5, 1967, he declared the formation of the Shanghai Commune. Red Guard and worker organizations opposing Zhang were excluded from the commune, and he later admitted there had been considerable opposition.[60] His claim to represent the majority is suspect. Geng Jinzhang, whose fate I have been unable to ascertain, claimed the support of more organizations than Zhang. Moreover, many of the organizations that supported Zhang were Red Guard organizations based in Beijing, not Shanghai. Zhang had arranged, however, for the support of the People's Liberation Army. On the day the commune was proclaimed, speaking after Zhang, Liao Chenguo, commander of the Shanghai garrison of the PLA said: "The PLA units stationed in Shanghai have made all preparations. We will ruthlessly suppress anyone who dares to undermine the Shanghai People's Commune or the Proletarian Cultural Revolution."[61]

57. Hunter, 293.
58. Though Geng Jinzhang and Workers Second Regiment had not been on good terms with Zhang Chunqiao since the train incident, they had been Workers General Headquarters' most militant group.
59. Hunter, 244.
60. Zhang stated: "In February after repeated meetings, the 38 organizations recognized by all were to announce the seizure of power. To include the 38 means to have the majority of the organizations in Shanghai. All famous organizations joined and this was already better than other places. Just as the 38 organizations were ready to draft the document to establish the 'Shanghai Commune,' we discovered that another 25 organizations were also meeting to establish a 'New Shanghai Commune.' Now we faced the problem of two opposing factions. The 38 organizations were the minority and were not unified. Each called the other conservative. How do you cope with this kind of situation?" Cited in Alan P. Liu, *Political Culture and Group Conflict in China*, 64.
61. Cited in Walder, *Shanghai's January Revolution*, 61. In May 1967 Zhang was made First Political Commissar of the Nanjing Military Region, which includes Shanghai. See Chien Yu-shen, *China's Fading Revolution*, 139.

When Zhang found opponents still mounting a real challenge to his authority, he appealed to Mao, and only Mao's personal endorsement sealed his victory. Zhang literally raced representatives of Geng's group to Beijing, but the latter were not granted an interview with Mao. When Zhang returned to Shanghai on February 23, he addressed the city as Mao's personal envoy, even though Mao had vetoed the commune. He labeled Geng Jinzhang and his other opponents enemies of Mao and even made the fantastic claim that Geng was in league with Cao.[62] From beginning to end, the Shanghai Commune was directed from above, not below.

Mao endorsed Zhang Chunqiao, but he vetoed the commune. He not only told Zhang Chunqiao and Yao Wenyuan that the commune was inappropriate for China at this moment in history, but rejected the ideal of the Paris Commune. He said that it made no sense to change the names of organizations and the titles of individuals, as there would always be "heads," that "communes are too weak when it comes to suppressing counterrevolution," and that the commune model was inappropriate because there was a need for the Party as a leading force.[63]

Mao's actions demonstrated his affinity for the Leninist state system. There is no logic to the contention that he changed his mind or grew frightened and backed down after victory was at hand. He did not attempt to build democratic institutions, but sought to promote revolutionary virtue. Virtue, in this usage, refers to a charismatic quality, and charisma cannot be objectively defined or measured. So while Mao demanded an intense commitment to "revolutionary" values, such as leading an ascetic life, egalitarianism, and commitment to the collective, personal loyalty to Mao and adherence to his cult was the primary indicator of the rest of these values. The substance of virtue is not so important as the means by which it is tested and recognized, which in this case was by the arbitrary judgment of those already admitted to the charismatic community, that is, on the personal discretion of Mao and his chosen associates. Another possibility is that Mao wished to concentrate power in his own hands for largely personal purposes and cynically manipulated cadres and masses alike to achieve that end. In either case, personal loyalty to Mao or adher-

62. Various people interviewed in Shanghai in 1979 and 1980 proved unaware of Geng's current location or occupation but were certain that he was a "bad person."

63. Stuart Schram (ed.), *Chairman Mao Talks to the People*, 277–78; and *Miscellany of Mao Zedong Thought* (Joint Publications Research Service 616269-1 and 2).

ence to his cult was the most important measure of political merit, and his closest allies of the moment would have tremendous discretion.

Either way, Chinese society was the victim. Charismatic leadership is not a viable means of day-to-day administration, and therefore the state's grip on everyday affairs was weakened. Nonetheless, central authorities remained the final arbiters of local affairs, and their claim to charismatic virtue legitimated still more violent and arbitrary attacks on society. The real interests of groups like the contract workers were irrelevant to either a reign of virtue or Mao's personal power. The "winners" in the Cultural Revolution were not contract workers or other underprivileged Chinese, but people who learned to play the political game for personal advantage. Mass organizations representing groups like the contract workers might have offered civil society more autonomy, but they were manipulated and then suppressed. Mao had to die before the Chinese leadership could choose an alternate course.

THE NANJING INCIDENT

The Nanjing Incident was one of many public demonstrations held in cities across China during the Qingming Holiday in the spring of 1976.[64] In Nanjing and elsewhere people defied the orders of the Central Committee of the Communist Party of China and went into the streets to mourn the late premier, Zhou Enlai. In several cities, mourning for Zhou developed into public criticism of the current leadership of the Chinese Communist Party, especially of Jiang Qing and Zhang Chunqiao. These demonstrations reached a climax in Beijing's Tiananmen Square, the symbolic center of China, where very large numbers of people brought funeral wreaths for Zhou, wrote

64. Tiananmen-style incidents took place in many cities. In Jiangsu province alone, incidents were reported in Changzhou, Wuxi, and Yangzhou, and in the Huaihai area. ("All the Province's People Acclaim the Declaration that the Nanjing Incident Was a Completely Revolutionary Action" [Quan sheng renmin huanhu xuanbu Nanjing shijian wanquan shi geming xingdong], *Xinhua Ribao*, 19 Nov. 1978, p. 1). In Zhejiang province there were incidents in Hangzhou, Zhoushan, Jiaxing, Ningbo, Taizhou, and Shaoxing (Keith Forster, "The 1976 Ch'ing-ming Incident in Hangchow"; "Proclaim the Qingming Festival Hangzhou, Zhengzhou Mass Movements All Are Revolutionary Action" [Xuanbu qing ming jie Hangzhou Zhengzhou qunzhong huodong dou shi geming xingdong], *Xinhua Ribao*, 21 Nov. 1978). Other incidents were reported in Zhangzhou, Xiamen, Taiyuan, and Xian (ibid. and interview with Xiamen resident). Even in Shanghai, Zhang Chunqiao's political base, a couple of workers raised a flag bearing Zhou Enlai's picture in Culture Square only to be promptly arrested (interview with Shanghai resident).

commemorative poetry, and spoke out against Jiang and Zhang. They were soon driven from the square at gunpoint and possibly suffered loss of life. The Central Committee denounced the demonstrations as a counterrevolutionary conspiracy instigated by Deng Xiaoping, and the country was mobilized to condemn Deng and the "counterrevolutionary political incidents." Huge demonstrations and mass meetings were organized to support "the Central Committee led by Chairman Mao" and to condemn Deng Xiaoping, the Tiananmen Incident, and in Nanjing, the Nanjing Counterrevolutionary Incident. Some of the activists in the prior demonstrations were arrested and jailed, and many more were "investigated" and detained.

The Nanjing Incident and the Shanghai Commune illustrate the same pattern of politics. Both incidents were marked by the emergence of relatively autonomous organizations articulating demands previously suppressed by the state. People in Nanjing harbored a deep resentment of the leadership at all levels, not least for organizing the Cultural Revolution's costly political movements. The state was able to block public discussion of these problems until several factors coincided: the death of a popular leader, the presence of lower-level officials sympathetic to popular concerns, and a propitious holiday. At that moment, a protest movement quickly blossomed. In both cases state power holders were promptly able to mobilize overwhelming political strength to suppress the newly organized groups and their demands and ideas. And while repression in Nanjing was organized through the Party and everyday Leninist organization rather than the military, it was no less effective. Both cases suggest that China's Leninist state is able to dominate society but unable to shape society according to its dictates.

Because the Nanjing Incident was a protest against the use of state power during the Cultural Revolution, an outline of the course of the Cultural Revolution in Nanjing is pertinent. The "winner" of the first years of Nanjing's Cultural Revolution was General Xu Shiyou, commander of the Nanjing Military Region and a veteran revolutionary with a long and colorful past.[65] While the January Storm raged in

---

65. Xu was born of humble parents in 1906. In his youth he was a vagabond for awhile, but eventually graduated from the Shao Lin Monastery, a famous school of martial arts, and joined the army of warlord Wu Peifu (Dennis Bloodworth and Chang Ping, *Heirs Apparent*, 85–86). He had joined the Red Army by 1927 and evidently served in the Ouyuwan Soviet under the command of Xu Xiangqian and Zhang Guotao (David Lampton, "Xu Shi-You: A Soldier's Soldier." Many thanks to Professor Lampton for allowing me to read an early draft). In 1935, in the midst of the Long March, columns of the Red Army commanded by Mao and Zhang Guotao parted in acrimo-

Shanghai, the Jiangsu Provincial Committee recruited some ten thousand supporters from the countryside around Nanjing and brought them into the city to attack the "revolutionary rebels." Despite Mao's orders to the military to support "the revolutionary left," General Xu's troops supported the attack on the rebels. Some fifty rebels were killed, nine hundred wounded, and six thousand arrested.[66] Xu survived the vicissitudes of the next year to become chairman of the Jiangsu Provincial Revolutionary Committee when this body became the provincial government in March 1968.[67] In this position Xu's immediate antagonists were "revolutionary rebels" like Zhang Chunqiao, but Xu did not allow former provincial leaders like Xu Jiadun to return to power.[68]

---

nious circumstances. Zhang's troops arrived in Yan'an in late 1936 in desperate circumstances. In early 1937 Mao launched a campaign against Zhang Guotao and his supporters. Xu actively opposed Mao and was arrested (ibid.). Xu claims to have been pardoned by Mao in person. See "Chairman Mao Will Always Live in Our Hearts" (Mao zhuxi yongyuan huo zai womende xinzhong), *Renmin Ribao*, 8 Sept. 1978, p. 2. Xu went on to Shandong where he remained until his promotion to commander of the Nanjing Military Region, which includes Jiangsu, Zhejiang, Anhui, and Shanghai and was therefore one of the most important of China's thirteen military regions in 1954. See W. Bartke, *Who's Who in the People's Republic of China* (New York: M. E. Sharp, 1981).

66. For a brief account of these events, see Lampton, 229–35, and Bloodworth and Ping, 94.

67. Bartke, 10–15. Xu and other regional military commanders came under attack following the Wuhan mutiny of General Chen Zaitao in July 1967. Wang Li, one of the kidnapped emissaries, eventually returned to Beijing a hero, and the mutiny was soon used to justify attacks on the military. Chen Zaitao was arrested and brought to Beijing. Xu faced considerable opposition (Chien Yu-shen, *China's Fading Revolution*, 47–48). Beijing Red Guards, including Kuai Dafu, who was later associated with the "May 16" conspiracy, came to Nanjing to attack Xu (Jaap Van Ginneken, *Lin Piao*, 123–24; Daubier, *History*, 223). While Jiang Qing was a leading proponent of attacks on the military, there were also conflicts between the General Staff of the People's Liberation Army and the regional commanders (H. Nelson, "Military Forces in the Cultural Revolution"). Both Lin Biao, then minister of defense, and Yang Chengwu, acting chief of staff, are alleged to have made threats against Xu (Lampton, 51; and Chien, 100–5). But the balance of forces changed in late August and early September. Despite Mao's former endorsement of the attacks on the military, various national publications began to argue that the real danger came from those who were attacking the military, who formed an alleged "May 16" conspiracy (Barry Burton, "The Cultural Revolution's Ultraleft Conspiracy: The 'May 16' Group"). Jiang Qing publicly reversed her position on September 5 and condemned the attacks on the military (Milton, 285–87). Wang Li, a hero two months before and a member of the Cultural Revolution Group, was implicated in the "May 16" conspiracy and relieved of his offices (Daubier, 215–16). While Xu had had difficult times, he emerged with the personal endorsement of Zhou Enlai (Lampton, 52). These events suggest that Xu had every reason to fear "May 16" and to hate Jiang Qing and Lin Biao, but he certainly did not eschew their campaign-style politics.

68. Zhang was the political commissar of Xu's military district, and the two were known to quarrel. See Lampton.

General Xu used the power he had won in an arbitrary and brutal manner, as if to demonstrate the autonomy of the state. He proved a murderous leader, no less willing than his opponents to launch fearful political campaigns. The most significant of these was the year-long campaign to "drag out May 16" (*qingcha wu-shiliu*), which began in May 1970.[69] "May 16" was purportedly a national "ultraleft" conspiracy bent on assassinating leaders like Xu. It was eventually admitted that no "May 16" organization existed in Nanjing in 1970, and probably no such group existed then anywhere in China.[70] Nonetheless, tens of thousands of people were implicated in the conspiracy in Jiangsu alone, with results including death, incarceration, exile, and loss of reputation and livelihood. Wu Dasheng, a military man, directed the campaign at the provincial level, and General Xu transferred Wang Yong from a military propaganda unit to direct the campaign at Nanjing University. Wang evidently did his job well, as Nanjing University became a focus of the campaign.[71] The university had been closed, and only about two thousand faculty and staff remained on campus. During the course of the campaign approximately thirteen of these people died, mostly suicides.[72] All faculty were confined to the campus. Two hundred people were more stringently detained, mostly in dormitory rooms, some of which were kept dark and divided into cubicles so tiny the detained could neither lie down nor stand up. Some persons interviewed claimed that torture was used to extract confessions. About a thousand people were charged as "May 16" conspirators on the campus alone. Those implicated but

69. Chen Ruoxi's (Chen Jo-hsi) short story "Jen Hsiu-lan" is a moving account of the social costs of this campaign in Nanjing. See Chen Jo-hsi, "Jen Hsiu-lan," in *The Execution of Mayor Yin*, 115–36.

70. The purpose of the campaign is thus not clear. Possibly it was connected with Lin Biao's attempted coup d'état. Following the criticisms of 1967, "May 16" was not an issue for two years. It resurfaced in criticisms of Chen Boda and Lin Biao following the Second Plenum of the Ninth Party Congress held in Lushan in August 1970. Chen Boda evidently proposed to the Plenum that Mao fill the vacant position of head of state. This was interpreted by others as a means of preparing for Lin Biao's eventual succession to this post (Van Ginneken, 214–16). The media revived criticism of "May 16" and implicated Chen Boda (Burton, "Ultraleft Conspiracy," 1049). Mao personally criticized "May 16" in (*neibu*) documents read only by Party cadres (interview with Nanjing cadres). Lin's attempted coup occurred shortly thereafter. While this might explain why "May 16" was an issue, it hardly explains the broad scope of the campaign.

71. Wang was the most recent in a series of military officers who took charge of the university after its former president, Kuang Yaming, was purged in July 1966.

72. This was nearly half of the twenty-seven people who died at Nanjing University during the entire Cultural Revolution. This information was gathered in various interviews in Nanjing.

not incarcerated were liable to be sent to labor reform camps or "sent down" to the countryside.[73] In all of Jiangsu over a hundred thousand individuals were accused of being "May 16" elements.[74] By the time half the campus population had been accused of taking part in the "May 16" conspiracy, let alone the large numbers off campus, the accusations grew implausible. After a year the campaign died down, but Xu remained the most important man in Jiangsu.

Society had little recourse until General Xu's superiors moved him to another province. Until today, General Xu has not been called to account for his deeds, and as long as he remained in Nanjing those accused of participating in the fictional conspiracy could not be rehabilitated and the campaign to eliminate the conspiracy could not be publicly criticized. Moreover, Xu's hated subordinates, Wu Dasheng and Wang Yong, remained in office. The situation finally began to improve with Deng Xiaoping's rehabilitation in 1973.[75] In March 1974, with the support of Peng Chong, a veteran provincial leader and at that time the second-ranking leader of the Jiangsu provincial revolutionary committee, Zhang De arrived at Nanjing University to take charge of the propaganda department. In 1974 "May 16" victims began to be rehabilitated. Eventually some four hundred individuals were exonerated. In 1975 Xu Shiyou was transferred to the Guangzhou Military Region in a general rotation of regional military commanders. In the same year, with Deng's help, Zhou Lin was appointed chairman of Nanjing University's revolutionary committee.[76] In April 1975 Wang Yong, leader of the "May 16" campaign at Nanjing University, delivered a self-criticism and was transferred to head Nanjing City's Environmental Protection Bureau. Zhou Lin and Zhang De attempted to "rectify" others, such as Wu Xiangdong, the head of the University Committee's office. But Wu Xiangdong was supported by Wu Dasheng, the leader of the provincial campaign, who remained on the provincial revolutionary committee despite Xu's departure.[77]

73. Many were sent to the extremely poor northern portion of Jiangsu, where, as one interlocutor stated, chickens were worth more than people because an egg was worth more than a day's wages.

74. These figures are rough estimates derived from interviews with witnesses.

75. In April 1973 Zhou Enlai introduced Deng as a vice-premier of the State Council; in August of the same year he was elected to the Central Committee of the Party, and in January 1975 he became vice-chairman of the Party, first vice-premier, and vice-chairman of the Central Committee on Military Affairs (Chi Hsin, *Teng Hsiao-Ping*, 263).

76. Zhou Lin eventually became a vice-minister of education.

77. Interview with Nanjing cadres.

Later in 1975 Deng Xiaoping encountered stiff opposition from Mao and Mao's supporters. During the early part of the year, Zhou Enlai protected Deng, and together they promoted policies like the Four Modernizations, which promised economic growth and a political relaxation.[78] At the same time members of the Jiang Qing group, especially Zhang Chunqiao and Wang Hongwen, gained positions of roughly equal rank. Their policies continued to emphasize strict standards of political virtue and the maintaining of a sharp struggle against "capitalist-roaders."[79] In November the Jiang Qing faction went on the offensive. Mao instructed students at Qinghua University in Beijing to "debate" educational policies, and the media widely publicized their claim that the Four Modernizations was a plot to "kill socialist new things."[80]

This course of events led many in society to fear that some state leaders were about to initiate yet another political movement. Zhou Enlai's death in January 1976 seemed an opportunity for Jiang Qing and her allies to purge his supporters and launch another violent campaign for political virtue. During the televised broadcast of Zhou's funeral, many people observed that Jiang Qing did not take off her

78. Many people in Nanjing claimed that despite difficult circumstances, Deng had a favorable impact. One cadre, without realizing the irony in his remark, commented that Deng had made the trains run on time, and went on to discourse about the difficulties of coping with unscheduled transportation. Regardless of Deng's attempted reforms, by most reports Nanjing remained chaotic. Large numbers of people returned from the countryside without authorization. Many of those sent down from Nanjing had been sent to northern Anhui and northern Jiangsu, one of China's poorest regions, and found life so difficult that they had little to lose in returning to Nanjing even if they lacked employment and housing. Five years later, the city still had not succeeded in finding accommodations for all of the "returnees," and many were still living in makeshift huts. In 1975 there were large numbers of destitute people sleeping at the train stations or in the streets. They worked the streets, begging, staging impromptu acrobatics, music, and story-telling, selling handicrafts; some engaged in prostitution. I also heard reports of mass raids on vegetable markets. Many "returnees" sought recompense by writing big-character posters or marching in informal delegations to governmental headquarters. They were joined in this by sundry groups of peasants coming from the surrounding suburbs and countryside to make their problems known (various interviews in Nanjing).

79. I will consider the differences in line between the two groups in greater detail in chapter 3. Tsou Tang summarizes their differences as follows: "While the ultra-leftists were formulating the theory of 'bourgeois right' and 'all-round dictatorship over the bourgeoisie,' the veteran Party leaders preoccupied themselves with the solution of the concrete problems of industrial management and production, science and technology, and foreign policy and trade" (Tsou Tang, "Mao Tse-tung Thought, The Last Struggle for Succession and the Post-Mao Era," China Quarterly 71 [September 1977]: 514).

80. The students said: "The rightist wind is using the four modernizations as a weapon with which to kill the socialist new things and attack the proletariat. This proves that it is not aimed at modernization, but at capitalism restoration. Their desire for the satellite to go into the heavens is just a front: their real intention is to let the red flag fall to the ground" (Chi Hsin, The Case of the Gang of Four, 151).

cap.[81] Moreover, the Central Committee banned memorial meetings for Zhou or even the wearing of the black armbands customarily worn by the bereaved.[82] Mao was quoted as saying that the "capitalist class is right inside the Communist Party," words that must have been chilling to Deng Xiaoping, and that "the rightist reversal of verdicts does not gain the people's heart," words that must have been chilling to victims of political campaigns. Though Deng's name was not mentioned in public media, he was incessantly criticized under the code name "unrepentant capitalist-roader." Students at Nanjing University saw other, more arcane, signs that persuaded them that an anti-Zhou campaign was about to be launched.[83] Students and staff at Nanjing University indicated their reaction to these developments in two contrasting meetings. On January 12, defying the Central Committee's wishes, the university held a memorial meeting for Zhou Enlai, which was extremely emotional.[84] A meeting held on March 18 to criticize Deng was attended with little enthusiasm.[85]

As with the Shanghai Commune, only special circumstances made it possible for society to assume the initiative. The Nanjing Incident could not have occurred without the coincidence of Zhou's death, the Qingming Holiday, and the prior posting of sympathetic lower-level officials. The Qingming Holiday, which fell on April 5 in 1976, is the traditional time to honor ancestors by sweeping their tombs. In Nanjing students also honored the occasion by marching to Yuhuatai, a

81. Ibid., 32.

82. Ting Wang, *Chairman Hua*, 103.

83. These included the following: On February 6, *Reference Materials* (Cankao Ziliao), an "internal" newspaper with a limited circulation, reprinted an article from a Hong Kong paper that attributed complicity in the 1927 slayings of Communist sympathizers by the Guomindang to Wu Hao, a pseudonym once used by Zhou. On March 3, *Wenhui Bao*, a Shanghai daily, printed an article on Lei Feng that included various tributes to Lei, but left out Zhou's, which had been printed in other versions of the article in other papers. On February 25, *Wenhui Bao* printed an article that referred in passing to the "biggest capitalist-roader" behind the "unrepentant capitalist-roader," which, if Deng is understood to be the "unrepentant capitalist-roader," indicated that Zhou was soon to be labeled a counterrevolutionary. An article from *Renmin Ribao* of 14 Jan. 1976 entitled "Great Debate Brings Great Change" (Da bianlun dailai da bianhua) seemed to suggest that the debate at Qinghua indicated that major changes in policy would soon be occurring.

84. Gennie and Kam Louie, "Role of Nanjing University in the Nanjing Incident," *China Quarterly*, no. 86, p. 32. Kam Louie was extremely helpful to me in supplying ideas on how to begin work on the Nanjing Incident in Nanjing. Possibly, this meeting was technically not a breach of organizational discipline, as the ban may not yet have reached the university in written form. Nonetheless, the intentions of higher levels and the meeting's significance were apparent. Zhang De was the key speaker at this meeting.

85. Ibid., p. 34.

former Nationalist execution ground, now a park south of the city, to honor martyrs. In addition, Zhou had resided in Nanjing at Meiyuan. Consequently, upon the approach of Qingming in 1976, several groups in Nanjing began to contemplate marches on Yuhuatai or Meiyuan to honor Zhou Enlai.

The tacit support of lower-level leaders like Zhang De and Zhou Lin was especially important to those trying to organize marches.[86] The first successful march illustrates the kind of informal contacts necessary to organize social action. Li Xining, secretary of Nanjing University's Mathematics Department's branch of the Youth League, established a small committee to effect liaison with other departments and find desired supplies, such as a car, a megaphone, and a large portrait of Zhou. This committee included several people with formal authority at the grass-roots level, such as the student head of the departmental branch of the university's student association, the secretary of the student Party branch of the computer science section of the Mathematics Department, and the secretary of the departmental branch of the Youth League. At first they attempted to follow official procedures. They reported to the University Youth League plans to march to Yuhuatai on April 5 and requested large portraits of Zhou from the university's propaganda department.[87] After agreeing to the loan of the portraits, the propaganda department recanted. When the Youth League reported the students' plans to the university Party office, the office manager, Wu Xiangdong, attempted to persuade Li Xining to cancel the march, but Li insisted on going ahead. Wu lacked the authority to block the march, and given the presence of Zhou Lin and Zhang De on the University Committee, he could not obtain the committee's support. Wu appealed to the Provincial Revolutionary Committee, which directly supervised Nanjing University. Yang Guangli, then a leading figure in the Provincial Revolutionary Committee with ties to the Jiang Qing group, prepared to issue formal instructions to cancel the march, but students learned of his impending action through an informal connection to the Provincial Committee, and Li promptly rescheduled the march to depart early

86. On March 24 and 25 student delegations set out for these destinations but were turned away by the authorities. One of these delegations consisted of about four hundred students from the Jiangsu New Medical College (ibid., pp. 32–33). The other included about fifty students from Nanjing University's History Department (Tang Jianzhong and Li Liangyu, "Unforgettable March 29").

87. Interview with participants in the Nanjing Incident.

the next morning before Yang could act officially.[88] At the break of day on March 28 about three hundred students marched off campus and through the center of the city to Meiyuan, carrying a large wreath with a portrait of Zhou Enlai.

When the opportunity did arise, the whole of society responded. For the next few days the city was jammed with crowds, slogans, pamphlets, posters, and speeches mourning Zhou Enlai and protesting against Jiang Qing and Zhang Chunqiao. Other delegations from the university, other schools, factories, and various units marched through the city to Yuhuatai and Meiyuan, often attracting large numbers of followers as they went.[89] On March 29 students at Nanjing University posted a copy of an article from *Wenhui Bao* that seemed to imply that Zhou was the "biggest capitalist-roader," underlined the offending phrase, and commented, "Look at this and reflect. What does it show?" The math students posted two large slogans reading "We will use our blood to protect the red land won by countless revolutionary martyrs and predecessors" and "Beware Khrushchev-type careerists and conspirators who want to seize power from the Party and state."[90] Large crowds jammed into the university to read these and other posters.[91] Student activists soon moved on to the city's three main squares, and large crowds followed to read posters and listen to speeches. As the crowds grew so large that traffic was blocked, the activists grew increasingly bold. For example, on March 30 Xu Tongxin, a soldier, posted a leaflet that concluded: "Drag out and publicly expose the Khrushchev-style careerist, con-

88. Ibid.
89. For example, on March 29 Zhang De approved a march to Yuhuatai by the Foreign Languages Department and two other departments who carried banners proclaiming "Attack whoever attacks Zhou" (Tang and Liang). On March 31 Chen Banghui, a young worker, Party member, and union functionary at the Nanjing Mechanical Instrument and Meter Factory, together with the factory Youth League Secretary, organized a march to Yuhuatai in which all the factory's workers participated. At Yuhuatai, Chen played a tape of the eulogy Deng Xiaoping delivered at Zhou's funeral ("Since Ancient Times the People Make History" [Zi gu renmin xie chunqiu], *Nanjing Bao*, 24 Nov. 1978, p. 3). A delegation from the Red Flag Machine Tools Factory planned to include two hundred workers, but by the time it cleared the factory gates there were a thousand people, and marching through Xinjiekou Square the numbers mounted toward ten thousand ("Looking Back, Full Recollections" [Huishou zhu shiqing manhuai], *Nanjing Bao*, 24 Nov. 1978, p. 1).
90. As it was widely rumored that Zhang Chunqiao wanted to succeed Zhou as premier, this last was a reference to him.
91. Louie, "Role of Nanjing University," and interviews. Other posters mainly expressed grief and respect for Zhou, but a few also "remembered" Yang Kaihui, Mao's former wife, in a not very veiled criticism of Jiang Qing.

spirator, and two-faced Zhang Chunqiao."[92] Qin Shizuo, an old worker, Party member, union leader, and head of the survey section of the Nanjing Telegram No. 3 Branch Bureau, organized workers to make a flower wreath two meters in diameter with a portrait of Zhou Enlai in the middle and took it to Gulou Square. With the help of the crowd gathered there, the wreath was lifted onto the ledge over the door of the Gulou Grocery Store, a prominent and provocative location.[93] But students remained the most daring. On the afternoon of March 29, students from Nanjing University and Nanjing Telecommunications College went to the train station and, with the help of railway workers, painted slogans on trains and made speeches to travelers to broadcast their message to the entire country.[94]

Subsequent newspaper accounts attempting to condemn the incident inadvertently gave testimony to overwhelming popular support for the students. While they attributed the incident to "capitalist-roaders," they had difficulty finding evidence of popular antipathy to supposed "class enemies"[95] and had to admit that there were as many as ten thousand people in the squares and that "comrades with revolutionary anger" who tried to "restore order" were repulsed and beaten by the crowds.[96]

Nonetheless, the incident was over by April 1, and within three weeks the central authorities had pressured local authorities into mounting an overwhelming response. On April 7 the central authorities declared the Tiananmen Incident a "counterrevolutionary political incident" organized by Deng Xiaoping. Deng was labeled a "capitalist-roader" and relieved of his offices. Peng Chong, represent-

92. "Battlefield Chrysanthemums" (Zhandi huanghua), *Nanjing Bao*, 8 Oct. 1978, p. 2.

93. "A Lofty Floral Wreath Terrifies the Enemy" (Huaquan weiran di danhan), *Nanjing Bao*, 8 Oct. 1978, p. 3.

94. Workers at the train stations supported the students by offering them paint and tar to replace the ink they had originally used, so the slogans would be indelible. Other students went to a long-distance bus station ("A Warrior Cries Out for Truth" [Wei zhenli er nahan de zhanshi], *Nanjing Bao*, 6 Oct. 1978, pp. 2–3).

95. Later awards meetings listed as heroes two or three Party secretaries who had dissuaded workers or students from participating in the incident, police who had gone out to the squares to investigate, and street-cleaning crews who had cleaned up the mess. This last indicates that it was difficult to find people willing to take down the "counterrevolutionary slogans" ("Nanjing Committee Convenes 10,000 Person Mass Meeting to Award Advanced Individuals" [Nanjing shiwei zhaokai wan ren da hui biaoyang xianjin], *Xinhua Ribao*, 14 May 1976, pp. 1, 4).

96. "Thoroughly Smash Nanjing Counterrevolutionary Political Incident" (Chedi fensui Nanjing fangeming zhengzhi shijian), *Xinhua Ribao*, 12 May 1976, pp. 1, 4.

ing the Jiangsu Provincial Committee, conveyed this message to a mass meeting in Nanjing, and 200,000 soldiers and citizens marched to support the Central Committee.[97] There was no public response to the Nanjing Incident for two more weeks, but thereafter officials organized a massive campaign. On April 21 Yang Guangli, the Provincial Committee member who had earlier attempted to block the math students' march, chaired a meeting sponsored jointly by the Nanjing Military Region and the Jiangsu Provincial Party. Simultaneous meetings were held at 122 locations with an electronic linkup so that about 150,000 Party members could listen.[98] The main speaker was Peng Chong. He applied the Central Committee's criticism of the Tiananmen Incident to the Nanjing Incident, urging loyalty to "Chairman Mao and the Party Central Committee led by Mao" and labeling Deng Xiaoping and participants in both incidents opponents of Mao and counterrevolutionaries. Peng declared that everyone should study the spirit of the worker militia, the police, and the security guards who had cleared Tiananmen Square.[99]

For the next month the Party mobilized the masses to criticize the incident and its supporters, which amounted to organizing the city to repress itself. At units across the city there were mass meetings where leaders repeated the official explanation of the incident, which were followed by marches through the streets to show solidarity with "Chairman Mao and the Party Central Committee led by Chairman Mao." For example, immediately following the Provincial Party and Regional Military meeting, Nanjing University, despite having been the center of the incident, held a meeting of six thousand people, led

97. "200,000 Military and Masses Meet and Demonstrate, Resolutely Support the Party Central Committee's Resolution, Angrily Denounce Crimes of the Unrepentant Capitalist Roader Deng Xiaoping" (Nanjing ershiwan jun-min jihui youxing jianjue yonghu dang zhongyang jueyi fennu shengtao bu ken gaihui de zou zi pai Deng Xiaoping de fandong zuixing), *Xinhua Ribao*, 9 Apr. 1976. In the atmosphere prevailing during the campaign to condemn the Nanjing and Tiananmen movements, even Party members who had seemingly supported the incidents were compelled to criticize them publicly. One person reported that during that time it was not safe to talk about political issues with a spouse.

98. "Push Criticism of Deng and Oppose Rightist Reversal of Verdicts to a New High Tide. Thoroughly Expose Nanjing Counterrevolutionary Political Incident. Suppress Counterrevolution" (Ba pi deng fanji youqing fan an feng douzheng tuixing xin gaochao. Che cha Nanjing fangeming zhengzhi shijian zhenya fangeming), *Xinhua Ribao*, 22 Apr. 1976, pp. 1–2.

99. Ibid. According to some accounts, thousands of people were killed or injured when the police swept the demonstrators from Tiananmen Square. See Ting Wang, *Chairman Hua*, 104–5.

by Zhou Lin.[100] A few days later the Nanjing Workers Militia, a force associated with the Jiang Qing group, demonstrated, carrying arms.[101] Investigations and arrests followed. Though only about twenty people were arrested, approximately three hundred people were investigated.[102] "Investigation" included confining people to the premises of their unit (place of employment), organizing "struggle sessions" against them, and demanding self-criticisms.

At the elite level, factional struggle persisted. According to one report, Wu Dasheng and Yang Guangli on the Provincial Committee sought to replace Zhou Lin with Wu Xiangdong. To this end, they worked at discrediting Zhang De as a "backstage plotter" (*muhou cehua ren*) in the hope that disgracing him would cast a shadow on Zhou Lin. They succeeded in discrediting Zhang, for not only had he approved the march of the Foreign Languages Department to Yuhuatai, but also his son, studying at the Telecommunications College, had taken an active role in those demonstrations. Zhou Lin, however, who had remained aloof from the incident, or who had at least managed to conceal his involvement, remained unimplicated.

Rehabilitations did not resume until the fall of 1978, when the Central Committee reversed the verdict on both the Tiananmen and the Nanjing incidents. At that time the arrested activists were released. However, the relationship between the grass-roots activists and the reform leadership remained complex.[103] Some of the activists returned to the university and promising careers while others remained in political limbo. Although activists and the new leadership had both been opponents of the Gang of Four, the new leadership was not willing to allow activists the right to speak freely or to organize. On the other side, a few of the worst tyrants and murderers were arrested and disgraced. Others, such as Xu Shiyou, may lack their former power, but have not been brought to account publicly for their deeds.

100. "Deeply Criticize Deng Xiaoping, Oppose Rightist Reversal of Verdicts" (Shenru pipan Deng Xiaoping fanji youqing fan an feng), *Xinhua Ribao*, 23 Apr. 1976, p. 1. Other major secondary schools in the city met concurrently. Party members of the Workers Hospital upon returning from the provincial meeting organized all hospital staff to attend meetings and march (*Xinhua Ribao*, 27 Apr. 1976).

101. "Nanjing Workers Militia Holds Mass Rally and Armed Demonstration" (Nanjing gongren minbing jihui wuzhuang youxing shiwei), *Xinhua Ribao*, 26 Apr. 1976.

102. Interview with Nanjing cadre.

103. Stanley Rosen, "Guangzhou's Democracy Movement in Cultural Revolution Perspective," provides a first-rate look at this relationship in Guangzhou.

Consequently, the Nanjing Incident was not the end of the Nanjing student movement. In May 1984 there was yet another incident at Nanjing University. The university's loss of academic prestige, the consequent loss of funding, and the failure of the leadership to eliminate "leftism" disappointed students, who wrote big-character posters and took part in critical discussions. Fifteen hundred students marched across the city to complain to the provincial governor but were refused admittance. Once again, lower levels of official authority, such as the Students' Association, were sympathetic, but again the overwhelming weight of the Party proved superior to social concerns.[104] Demonstrations began anew in December 1986 in conjunction with a wave of student demonstrations across the nation. Students first put up big-character posters on campus, calling for a more democratic political system and also raising issues pertaining to the university. Thereafter they took to the streets, attracting crowds that numbered in the thousands and blocked thoroughfares.[105] In December 1988 Nanjing students again took to the streets, and they led massive demonstrations in the spring of 1989.

The strength and autonomy of China's Leninist state were conclusively demonstrated both in the campaign to "drag out May 16" and in the repression that followed the Nanjing Incident. Although very large numbers of people were mobilized to participate in each of these events, increasing political participation was not equivalent to democratization. These events are a tribute to the power of Leninist states to manipulate and intimidate. And yet these massive movements failed, despite their terrible cost. Large numbers of people were not persuaded and did not remain intimidated. At a special moment they were able to voice their concerns. The Leninist state's organization was not and cannot be impervious. Growing quickly from its humble beginnings, the Nanjing Incident overtook the authorities and engulfed the city. But it was quickly exhausted, and real change was possible only when changes occurred among the leaders of state. In sum, the state could dominate society, but it never gained hegemony.

104. See Ke Pu and Chen Yi-ko, "Origin and Development of Unrest at Nanjing University."
105. "Reportage on Nanjing Student Demonstrations," FBIS-86-250, 30 Dec. 1986, pp. O8–13.

CONCLUSION

The Cultural Revolution was not a break with the Leninist state but rather another attempt to impose revolution from above. Mao's slogan "politics in command" may have been his means of calling attention to the decline of virtue in everyday Leninist politics, but in practice "politics in command" meant that self-appointed leaders claimed the exclusive right to define political ideals and to impose them on society. "Politics in command" removed already limited institutional restraints from the exercise of state power and created an arbitrary, manipulative, and violent political system. Moreover, it would have been impossible for Mao to impose the Cultural Revolution without the prior foundation of the Leninist state. Despite mass participation, the Cultural Revolution was closely linked with the structures of the Leninist state. Without the state's prior domination of the economy and communications, without its neighborhood organization, without the *nomenklatura* system, or without the secret police, it is unlikely that Mao's cult of personality could have grown to such extreme proportions that he could launch the Cultural Revolution in the face of opposition from so many quarters. Cults of personality are relatively commonplace in the history of Leninist systems, as are violent attacks on society. Mao did not intend to replace these structures, as was demonstrated by his verdict on the Shanghai Commune.

This attempt at revolution from above was not only harmful to society but destructive to the state as well. It is widely recognized that the Cultural Revolution was an economic failure. The Cultural Revolution also created a political crisis. The tremendous expenditure of power, combined with the terrible human cost and the visible failure to attain any desirable results, severely depleted the state's store of legitimacy and diminished its ability to govern. At the end of the Cultural Revolution the state was left with an ideology composed of hollow symbols that pointed in a direction that no one wanted to go. A decade of "power seizures," violent factional struggles, and high-intensity politics crippled the state's institutional infrastructure while training society in the art of covert resistance. In these circumstances, the failure to vigorously pursue fundamental reforms could have had very grave consequences.

The Cultural Revolution defined and enforced an ideology that could not grapple with real problems. The symbols of the Cultural

Revolution, such as "class struggle," "revolution," "the Great Helmsman," were apparently very idealistic and had at first held out the promise of helping groups like contract workers improve their lives. But they were subsequently invoked to suppress the contract workers, students in Nanjing, and countless other Chinese with equally reasonable ambitions and, in practice, were invoked to legitimate the self-serving and often destructive actions of individual leaders. This gap produced a profound cynicism, to which subsequent generations have fallen captive. Moreover, the ideology of the Cultural Revolution was a closed system that administered severe sanctions for those who pushed beyond its limits, even while the most pressing problems, like the economy and the political crisis, were beyond those limits. The result was that as long as the state held to those symbols, it was blinded, unable to perceive or ameliorate real problems, and faced with growing numbers of nonbelievers.

The Cultural Revolution was equally destructive to the state's organizational infrastructure. Immediately following the revolution, Leninist state organization made it possible for the Party to restore social order, set the economy back on its feet, and reform the land-tenure system. Nonetheless, the building of rational-legal authority has been a problem for Leninist states. The monolithic and hierarchical character of Leninist organization enables leaders at all levels to use their power arbitrarily and to achieve personal purposes without fear that those beneath them will be able to appeal through other channels. Even in the midst of the Cultural Revolution, Zhang Chunqiao's exclusive access to Mao doomed his opponents. Consequently, under the best of circumstances, Leninist organization has a tendency to decay into an agglomeration of local dictators with personal, not legal, authority. This results in declining administrative capacity and an inability to impose official goals on individual cadres. The Cultural Revolution greatly accelerated these tendencies. Mao legitimated the ignoring of official duties and violent insubordination and crippled ordinary means of enforcing rules and procedures. The result of the Cultural Revolution was that the Party and the state suffered a decline not only in their ability to govern the nation but even in their ability to regulate themselves.

During the Cultural Revolution society did not passively follow instructions from above, but responded in terms of its real interests and opportunities. No amount of repression or terror could turn society into the blank sheet of paper that Mao imagined he could write on.

Terror and organized repression only limited the opportunities to speak out and did not eliminate the issues that people wanted to discuss. When opportunities did arise, like the early invitation to the contract workers or the death of Zhou, the response was all the more swift and dramatic for having been repressed. Individuals responded to real opportunities to pursue their own goals, whether these were perceived in terms of political ideals, as in the Nanjing students' protest against the central leadership or the contract workers' attempt to improve their standard of living. In a limited sense, the brief opportunity to organize and speak out provided opportunities for society to learn a measure of autonomy. A small number of former Cultural Revolution activists went on to participate in the post-Mao democracy movement.[106]

In sum, the Cultural Revolution demonstrated the existence of a chasm between the Chinese state and Chinese society. On the one hand, state leaders like Mao or Zhang Chunqiao exercised considerable personal autonomy, owing in part to Mao's personal charisma, but also rooted in the vertical structure of Leninist state institutions. On the other hand, the mobilization of groups like the contract workers demonstrated the existence of long-standing grievances in civil society. However, the violent conflicts of the Cultural Revolution allowed civil society little chance to institutionalize autonomy and at the same time diminished the state's capacity to govern itself. The result was a diffusion of state power to lower levels in the state hierarchy without the development of a more autonomous civil society.

Once Mao died, new leaders saw the necessity of reform. Reform was necessary not only because of international economic competition, or because a new generation of leaders had a preference for development-oriented policies, but because the politics of the Cultural Revolution weakened the state and alienated society. Not just economic reform but political reform was necessary to rescue the state from the tragic policies chosen by its own leaders. The state had to regain control over its own staff and open channels of communication with society. Considering the damage that had been done, not least to the state itself, this would not be an easy task.

106. Rosen, "Guangzhou's Democracy Movement."

CHAPTER TWO

Patrimonial Rulership in China's Leninist State

States are not just strong or weak, but have specific strengths and weaknesses. Leninist states are very powerful, yet they are unable to accomplish some of their most basic goals. In the preceding chapter I argued that Mao was able to use Leninist state power to launch the Great Leap Forward and the Cultural Revolution but was unable to achieve his ends in either movement. In subsequent chapters I will argue that Leninist states are able to constrain social autonomy but have difficulty in implementing rationalizing reforms. To describe and understand these strengths and weaknesses, I will utilize Max Weber's ideal types of rulership.[1]

Most Western analysts of China implicitly use only two of Max Weber's three main ideal types. For example, the post-Mao reforms are widely considered a form of "modernization," a category that roughly equates with Max Weber's ideal type of rational-legal rulership. Modernization is often conceived as the opposite of "revolution," a category that roughly corresponds with Weber's ideal type of charismatic rulership. This dichotomy really exists. Mao did draw on his personal charisma, which was in turn rooted in the Party's victory in the revolution. Post-Mao reforms have tried to strengthen laws and improve the technical capacity of formal organizations. This contrast

1. My intention in using "rulership" instead of "authority," "legitimacy," or "domination" is to emphasize that Weber's ideal types encompass both ideas and behavior and not just attitudes and values.

fails, however, to consider a wide range of problems that contemporary Chinese refer to as "feudalism" or "feudal remnants." "Feudalism" refers to various corrupt and arbitrary patterns of authority that are prevalent in contemporary China. In this chapter I will argue that these problems deserve serious attention and that interpreting "feudalism" as patrimonialism, the third of Weber's ideal types, puts "modernization" and "revolution" in a new context.

Patrimonial rulership is an integral aspect of Leninist states. Theories that attribute patrimonialism to political culture or to the persistence of traditional society are helpful. The Chinese state was established in the midst of a society that emphasized personal relationships, and the state has since attempted to transform society. There is also strong empirical evidence to support rational-actor theories that explain corruption as a rationally calculated response to rigid and inefficient state bureaucracy. Theories that view patrimonial rulership either as an unfortunate historical remnant or as a reasonable response to the state cannot adequately account for the importance of patrimonial rulership in Leninist states. Leninist state organization is formally rational-legal. But the attempt to build pervasive and monolithic formal organization generates "organized dependency."[2] It awards officials personal discretion over a wide range of goods and services necessary for their subordinates' everyday lives. This dependency insures that the state can mobilize and constrain the many individuals enmeshed within its networks. Patrimonial rulership limits the state's technical capacity, however. Mao's style of politics could rely consequently on the strengths of Leninist states, even while he dismembered institutions, alienated society, and ruined the economy, but reformers have had to wrestle with the state even as they seek to remedy the problems Mao left behind.

Failure to account for patrimonial rulership obscures the most important obstacles to reform. Although reformers have been able to identify what reforms need to be implemented and even gain the official endorsement of Party plenums, they still have found themselves unable to implement reforms. Patrimonial rulership establishes a vast multilayered pyramid of personal relationships. Decisions and instructions filter down through countless personal connections and are systematically diluted to serve individual interests along the way. Information must return through the same networks and is systemat-

2. Andrew Walder, *Communist Neo-Traditionalism: Work and Authority in Chinese Industry*.

ically edited to protect local interests. Reformers in China and the Soviet Union initially emphasized economic reform, but in practice they have found that patrimonial rulership makes the implementation of economic reform difficult and distorts the results. Consequently, in both countries, some reformers have turned toward political reform as the key to all other reforms.

Accounting for patrimonial rulership redefines the revolution. If our only categories are revolution and modernization, then, whether in praise or in condemnation, the revolutionary victory of the Communist Party in 1949 and the Cultural Revolution are linked as charismatic events, and post-Mao "modernization" is the negation of both. If, as many Chinese argue, the revolution in 1949 was supposed to be against "feudalism," but unfortunately the Cultural Revolution strengthened "feudalism," then post-Mao "modernization" is not the opposite of "revolution" but its continuation by different means under different circumstances. In the long run, the Party's ability to deal with the issues posed by patrimonial rulership will be as decisive as any issue in modern Chinese history.

PATRIMONIAL AND RATIONAL-LEGAL RULERSHIP

Max Weber develops the concept of patrimonial rulership by contrasting it with other types of rulership.[3] Each of his three main ideal types encompasses "beliefs in legitimacy" and "the actual operating modes and administrative arrangements."[4] They do not occur in "pure" forms but always exist in conjunction with other forms of rulership.[5] He defines charismatic rulership as uniquely revolutionary and contrasts patrimonial rulership and rational-legal rulership as alternate forms of everyday rulership.

In rational-legal authority, which Weber also calls bureaucracy, human beings are dominated by large impersonal organizations. They spend their lives working at tasks that have little intrinsic meaning but that make sense in terms of the organization's goals. In a bureaucratic setting, "entrance into an office, including one in the private economy, is considered an acceptance of a specific duty of fe-

---

3. See Weber, *Economy and Society,* 212–40, 956–1070.
4. Guenther Roth, "Personal Rulership, Patrimonialism and Empire Building," 157.
5. Weber, *Economy and Society,* 217 and 262.

alty to the purpose of the office in return for the grant of a secure existence."[6] Hiring and promotion are based on merit, that is, on technical ability to do the job, sometimes measured by examination. In theory, all aspects of administration are guided by written rules, including each official's rights, duties, and relationships with other officials. In theory, there is even an official appeals procedure that allows for the arbitration of grievances according to a formal code, and the office maintains extensive records of its operation.

The legalistic organization of bureaucracies makes them relatively stable and predictable and allows them to coordinate the efforts of large numbers of diverse technical experts. Weber argued that this was the foundation of modern capitalism, which he saw as the pursuit of "forever renewed profit, by means of continuous, rational capitalistic enterprises"—not merely the private ownership of the means of production.[7] He could argue, therefore, that socialism must also be bureaucratic, at least as long as it also seeks technical efficiency and universalistic administration.[8] In either case, rational-legal authority achieves a technical efficiency at the cost of impersonality and alienation.

In contrast, patrimonial authority is based "on a strictly personal loyalty."[9] Weber states: "The patrimonial office lacks above all the bureaucratic separation of the 'private' and the 'official' sphere."[10] Patrimonial officials typically do not consider the functions of their office duties they are obligated to undertake, but favors that can be dispensed according to personal discretion.[11] Private profit from the performance of public duty is the norm. Recruitment and promotion are based not on merit or examination but on personal relationships with other officials. There is no impartial appeals process. Extensive records are not maintained, and decisions tend to be made on an ad hoc basis. Authority in a patrimonial organization depends primarily on personal relationships, not technical competence. In this environment organizational goals are diluted by the personal goals of the

---

6. Ibid., 959.
7. Weber, *The Protestant Ethic and the Spirit of Capitalism*, 17.
8. Ernest Kilker, "Max Weber and the Possibilities for Socialism," 31–37.
9. Weber, *Economy and Society*, 1006.
10. Ibid., 1028.
11. Weber states: "Practically everything depends explicitly upon the personal considerations; upon the attitude toward the concrete applicant and his concrete request and upon purely personal connections, favors, promises and privileges" (ibid., 1041).

staff. Patrimonial organization is therefore inefficient in technical terms but is sometimes far more humane than bureaucracy.[12]

THE EXTENT OF
PATRIMONIAL RULERSHIP

One of the most difficult problems facing research on patrimonial rulership is the documentation of its actual importance. First, there is a conceptual problem. Weber's ideal types are not exclusive categories but are all present in different degrees and in different relationships in all states. The most significant problem is not to demonstrate that China is patrimonial but to determine how, when, and to what degree political institutions and relationships are structured in patrimonial terms. Nonetheless, some measure of the extent of patrimonial rulership is required to justify invoking the concept. This raises a second problem: it is difficult to measure empirically the extent of patrimonial rulership. Virtually all modern states are formally committed to universalistic or rational-legal principles of administration, and patrimonial rulership is consequently seen as embarrassingly close to corruption. It is difficult to measure empirically the extent of corruption anywhere. Leninist states impose additional restraints on research and information on the exercise of political power.

Wayne Di Franceisco and Zvi Gitelman have undertaken the most successful empirical measure of the extent of patrimonial rulership in a Leninist state. Their approach to the problem of conducting research inside Leninist states was to interview émigrés. They concluded that "bribery is not a last resort or an activity limited to society's marginal elements, but seems to be accepted by a large number of people as a common way of handling difficult situations" and reported that a plurality of respondents argue that "connections" are the best way to influence a government decision.[13] Interviewing émigrés is not a first choice, but this finding strongly suggests that in the Soviet Union many people approach political questions in patrimonial terms.

12. Most contemporary literature on patrimonial rulership is not explicitly Weberian, but instead uses the framework of "patron-client" relationships. For a comprehensive bibliography of this literature, see S. N. Eisenstadt and L. Roniger, *Patrons, Clients, and Friends: Interpersonal Relations and the Structure of Trust in Society.*
13. Di Franceisco and Gitelman, "Soviet Political Culture and 'Covert Participation' in Policy Implementation," 603–21.

In China widespread concern about corruption indicates that patrimonial rulership is important. Corruption indicates that private interests and personal relationships take precedence over rules and universalistic criteria that characterize patrimonial interaction. Corruption has been widely discussed in the post-Mao Chinese press, although usually episodically and to serve moral or political ends. Corruption has also been a frequent topic in "new realism" literature. Of course, fiction cannot be understood as fact, but literature is one of the least restricted forms of expression in China. Some relevant research has been conducted by Chinese academics, which I will discuss later. In a few select areas, detailed studies by Western academics are available. Finally, the leadership itself has estimated that "Party style" is a vital problem. Taken as a whole, these sources indicate that patrimonial rulership is pervasive.

Corruption has been an issue in Chinese Communist politics since at least 1949.[14] The People's Republic has a long history of anticorruption campaigns, beginning with the Sanfan-Wufan (3-Anti 5-Anti) campaign of 1952, which was in part oriented against social corruption but also concerned corruption within the ranks of the Party. Corruption was again a major focus of the Socialist Education movement and the Four Cleans campaign of the early 1960s. In the early 1970s the little reported or studied but large and violent Yida-Sanfan campaign focused once more on corruption. In the 1980s Party rectification has once more taken corruption as a central theme. Some episodic reports also suggest that corruption has a long history in individual localities, with corrupt local officials being displaced in one campaign but retaining behind-the-scenes influence and returning in a subsequent campaign.[15]

---

14. While this did not necessarily indicate corruption, intellectuals in the Yan'an Base Area complained that cadres received special privileges, including extra food rations. Wang Shiwei, who was later executed, wrote a *zawen* titled "Wild Lily" that dealt extensively with the system of ranks in supposedly egalitarian Yan'an. He states that there were five grades for food distribution and three for clothing (Wang Shiwei, "Wild Lily"). Wang states that one of the justifications given for this system of ranks was that the Soviet Union had such a system. Under Stalin there were various forms of "proto-corruption." Party members were rewarded with money and gifts, which were perhaps not illegal but were nonetheless kept secret. Several authors have argued that this provided the foundation for less ambiguous forms of corruption later. See, for example, Mervyn Mathews, *Privilege in the Soviet Union*, and Roy A. Medvedev, *Let History Judge*, 540. A similar argument could trace the origins of corruption in the CCP to the Yan'an period.

15. See, for example, "Local Factionalism Problem in Neiqiu County Receives Strict Handling" (Neiqiu xian difang zongpaizhuyi wenti shoudao yansu chuli), *Renmin*

The Chinese press has reported that many aspects of life in China are touched by corrupt dealings. Wojtek Zafanolli's study of China's second economy is the most complete attempt to survey press reports known to me. He reports a black market, questionable land dealings, illegal imports and exports, a parallel financial market, and extensive irregularities in individual localities and units. He finds the abuse of public property so widespread that he concludes that the concept of "state property" has legal connotations but is economically meaningless.[16] Episodic reports indicate that tax evasion, improper accounting, and violations of price controls are commonplace.[17] In general, "control and accounting" in Chinese commerce and industry remain weak and ineffective.[18] Other reports complain of extensive corrup-

---

Ribao (8 Nov. 1983): 5, and "Leader of Work Team of Central Discipline Inspection Commission Answers Questions," *Guangming Ribao*, 15 Jan. 1984, pp. 1, 4, trans. in FBIS-CHI-84-019, 27 Jan. 1984, pp. K7–11.

16. Zafanolli, "China's Second Economy: Second Nature?"

17. *Renmin Ribao* states that taxes account for 50 percent of the state's revenues, but serious problems remain in collecting taxes. See "Support Tax Departments in Levying Taxes According to Law," *Renmin Ribao*, 6 May 1981, p. 2, trans in FBIS-CHI-81-91, 13 May 1981, pp. K23–24. Investigations undertaken by tax departments in several provinces in 1981 uncovered tens of millions of yuan in unpaid taxes. See "Shaanxi Committee Demands Thorough Tax Inspection," *Shaanxi Ribao*, 6 Aug. 1981, trans. in FBIS-CHI-81-165, 26 Aug. 1981, p. T1; "Jiangsu Commentator Urges Tax Evasion Investigation," Jiangsu Radio, 23 July 1981, trans. in FBIS-CHI-81-142, 24 July 1981, p. O2; "Hubei Tax Evasion," Hubei Radio, 23 July 1981, trans. in FBIS-CHI-81-144, 28 July 1981, p. P4; "Jilin Scores Well in Solving Tax Evasion Cases," Jilin Radio, 10 Aug. 1981, trans. in FBIS-CHI-81-162, 21 Aug. 1981, p. S1; and "Investigate and Reform Strict Financial Regulations" (Bancha-bangai yange cai-jing jilu), *Nanjing Ribao*, 11 Oct. 79, p. 1.

In one episode, a petrochemical works in Jinan was cited for defrauding the state of 4.5 million yuan in one year, which meant that it had remitted only 12.5 percent of its lawful taxes. The firm had misrepresented the costs of various materials, recorded as productive expenditures nonproductive expenditures such as welfare benefits, and illegally purchased luxuries, such as a large motor pool, and gifts for cadres, such as silk and calculators. Moreover, petty-cash boxes throughout the plant funded by sales of spare parts and scrap were widely abused by cadres. See "Official Raps Funds Misuse at Jinan Plant," Beijing Xinhua Service, 28 July 1981, trans. in FBIS-CHI-81-145, 29 July 1981, pp. K1–2. One report from Guangdong province cited "several hundred cases" of tax collection cadres being beaten up in the course of their duties. See Guangdong Provincial Service, 24 Aug. 1985, trans. in FBIS-CHI-85-165, 26 Aug. 1985, p. P2.

18. Lax accounting has been cited as the cause of enormous losses to the state, as in the examples of tax fraud above. Nanjing officials estimated that over one-third of all thefts occurring in the city were "inside jobs" and that weak management and accounting procedures not only made abuses like these easier to conduct but also made them more difficult to track down. See "Internal Problems Stand Out" (Neibu wenti tuchu), *Nanjing Ribao*, 4 Mar. 1981, p. 4. Examples of embezzlement include a vegetable market manager who skimmed 40,000 yuan out of the market's funds over a ten-year period; a worker at a grain station who had pocketed 1,600 *jin* of grain-ration coupons and an unknown amount of cash; an accountant working for a food products company

tion in particular sectors of the economy, such as the Central Discipline Inspection Commission's announcement that "economic crime is rampant in grain departments."[19] A provincial secretary stated that reported episodes were not isolated but were part of a general pattern:

> Cases of power abuse . . . are not isolated. . . . Those in charge of highways abuse their power to flag down cars; those in charge of water shut off water supply at will; those in charge of taxes increase taxes and fines at will. Even in departments in charge of land planning, housing management, administration of justice, and public security, there are some people who would use the power given them by the people for personal gain. If these "highway lords," "water lords," and "housing lords" were allowed to continue practicing their philosophy that "those who live near a mountain live off the mountain, those who live near water live off the water," they would inevitably cause serious damage to the interests of the state and the people and [would] corrupt social practices.[20]

Episodic reports indicate that corruption takes place at all levels of Chinese society and occasionally on a grand scale. In the best-known episode, authorities on Hainan Island illegally imported 79,000 automobiles in fifteen months, which was more than the nation officially

---

who manipulated accounts around a period of decreased prices for holidays to make a small personal profit; and, in Beijing, a unit leader at a small retail store who was simply lifting money out of the till from time to time. See "Big Embezzler Zhang Liming Receives Legal Sanctions" (Da tanwu fan Zhang Liming shou falu zhicai), *Nanjing Ribao*, 14 Jan. 1980, p. 4; "Theft of Grain Ration Coupons Receives Punishment" (Touqie liangpiao shou chengban), *Nanjing Ribao*, 11 Nov. 1979; "Manager Wang Dexi Receives Punishment" (Yingye Yuan Dexi shou chu-fen), *Nanjing Ribao*, 11 Nov. 1979; "Thief of Cash Caught in the Act" (Dangchang zhuahuo tou na huokuan de qiezei), *Beijing Wanbao*, 22 Aug. 1980, p. 2. Reported incidents of internal thievery included a bank clerk who assisted another man in withdrawing funds with a stolen passbook; a man working for the Nanjing Broadcasting Equipment Factory Supply and Marketing Section who stole and resold privately to other units equipment worth over 12,000 yuan; a postal carrier who rifled mails for which he was responsible, for over 550 yuan; and a worker at a county department store who stole parts from the store to build his own television. See "Thief of Equipment Yang Jianting Has Been Sentenced to Five Years" (Yang Jianting daoqie qicai bei pan xing wu nian), *Nanjing Ribao*, 15 Aug. 1980; "Li Maohong Sentenced" (Li Maohong bei pan xing), *Nanjing Ribao*, 16 Jan. 1980, p. 4; "Relevant Departments Point Out That This Factory Has Many Loopholes" (Youguan bumen tichu zhege chang de loudong hen duo), *Beijing Wanbao*, 24 July 1980; "Xuanwu District Investigators Break an Important Embezzlement Case" (Xuanwuchu jianchayuan chaqing yijian zhongda tanwu an), *Nanjing Ribao*, 2 Jan. 1980; "Criminal Tracked Down" (Chahuo zuifan), *Nanjing Ribao*, 16 Jan. 1980.

19. This report cites 14,700 criminal cases and the embezzlement of 35 million *jin* of grain and edible oil and over 15 million yuan (Beijing Xinhua Service, 17 Jan. 1984, trans. in FBIS-CHI-84-018, 26 Jan. 1984, pp. K2–5).

20. Bai Jinian, secretary of the Shaanxi Provincial CPC Committee, cited in Beijing Xinhua Service, 28 Apr. 1986, trans. in FBIS-CHI-86-085, 2 May 1986, pp. T1–2.

planned to import in a year, and for financing, illegally obtained 540 million U.S. dollars in foreign exchange, whereas their official allotment was only 40 million U.S. dollars.[21] Both disposing of the automobiles and obtaining the foreign exchange must have been nationwide operations. Reports also complain of smaller-scale abuses at lower levels, such as gas company repairmen receiving gifts for services, or schools demanding bribes to admit new students.[22]

Corruption has been a prominent theme in post-Mao "new realism" literature. There are so many examples that it is possible to list only a few representative samples. In Jiang Zilong's "Pages from a Factory Secretary's Diary," a factory manager uses corrupt means to build morale and boost production. At the end of the story, a bit drunk, he compares himself with an honest subordinate:

> I know you must think I'm slick as a snake. But I wasn't born like that. The longer you muddle along in this society, the smarter you become. . . . The more complex the society, the sharper the people. Liu's a good man, but . . . If I'd listened to Liu and run the factory in a rigid way, production would have dropped. I'd have offended the workers and there'd be no profit. The state and our leaders wouldn't have been happy about it. Don't think I'm glad.[23]

Other short stories tell of a young man who obtains tremendous privileges by impersonating the son of a cadre,[24] of a slick operator who

21. *Nanfang Ribao*, 4 Aug. 1985, pp. 1, 2, trans. in FBIS-CHI-85-153, 8 Aug. 1985, pp. P1–9, and Niu Zhengwu, "Hainan: The Future Remains Bright," *Liaowang* 33 (19 Aug. 1985), pp. 19–20, trans. in FBIS-CHI-85-172, pp. K6–10.

22. "Personal Considerations Not Yielded to in Installing and Repairing Gas Equipment" (Jie zhuang meiqi bu xun siqing), *Wen Hui Bao*, 26 Dec. 1980, p. 1. The problem with school admissions was reported in a series on the problems encountered when residents moved into a new apartment block. From a Chinese perspective, most serious was the refusal of the manager of the local grain station to provide them with grain. See "Manager's Corruption Bravely Reported" (Dadan jianju jingli tanwu zui), *Beijing Wanbao*, 3 July 1980, p. 2; "Measures Adopted to Guarantee Newly Moved Families' Grain Supply" (Caiqu cuoshi qiebao xin qian hu liangshi gongying), *Beijing Wanbao*, 8 June 1980, p. 1; "Work Style Does Not Gain People's Hearts" (Zuofeng bude renxin), *Beijing Wanbao*, 3 June 1980, p. 1; "Is This According to Policy?" (Zhe fuhe zhengce ma?), *Beijing Wanbao*, 29 May 1980, p. 1.

23. Jiang Zilong, "Pages from a Factory Secretary's Diary," in Jiang Zilong, *All the Colors of the Rainbow*. In the same collection, "Manager Qiao" and "More on Manager Qiao" also portray a freewheeling factory manager. In one of the most intriguing episodes in the Manager Qiao series, the truly corrupt antagonists leak information about one of Manager Qiao's indiscretions to the press, and the resulting "episodic report" actually serves to cover up the worst transgressions. This suggests that while episodic reports may not be an entirely accurate source of information, perhaps they downplay corruption as much as they exaggerate it.

24. Sha Yexin, Li Shoucheng, Yao Mingde, "If I Were For Real."

obtains anything he wants while the family of an honest intellectual lead miserable lives in a cramped apartment,[25] and of a peasant's life-long quest to build his family a home, which is checked by every change in the political wind and succeeds at last only by bribing all and sundry.[26]

Liu Binyan's reportage literature (*baogao wenxue*) provides detailed accounts of extensive corruption. Reportage literature is not quite investigative journalism,[27] but Liu's case studies offer vivid descriptions of how formal public hierarchies are displaced by informal covert networks or webs of personal relationships. In his best-known piece, "People or Monsters," an entire county is dominated by one woman. Her power base is a coal company, which she came to control through factional struggles during the Cultural Revolution. Thereafter, she traded favors to amass tremendous power and embezzled her way to wealth. Those who dared to criticize her or who attempted to report her doings to higher authorities were defamed, arrested, and tortured.[28]

The post-Mao leadership has consistently concerned itself with corruption. Premier Zhao Ziyang stated:

25. Liu Xinwu, "The Overpass."

26. Gao Xiaosheng, "Li Shunda Builds a House." In another pertinent example, Wang Meng, subsequently promoted to minister of culture, wrote of an honest barber who renders life-saving assistance to a ranking cadre during the Cultural Revolution while the cadre is in deep political difficulties. The cadre vows that if he is ever returned to power he will implement reforms, but when he is returned to power, the barber discovers him to be obsessed with cultivating his superiors and distributing luxury goods at bargain prices. The barber concludes that his cadre friend is far superior to the Cultural Revolution cadres and that hotheaded attempts to rectify his behavior will only lead to a return to the bad old days. It therefore falls on the barber and other citizens to constantly but gently remind their leaders of their promises and duties. See Wang Meng, "The Barber's Tale."

27. Liu is often accused of distorting the facts, although he himself claims to employ careful interview techniques. See the "Prologue" to *Because I Love* (Yinwei wo ai), 1–5.

28. See Liu Binyan, "People or Monsters," as well as other in-depth reports, including "Let Me Tell You Some Secret," and, with Li Guosheng, "An Invisible Machine—A Negative Example of Perfunctorily Carrying Out Party Rectification." Another recent essay by Liu, "A Second Kind of Loyalty," offers several examples of individuals wrongly accused of political crimes who subsequently suffer years or decades of privation. In each case the protagonist heroically struggles to make some meaningful contribution to society, but finds every avenue blocked by political prejudices and personal animosities. Liu contrasts this "second kind of loyalty," which is loyalty to principles or to the Party's public purposes, with the blind loyalty of the Lei Feng type of model workers and implicitly with the personal loyalties that undergird the webs he describes elsewhere. The conclusion is that too often the first kind of loyalty is rewarded while the second is punished, which Liu's recent loss of Party membership ironically confirms.

Today, smuggling, peddling smuggled goods, speculation, swindling, corruption, accepting bribes, and other crimes in the economic sphere are
much more serious than during the movements to oppose the three and
five evils in 1953. The inroads of such crimes on our Party organizations
and cadres' contingents are quite serious. This situation, if not struggled
against immediately with determination, will develop from bad to worse
in certain localities and will be unstoppable in two or three years.[29]

Accounts like these do not prove that China is corrupt or patrimonial, but it was not my intent to do so. Instead, they suggest that
in many different spheres of Chinese life, personal relationships are
more important than rules, and particularistic norms are more important than universalistic norms. This is an important step toward
understanding the strengths and weaknesses of Leninist states, but it
needs to be refined through a consideration of why patrimonialism is
important.

POLITICAL CULTURE

Why is patrimonial rulership important in China? I will consider
three possibilities: first, patrimonialism stems from Chinese society,
especially from long-standing cultural traditions; second, patrimonialism, and especially corruption, is a rational response to rigid and inefficient bureaucracy; and third, patrimonial rulership is an integral
aspect of China's Leninist state. I find important truths in each of
these arguments and will not attempt to reach an absolute or unilat-
eral conclusion.

The first group of arguments finds the sources of patrimonialism
and corruption in Chinese society. A Western version of this argument is based on political culture theory and draws heavily on Talcott
Parsons' argument that shared values hold social systems together.[30]
Political culture theory argues that even when institutions change,
traditional values will continue to influence behavior. For example,
Samuel Huntington argues that corruption is "not so much the result
of the deviance of behavior from accepted norms as it is the deviance

29. From *Renmin Ribao*, 30 Mar. 1982, trans. in FBIS-CHI-82-063, 1 Apr. 1982,
p. K5.
30. For an example of the work of Talcott Parsons, see *The System of Modern
Societies* (Englewood Cliffs, N.J., 1971). Parsons' argument owes much to Weber, although Parsons' emphasis on the centrality of values and his neglect of history would
surely have been rejected by Weber, who rejected mono-causal arguments, whether they
were based on economics or on values.

of norms from established patterns of behavior.[31] In other words, when a modernizing state imposes new norms for social behavior, previously accepted practices are redefined as "corruption."[32] Although Huntington argues that a strong state is a powerful agent of change, those who apply political-culture theory to the study of communism have generally concluded that these very strong states have not been able to transform traditional culture radically.[33]

Chinese scholars similarly criticize the persistence of "feudalism" (*fengjianzhuyi*) in Chinese culture. The general thrust of this argument is that remnants of China's long "feudal" period have persisted into the period of socialism. Feudal remnants include a wide range of corrupt and arbitrary abuses of power, such as commands issued by cadres without regard for others' opinions, assumption by cadres that their official status entitles them to special privileges, increased indifference and inefficiency among bureaucracies, and social susceptibility to cults of personality based on individuals who act like emperors.[34] Cast in this light, leaders such as the Gang of Four and innumerable lesser but nonetheless corrupt and dictatorial officials are the latest representatives of a long line of "reactionary diehards" stretching from the Qin emperor to the dowager-empress.[35] Chinese reformers argue that because feudalism persisted for so long in China—about

31. Huntington, *Political Order in Changing Societies*, 50.
32. W. F. Wertheim has described a classic example of this process. When the Dutch attempted to export the Napoleonic Code to the Dutch Indies, various long-standing practices that demonstrated a lack of separation of personal and office life in the colonial administration persisted, but became illegal. See Wertheim, "Sociological Aspects of Corruption in Southeast Asia." Wertheim's optimism about the Sanfan-Wufan campaign proved misplaced.
33. Gabriel A. Almond, "Communism and Political Culture Theory." Alfred Meyer makes a substantively similar argument in somewhat different terms in "Communist Revolutions and Cultural Change." Stephen White among others has applied this methodology to the Soviet Union and concludes, for example, that the lack of democratic institutions, and development through "revolution from above," are deeply established cultural patterns with little to do with Marxism. See White, "Soviet Political Culture Reassessed." Among others, Lloyd Eastman and Lucian Pye have applied these arguments to China. See Eastman, *The Abortive Revolution: China Under Nationalist Rule, 1927–37*, esp. chap. 7, "Social Traits and Political Behavior in Kuomintang China," 238–313. Recent works by Lucian Pye include *The Dynamics of Chinese Politics;* "Nuances in Chinese Political Culture," with Nathan Leites; "On Chinese Pragmatism in the 1980's."
34. The first three are often described, respectively, as "what one person says goes" (*yige ren shuole xuanle*), "becoming privileged" (*teshuhua*), and "bureaucratism" (*guanliaozhuyi*).
35. Lan Ling, "Getting to the Bottom of 'What One Person Says Goes' "; also Li Kan, "The Nature of the Feudal Diehard Faction and the Characteristics of Its Thought."

two thousand years from the Qin or Han dynasty to the Opium War—it has a lasting influence. Yuan Shi wrote: "The tragic fate suffered by the Chinese people was seldom seen in the world. This is because feudalism emerged early and lasted long."[36]

Like the political-culture argument, the critique of feudalism finds the sources of contemporary problems in the persistence of something old. In proper Marxist form, however, the critique of feudalism explains that the persistence of feudal superstructure is based on the survival of small-scale peasant production. In much the same tone as Marx's "sack of potatoes" argument,[37] Xu Sheng and Zhou Jizhi argue that peasants cannot change the nature of society, for they are not representatives of a new means of production. Therefore peasant revolutions could not end feudalism, and in practice the widespread destruction they caused delayed precapitalist accumulation.[38] However, because peasant production was organized in relatively autonomous and self-sufficient households, it could be reestablished following any period of havoc. Viewed in these materialist terms, Mao's attempt to transform China's social and political superstructure before achieving a transformation of the economic base was a tragic mistake that not only delayed economic growth but also retarded the development of progressive socialist values such as democracy.[39]

Wei Keming and others locate the link between feudal economics and culture in the persistence of attitudes generated by the structure of peasant families.[40] Zhang Pufan argues that the current authoritar-

36. Yuan Shi, "The Ideology of Special Privileges Is the Ideology of Decadent Exploiting Classes."

37. In the "Eighteenth Brumaire of Louis Napoleon" (pp. 320–21) Marx argues that peasants' "mode of production isolates them from one another"—like a sack of potatoes—and that peasants are therefore incapable of leading society toward historical progress.

38. Xu Sheng, "Are Peasant Wars the Only Direct Impetus of Development in Feudal Society?" Also Zhou Jizhi, "The Basic Characteristics of the Development of Chinese Feudal Society."

39. Zhou Jizhi writes: "The creation of the feudal millstone . . . cannot be completely imputed to past history. . . . After liberating the whole country, we did not emphasize the method of developing the productive forces to transform the structure of the natural economy, but instead concentrated on continuous transformation of the relations of production, increasing the extent of public ownership to promote the socialist transformation of the economy. Relevant to this, we also did not fully attend to the task of developing socialist democracy and strengthening the dictatorship of the proletariat, thereby continuously running many political movements that were divorced from the demands of economic development." See Zhou Jizhi, "Chinese Feudal Society."

40. Wei Keming, "The Evil Legacy of the Patriarchal System Cannot Be Neglected."

ian and arbitrary work-style of some cadres is based on the model of the peasant patriarch.[41] Tong Chao and others argue that some cadres' expectations of being accorded "special privileges" are remnants of the feudal system of ranks and privileges and the clan system.[42] Traditional family structure is also linked to the "politics of the emperor's relatives on his wife's side of his family" (waiqi), which is seen as the antecedent of the use by some cadres (including Mao) of their official position to promote their relatives to positions of power.[43] Other "feudal remnants" are linked to what Marx calls the "idiocy of rural life." Wang Zhizhong claims that "obscurantism" (mengmeizhuyi), or social susceptibility to wildly unscientific beliefs, such as the superstitions of the Boxers, is the background to the social acceptance of the ideology of the Gang of Four.[44] Elsewhere the problem of the deification of individuals is considered in a similar light.[45]

The critique of feudalism also shares with the political-culture approach the argument that the new state has tried to change culture with limited success. It argues that Chinese history was different from European history because of the lack of a strong bourgeoisie. The reforms that followed bourgeois revolutions in the West, such as "equality before the law" and democracy, are viewed as progressive challenges to feudal hierarchy, despotism, and nepotism. Li Genhe and Lin Qun note that the Chinese bourgeoisie was never strong enough to rule on its own, but had to form alliances with other classes.[46] While Marx argued that imperialism would end the stagnation of Asiatic societies, Chinese now argue that the foreign bourgeoisie also had a limited influence. Li Shu writes:

41. Zhang Pufan, "Patriarchal Leadership Style Is a Pernicious Vestige of Feudalism."
42. See Tong Chao, "Criticizing the System of Powerful Families and Feudal Special Privileges"; Xue Mudao, "The Systems of Stratification and Special Privileges of Feudal Society"; Ye Linsheng, "On Special Privileges and the Growth of Family Power in Feudal Bureaucracy"; Zheng Changgan, "Feudal Society's Patriarchal Clan System"; and Zhang Shapo, Zhang Pufan, and Zeng Xuanyi, " 'The Big Official's Will' Cannot Replace Law."
43. Zhou Xinqiang, "Female Relatives of the Emperor in the Feudal Era and Their Disaster."
44. Wang Zhizhong, "Feudal Obscurantism and the Yihetuan Movement."
45. Special Commentator, "The Deep Lessons from the Deification of an Individual" (Shenhua geren de shenke jiaoxun), Renmin Ribao, 4 July 1980; also Xinhua Yuebao 9 (1980): 6–7.
46. Li Genhe and Lin Qun, "A Preliminary Study of the Struggle Against Feudal Remnants During the Period of Socialist Construction in Our Country."

> Semi-colonialism semi-feudalism, strictly speaking, was a special character-
> istic of large and medium cities along the coasts and rivers. The influence
> of foreign aggression on the extensive rural areas of the interior was indi-
> rect; to a large extent it was still the forces of feudalism ruling.[47]

Consequently, China never experienced the progressive aspects of bourgeois history, and the destruction of feudalism awaited the victory of the Chinese Communist Party—which Chinese writers assert has the capacity to far surpass the bourgeois version of human rights.[48] Nonetheless, Li and Lin argue that the Party failed to live up to its potential and in practice exacerbated the problem of feudalism:

> But, for a relatively long period, we lacked complete knowledge of the
> serious presence of feudal remnants, and took capitalism, originally com-
> pletely weak, for our most dangerous and only enemy. As a result, the
> danger of the dead forces of feudalism rekindling existed but was not seen,
> as if the struggle against them had been relaxed, while on the other hand,
> the danger of capitalist restoration was exaggerated without limit, leading
> to great blindness in the struggle against capitalism. In this way, feudal
> remnants were concealed in several aspects of society and in the people's
> consciousness, like a shadow following us, corrupting the socialist
> enterprise.[49]

They argue that the Gang of Four posed as socialists when they attacked capitalism but in fact were representatives of feudalism who attacked capitalism for the wrong reasons.[50]

This general approach makes some persuasive claims and provides a powerful explanation of contemporary Chinese political history. First, traditional Chinese society was personalistic. Second, this argument provides a framework for interpreting the Party history since 1949. Broadly speaking, the twists and turns in the state's revolution from above represent alternating charismatic and rational-legal strategies in a continuous struggle against patrimonialism.

For example, in the Sanfan-Wufan (3-Anti 5-Anti) campaign of 1952, the Party attempted to depersonalize and regularize relations between the state and society in order to expand the role of the new state. A. Doak Barnett pointed out that the scope of government had dramatically expanded:

---

47. Li Shu, "Destroying the Influence of Feudal Remnants Is an Important Requirement for China's Modernization."
48. Shu Bing, "On Human Rights and the Rights of Citizens" (Lun renquan yu
gongmin quan), *Guangming Ribao*, 19 June 1979; also *Xinhua Yuebao* 7 (1979): 4–9.
49. Li and Lin, "Struggle Against Feudal Remnants."
50. Ibid., 79.

The Communists now operate with an enormous (for China) national budget which in the past two years has expanded rapidly with increasing military expenditures resulting from the Korean War, a great enlargement of the bureaucracy and government payroll, and an extension of government activities into all spheres of national economic life.[51]

This had to be paid for, and the old system of tax collection was too personal and too unreliable. Barnett writes:

> Chinese businessmen for many years have operated in a relatively amoral atmosphere in which laws, rules, and regulations have been viewed mainly as obstacles to be evaded; and tax evasion, bribery, use of official connections, and sharp dealings have been common if not standard practice.[52]

The Communists used their extensive organization to pressure business and commercial leaders to repudiate their former ways. They not only mobilized their growing command of the economy and the public security forces, but also organized trade unions and recruited informers in most enterprises.[53] The number of people investigated and charged bears tribute to the capacity of the Communists' organization and the breadth of their vision. Bo Yibo said that 76 percent of merchants investigated were found guilty and that 4.5 percent of government personnel were punished.[54]

The post-Mao reforms are a continuation of the same struggle by different means. Over and over, studies of post-Mao political reform note the intent to "rationalize, legalize, and institutionalize the structures of the state and party."[55] Legal codes have been promulgated,

51. Barnett, *Communist China in the Early Years, 1945–55*, 157.

52. Ibid., 150. Kenneth Lieberthal writes that at the time of liberation in Tianjin, even in the most advanced sectors of the economy that engaged in interregional and international trading, contracts were not widely used. Business was conducted primarily among friends and by giving one's word. He suggests that official rates of taxation were regarded merely as the government's opening position in negotiations over how much tax a firm would pay. See Lieberthal, *Revolution and Tradition in Tientsin*, 19–21.

53. Lieberthal portrays the investigation of a Mr. Wang in some detail. The normal accouterments of procedural justice were lacking. Mr. Wang was forced to meet with a group of businessmen who put intense pressure on each other to repudiate their past practices. See Lieberthal, 126–49.

54. Chen and Chen, "The 'Three-Anti and Five-Anti' Movements in Communist China." In addition, Sanfan-Wufan had a severe economic impact. Barnett (p. 136) claims that during the campaign, trade between the PRC and Hong Kong fell by half.

55. Hong Yung Lee, "The Implications of Reform for Ideology, State, and Society in China." See also Harry Harding, "Political Development in Post-Mao China." While noting countervailing tendencies, Harding writes: "Chinese leaders have placed heavy

the judiciary has been strengthened and given more autonomy, efforts have been made to separate Party and governmental functions, administrative structures have been simplified, and there has been a tremendous turnover of staff, favoring younger and more technically competent cadres. Corruption and other "feudal remnants" have been roundly condemned. These changes have been implemented in an orderly way. Above all, post-Mao politics has maintained a consistent effort to insure that such movements aid rather than impede economic growth and has even sought to tailor political strategies to expedite economic growth.[56] Despite the scale of the current movement, the previous record indicates that it is too early to predict success.

In sum, there is a strong case to be made for the political-culture explanation of corruption and patrimonial rulership. In Chinese debates it is not necessary to document the existence of "feudal remnants," it is only necessary to explain why they exist, whose fault they are, and what can be done about them. China's traditional political culture really did contain elements that appear corrupt by standards that the Party has subsequently attempted to implement. The Party has persistently employed a range of strategies to eliminate patrimonialism.

There is an important problem with this approach. Why has patrimonialism persisted despite the Party's efforts to eliminate it? Is it, as the critiques of feudalism often suggest, that the Party has adopted inappropriate strategies? Or are there more fundamental problems?

A RATIONAL-ACTION
APPROACH TO CORRUPTION

An alternate approach to the study of corruption is based on a rational-actor model of politics. The fundamental metaphor for this model is an economic market in which individuals choose between alternatives based on their own calculation of their best interest.[57] In

---

emphasis on the development of regular bureaucratic procedures and institutional processes" (13). Brantly Womack writes: "The thrust of democratic reform is to strengthen democratic institutions and the rule of law" ("Modernization and Democratic Reform in China").

56. For an accessible Chinese interpretation of Chinese administrative reform as rationalization, see You Chunmei, "Current Administrative Reform in China."

57. For an excellent outline of the rational-actor model, see J. C. Harsanyi, "Rational-Choice Models of Political Behavior vs. Functionalist and Conformist Theories."

this metaphor, modern bureaucracies create "a system analogous to the mandatory pricing system . . . while corrupt bureaucratic systems more resemble the free market."[58] From this perspective, corruption is not "traditional" but is a calculated response to state institutions. This approach reverses the political culture approach's estimate of the state. Instead of arguing that the state is attempting to eliminate corruption but has failed, it suggests that the state has created conditions under which people choose corruption as the best alternative. It also suggests that corruption performs socially useful functions more efficiently than state structures do.

This approach to corruption provides powerful insights into the nature of corruption in contemporary China. The Party's limited success in eliminating corrupt practices indicates that the Party not only has been ineffective in fighting patrimonialism, but has created institutions that perpetuate patrimonial relationships in general and corruption in particular. The authoritarian character of the Party's rule often masks inefficiency and unmet needs, which individuals—rationally—seek to remedy through the most efficient means available. The Party, in turn, labels this "corrupt" to protect its own inefficient prerogatives.

While rational-actor theory is less attractive for being ahistorical, it is satisfying for rejecting elitist explanations. The political culture approach in general and Huntington in particular assign a positive active role to the state and a negative passive role to society—that is, society bears retrogressive values which the state is trying to modernize. The political culture model notes society's ability to passively resist the state, which is a welcome corrective to the totalitarian model. Nonetheless, the state remains the only active progressive force, and society bears the onus of sustaining unsavory authoritarian, inefficient, clientelistic, and corrupt values. Moreover, individuals are implicitly assumed to be dominated by values they did not choose and have little will or choice.[59]

58. Robert O. Tilman, "Emergence of Black-Market Bureaucracy: Administration, Development, and Corruption in the New States."

59. Another significant problem with the political culture argument is that its concept of culture is simplistic and static. Following Parsons and the political culture theorists of the 1960s, the political culture approach tends to reduce culture to a series of core values, which are presented like mathematical axioms or proverbs. Past the observation that traditional culture tends to persist, the political culture approach does not tell us why culture does not change, or what could change it. Cultures do change over time. For example, in earlier periods, both Britain and Sweden were far more patrimo-

Many aspects of corruption in China are well explained by the rational-actor model. In particular, the inadequacies of state planning are nearly a guarantee of corruption. Production quotas that do not correctly estimate social demand, prices that do not reflect costs or demand, and various forms of regulated markets create numerous opportunities and a tremendous demand for violations of normal procedures. Regulated markets and restricted and administered systems of distribution have long created a demand for "domestic smuggling." For example, William Hinton reports that in the late 1950s the failure of the state and cooperatives to provide for basic needs created opportunities for enormous profits, as in the case of a peasant who was able to earn "several hundred dollars in one night" merely by riding his bicycle to a nearby town and returning with a hundred catties of turnip seed to sell locally.[60] According to reports in local papers, similar activities abounded in the early 1980s. For example, in a case reported in Nanjing Ribao, price differentials between two markets encouraged "profiteers" to buy large quantities of vegetables in one market and illegally ship them to the other where they could be resold at a higher price.[61] In a case reported in Hunan Ribao, the artificially low price of fish encouraged "speculators" to purchase nearly a whole truckload of fresh fish as soon as it was delivered to a shop in Changsha. The shop price for the fish was 0.61 yuan per jin, but they were able to sell the fish on the street at 0.80–1.00 yuan per jin.[62]

nial than rational-legal, which is to say that by contemporary standards they would have been judged quite corrupt. Nonetheless, now these nations are among the least corrupt in the world. Mary McAuley presents these and other provocative criticisms in "Political Culture and Communist Politics: One Step Forward, Two Steps Back," in Political Culture and Communist Studies, 13–39. Perhaps further research on political culture could turn to definitions of culture like that of Clifford Geertz, which views culture as a symbolic system for communication and is thus more open-ended and tolerant of conflict than is Parsons' (Clifford Geertz, The Interpretation of Culture, New York, 1973) or Howard Wiarda's, which views culture as a pattern of historical development and is thus directly concerned with change (Howard J. Wiarda, "Law and Political Development in Latin America" and "Social Change and Political Development in Latin America," in Politics and Social Change in Latin America.

60. Hinton, Shenfan, 288. Following this observation, Hinton echoes the state's usual moralistic condemnation of "profiteers" when he states that the "returns [from speculation] were often way out of proportion to the contribution," and that speculation "had a demoralizing effect on those honest peasants who stayed home."

61. "Xu Youhua Receives Economic Sanctions," (Xu Youhua shou jingji zhicai), Nanjing Ribao, 3 May 1980, p. 1.

62. "Hunan Ribao on Illegal Profiteering," Hunan Ribao, 10 Aug. 1981, trans. in FBIS-CHI-81-56, 13 Aug. 1981, pp. P2–3. Shop workers do not necessarily discourage

Side payments like these are not confined to the retail sector but are an important part of Chinese commerce and industry. Producers are often required to make extra payments to acquire needed supplies, or to "pour oil on the machine to make it run smoothly." For example, the director of a county light-industry bureau in Anhui stated:

> Giving presents, offering bribes and going in through the back door have become means for our enterprises to procure materials and market unsalable products. To secure supplies and "find the rice to put on our stoves," our purchasing agents have rushed about here and there. Their traveling expenses, gift expenses, and entertainment expenses were astonishingly large amounts. In one and a half months this year, the No. 2 light-industry bureau spent more than 10,000 yuan for entertainment expenses, not including the money for sending presents and offering bribes. According to investigations, the county's arts and crafts plant spent more than 4,000 yuan in one and a half months this year on gifts. To market unsalable goods it is also necessary to offer bribes and send presents. In the national exhibition of arts and crafts . . . most of the exhibits displayed by the Jiashan County Arts and Crafts Plant were unsalable products. As a matter of fact, the quality of embroidered quilt covers it produced was inferior to that of Wuhu's. However, the plant had taken along many peanuts to be given away as presents, as it succeeded in selling more than 3,000 quilt covers while Wuhu only sold a little more than 600.[63]

Alternatively, those who have scarce commodities are well aware of their ability to "pluck feathers from a wild goose as it passes":

> Some people take advantage of their goods, materials, and power to set up barriers at every level and create obstacles willfully, deliberately make things difficult for others, indulge in the practice of "plucking feathers from a wild goose as it passes," and even hint at bribery, engage in extortion and racketeering and block the normal channels of commodity circulation. Anyone who does not invite people to dinner, send gifts, and offer bribes is held up, with the result that no raw materials will be sent to the enterprises concerned and their products will be unmarketable.[64]

---

these practices even if they do not receive kickbacks, as it quickly clears both stock and shoppers from their store.

63. "Corruption Still Serious Among Party Cadres," *Zhengming Ribao*, 24 July 1981, trans. in FBIS-CHI-81-144, 28 July 1981, pp. W2–3. In another typical case, the model manager of a factory in Shanghai producing materials needed in making plastic goods received a letter from a plastic plant offering a premium of 100 yuan per ton in addition to the regular price, for ten tons of raw materials, and noting that no receipt would have to be issued for the premium. ("Anyone Using This Kind of 'Back Door' Will Be Rebuffed" [Lai ce gao 'hou men' gege yao pengbi], *Jiefang Ribao*, 29 Jan. 1981, p. 1.)

64. "Beijing Ribao Examines 'Study of Relationships,'" *Beijing Ribao*, 29 Sept. 1981, FBIS-CHI-81-200, p. R1. Other examples of "pouring oil" and "plucking feath-

The point is that in a planned economy, planning is inevitably imperfect and corruption is therefore inevitable.

Just as corruption marketizes a planned economy, corruption can provide openings in a closed political system. Citizens who encounter problems with the state's rigid and cumbersome formal organization can turn to informal private channels to work out compromises. To repeat a Polish joke, "patronage is the last human emotion on the road to socialism." For example, a college graduate who is given a work assignment to a unit he does not want to join might be able to use informal channels to redirect his assignment—if he has the right *guanxi,* or connections.[65] This form of policy adjustment is available primarily to those who have something to trade or at least some relationship with someone who has. Hence opportunities of this sort are disproportionately available to cadres. Cadres are able to buy things not available on the open market,[66] obtain better housing for themselves and their children,[67] find jobs and obtain urban residence per-

---

ers" include the manager of a wholesale fruit stand in Shanghai who diverted 300 *jin* of bananas from the open market and sent them instead to various other units' leaderships to "coordinate relations" (*xiezhu guanxi*) (Letter to the Editor, *Jiefang Ribao*, 29 Jan. 1981, p. 3); a company that had to pass out quilts and tea to get machine parts ("Extortion of 'Commissions' Prohibited," *Beijing Review* 37, 14 Sept. 1981, p. 3); and a farm machinery company in Qinghai that sold tractors and tractor parts to customers who were not legally entitled to them, in return for an automobile frame, parts for a jeep, a jeep, large quantities of various building materials, and tons of rice and flour ("People's Daily Reports on Legal Violations," *Renmin Ribao,* 26 July 1978, p. 2, trans. in FBIS-CHI-78-82, 7 Aug. 1978, pp. E19–20).

65. I heard several accounts of students using personal relationships to change their job assignment. In another example of the same sort, *Nanjing Bao* reported a case of a worker whose unit was offering employment to the offspring of unit members, but only if they were of a certain age. This worker's unemployed son did not qualify, so the worker attempted to "fix" things by asking the police precinct captain to change the date on the son's birth certificate. As an inducement, he offered the captain a hen, twenty eggs, a carton of high-class cigarettes, and a package of cookies. As luck would have it, this captain was a model policeman and refused to help. See "Police Precinct Captain Refuses Gift" (Paichusuozhang jue shou liwu), *Nanjing Bao,* 14 Mar. 1979, p. 3.

66. In a classic example in Beijing, when a brewery truck was sighted delivering beer—which was difficult to obtain—to a restaurant, a long line formed at the front door of the restaurant. In fact, the beer was literally being sold out the back door of the restaurant and was not available to the general public. When a customer complained, he was told he could go all the way to the Central Committee and it would not make a difference, as the unit buying the beer had very good connections. "Manager Taking the Lead in Opening the Back Door Is Not Afraid of Complaints" (Daitou kai houmen jingli bu pa gaozhuang), *Beijing Wanbao,* 2 Aug. 1980, p. 1.

67. When one unit in Beijing built a 72-unit apartment building, only 19 of 547 workers' families applying for housing received an apartment. In addition to 31 units reserved for prior residents of the new building's site, 18 units were turned over to the unit that provided the investment capital, and 4 units were allocated for the care of old

mits for their children, obtain extra permits to have children,[68] and even exempt themselves and their children from the law.[69] One of the common "scams" in Chinese society demonstrates social perception of cadres' special status. There are many reports in the Chinese press of impostors, or *pianzi,* who pretend to be the son or daughter of a high-level cadre. People who believe the impostor's story offer meals, gifts, and money in hopes of receiving the benefits of the cadre-parent's privileges and connections. One young *pianzi* in Beijing took a taxi from downtown to Beijing University, a reasonably long and expensive ride. He told the taxi driver he was the son of a PLA officer, had lived abroad as an embassy worker, and was about to begin graduate school. The taxi driver sought to introduce the young man to his daughter in hopes of arranging a favorable marriage. The daughter was embarrassed and refused to meet the young man, but he nonetheless offered to buy high-quality furniture that his supposed father could obtain without ration coupons. The unfortunate taxi driver advanced him 300 yuan and he promptly disappeared.[70] While the state cautions people to be less gullible, impostors may even

cadres, which turned out to be apartments for various children and a chauffeur of the unit's leading cadres. See "Where Did 53 Apartments Go?" (53 danyuan nar qu le?), *Beijing Wanbao,* 4 Oct. 1980.

68. For an example, see "Resolutely Correct Improper Work Style, Enthusiastically Manage Affairs for the People" (Jianjue jiuzheng bu zheng zhi feng, recheng wei qunzhong ban shishi), *Renmin Ribao,* 25 June 1985, p. 4.

69. One of the most notorious cases of cadres influencing the course of formal justice occurred in Hangzhou, where from 1974 to 1978 a gang of young toughs raped or molested over a hundred women in addition to committing various thefts. The gang had been led by the two Xiong brothers, whose father had been a ranking cadre in Zhejiang province during that time. His connections had been sufficient to protect the gang from prosecution even in the case of such terrible crimes. These connections even protected the brothers for a time after the father, having fallen from grace, was transferred to another area (but not prosecuted). See "Hangzhou People's Court Legally Punishes the Two Xiong Criminals and Their Gang" (Hangzhou renmin fayuan yi fa chengchu liang Xiong deng zuifan), *Renmin Ribao,* 15 Nov. 1979, p. 1; and Su Bichun, "Witnessing the Trial of the Xiongs by West Lake" (Xizihu pang kan shen "Xiong"), *Democracy and Legal System* (Minzhu yu fazhi), no. 4 (1979): 28, 27.

70. "Con-Artist Caught" (Pianzi luo wang), *Beijing Wanbao,* 13 May 1980, p. 2. Other examples of *pianzi* include a young woman from a rural county near Nanjing who passed herself off as a cadre kid to ten eligible bachelors who gave her over 1,400 yuan and a watch as engagement presents ("Conned" [Shou jian pi], *Nanjing Ribao,* 14 Feb. 1980, p. 4). In another case a young man roamed up and down the rail line between Nanjing and Shanghai, taking over twenty people for 1,600 yuan. He claimed that his father was an important official in a PRC intelligence agency. He claimed to be able to find people work, or to have the connections to get young people who had been sent down back into the cities. Several parents fed and housed him and gave him various gifts. ("Not a Very Brilliant Hoax" [Bu gaoming de pianshu], *Nanjing Ribao,* 31 Aug. 1979, p. 4.)

arouse a sense of admiration if their victims are among the upper crust. A popular but controversial work of fiction asked whether such an impostor's activities would have been illegal "if he were for real."[71]

PATRIMONIAL RULERSHIP IN LENINIST STATES

How can it be that a Leninist state is on a quest to transform traditional culture and at the same time a primary source of patrimonial rulership? To answer this question, we must consider the nature of Leninist state institutions and their particular strengths and weaknesses. If Leninist state institutions encourage patrimonial rulership, then Leninist states may be structurally ill-suited to the pursuit of their founders' goals of transforming society.

Patrimonial rulership is of crucial importance in the normal workings of Leninist state institutions. In Tilman and Leff's rational-actor approach, corruption is a solution to the problem of bureaucracy that is too modern or too rational.[72] However, as Jan Pakulski writes, bureaucracy in socialist systems does not approximate Weber's ideal type of rational-legal rulership. As was noted earlier, Weber's ideal type of bureaucracy or rational-legal rulership has the following characteristics: continuous rule-bound conduct of business, specified spheres of competence, hierarchical organization, an appeals procedure, specialized training, separation of the organizations' property and personal property, and a system of written records.[73] Pakulski cites the following exceptions to these standards in Leninist organization: legal norms are not binding (not least in the employment of force), there is no effective appeals procedure, high officials have enormous arbitrary power, the substitution of "a second polity," or patronage system, as a functional equivalent of law or the market, and the incompatibility of the *nomenklatura* system with impersonal meritocratic appointments.[74] In other words, the so-called bureaucracy is not bureaucratic, at least by Weber's definition.

71. Sha Yexin, Li Shoucheng, and Yao Mingde, "If I Were For Real." See also Jin Dayong, "The Virus Under the Microscope" (Xianweijing xia de bingdu), *Democracy and Legal System* (Minzhu yu fazhi), no. 3 (1979): 39.
72. Tilman, "Black-Market Bureaucracy," and Leff, "Economic Development Through Bureaucratic Corruption."
73. Weber, *Economy and Society,* 218–19. See also 217–26 and 956–1006.
74. Pakulski, "Bureaucracy and the Soviet System."

Patrimonial rulership in socialist countries is not just a response to rational bureaucracy but a basic means of holding organization together.[75] Maria Hirszowicz argues that in the USSR the Party offers privileges in exchange for loyalty to the Party line.[76] In an intriguing analysis, Michael Urban argues that it is not appropriate to speak of ideological legitimacy in socialist systems, because the closed nature of communication in such systems does not allow citizens the chance to freely accept or reject the regime's claim to legitimacy. He argues that in the absence of ideological legitimacy, a widespread system of particularistic exchange is the alternate means of holding the system together.[77] For example, John Fraser quotes a young Chinese speaking on his reasons for joining the Communist Youth League, which is a stepping-stone to the Party:

> I have joined the Communist Youth League to please him [his father], but it is not anything I have any enthusiasm for. Most of the members have no idealism. They have simply joined, either because they had no choice, like me, or to seek advancement. It is just a question of access to power and position. They know what life is like for most people, and they want something better. I would say this characterizes the spirit of the Party today. There are some good people, who have a strong conception of a better society, but they are in a minority and find themselves compromised all the time.[78]

In theory, the rigid structure of "units" (*danwei*) in China and the system of promotion and appointments are forms of rational-legal organization that the Party can use for its official purposes. These structures create what Andrew Walder calls "organized dependency."[79] Most Chinese life takes place in the context of "units." All individuals belong to a unit, which is not only their employer but which may

75. James Scott argues that patronage frequently serves to build unity, in *Comparative Political Corruption*, 115–16, 124–31. Roth makes a similar argument. He states: "One of the major reasons for the predominance of personal rulership over legal-rational legislation and administration in the new states seems to lie in a social, cultural, and political heterogeneity of such magnitude that a more or less viable complementary and countervailing pluralism of the Western type, with its strong but not exclusive components of universality, does not appear feasible. Even the total victory of totalitarian minority merely leads to a highly centralized variant to personal governance under which the ruler has maximum discretion" ("Personal Rulership, Patrimonialism and Empire Building", 157).

76. See Hirszowicz, *The Bureaucratic Leviathan*, 87–102.

77. Urban, "Conceptualizing Political Power in the USSR: Patterns of Binding and Bonding."

78. Fraser, *The Chinese*, 298–99.

79. Walder, *Communist Neo-Traditionalism*.

also provide their housing, education for their children, cafeterias, stores, medical facilities, entertainment, special access to consumer goods, and more. Units not only control promotions but also approve marriages and grant authority to have children. Units are relatively closed systems, often literally walled off from the rest of society. Most important of all, like feudal serfs bound to an estate, Chinese have great difficulty in leaving their unit.[80] As Andrew Walder has pointed out, a unit's leaders have tremendous discretionary authority within their unit. Their ability to distribute benefits according to arbitrary or personal criteria enables them to exploit "the leading role of the Party" to promote personal advantage, and the careful distribution of such benefits builds the loyalties that hold units together.

China's equivalent to the Soviet system of *nomenklatura,* or close supervision by those at higher levels of appointments and promotions at lower levels, is called the appointment system (*weirenzhi*) and has a similar effect. This system is often cited as one of the most significant "feudal remnants." Lu Min, writing in the unofficial publication *Beijing Spring,* claimed that it was equivalent to the feudal system of conferring ranks.[81] Wu Min, writing in the official press, states:

> Under the conditions of the proletariat having seized political power, to implement the appointment system for a long period of time must give rise to a psychology of lower levels regarding upper levels with awe and finding themselves inferior, and some cadres must respond only to upper levels, ignoring the people's interests and aspirations. In this way, bureaucratism can emerge at the present historic period, and even in the proletarian Party and inside the revolutionary ranks feudal monarch-official or master-servant relations of personal dependence can still be revived.[82]

The Party's general system of consultation and implementation, the "mass line" ("from the masses to the masses") builds particularistic

80. Even promotions usually occur within units, or at least within hierarchies of units called systems (*xitong*). For example, Harvey Nelson writes that in the Chinese military, promotions almost always follow the chain of command upward, whereas in the U.S. military, promotions usually also involve lateral movement. See Nelson, *The Chinese Military System,* 142–43. Universities also often hire staff from their own graduating classes.

81. Lu Min, "Democracy or Bureaucracy." Another unofficial writer, Chen Erjian, argues that the "system of appointment to office" is one of the main pillars of the "coercive monopolization of power by the minority." See Chen Erjian, *Crossroads Socialism,* 99.

82. Wu Min, "Bureaucratism and the Appointment System."

criteria into the Party's normal procedures.[83] The mass line suggests that while the population may be polled and consulted, the Party reserves the exclusive right to make policy decisions. However, recognizing that it is impossible for high-level policymakers to anticipate all local contingencies, the mass line encourages further consultation at the stage of implementation. Individual localities or units can be granted particularistic exemptions from general policy. This means that the bulk of political bargaining occurs within the bureaucracy and is cast in particularistic terms. Individual needs and personal relationships are the substance of this style of politics. James Scott has described a similar situation in Thailand:

> The many anomalies of Thai administration are cast in a new light once we understand that, because the bureaucratic elite is the political elite, much of administration must be seen as politics. This perspective, suggested by Riggs, helps explain why a bureaucrat's influence and connections are more decisive for his success than his administrative skill or his technical competence. It also helps explain why loyalty is more highly rewarded than the ability to make technically "correct" decisions, and why, especially at higher echelons, merit or seniority criteria are less influential for career success than the quality of one's personal alliance network.[84]

The rational-action approach's suggestion that corruption is analogous to a "free market" is a useful argument in a general sense but, under closer scrutiny, is not entirely accurate in this case. Dennis O'Hearn states: "There are basic structural differences between the second economy and capitalist enterprise—differences arising from the role the second economy plays vis-à-vis the planned economy."[85] O'Hearn's argument is essentially that many of the inputs into the second economy are provided by the state without recompense. For example, those producing for the second economy often make covert use of firms formally owned by the state, and thus they experience very low capital costs. Similarly, raw materials are also "appropriated" from the state at little cost to the entrepreneur. Labor is somewhat the reverse—since workers usually are already paid a salary by the state, they may not need a further source of income, and the entrepreneur in the second economy may experience a sellers' market. Janos Kenedi makes much the same point in his delightful account of

---

83. For a description of the mass line, see Mark Selden, *The Yenan Way in Revolutionary China*.
84. Scott, *Comparative Political Corruption*, 62.
85. O'Hearn, "The Second Economy in Consumer Goods and Services."

building a home in Hungary. He distinguishes between three markets: the state market, in which prices are low but shortages and delays are endemic; the licensed private market, which offers high quality and prompt service but at high prices; and "moonlighters," who offer high quality, immediate delivery, and, since they work on state time and use state materials, the lowest prices of all.[86] The second economy may be necessary, but it also diminishes the rate of capital accumulation and raises costs. To the extent that second economies are based on thievery, the pressures for entrepreneurial efficiency are reduced. The more important point is that the planned economy and the second economy are not distinct entities but in actual practice are thoroughly interwoven. It is not just the planned economy that requires the second economy for its continued functioning; the second economy itself is still more parasitic.

The outcome of reform in China also belies the rational-actor model of corruption. If corruption is a result of a bureaucracy that prevents efficient market outcomes, then reforms that open up markets should reduce the level of corruption. There is no evidence that the current reforms in China have had this effect. Instead, some forms of corruption seem to have increased. This could be interpreted as evidence to support the political culture argument. Lucian Pye argues that new state policies reflect decreased commitment to the imposition of the new socialist culture, and a consequent resurgence in traditional culture.[87] But there is another possibility—that corruption is not just a means of making a rigid bureaucracy more efficient but is an integral part of that bureaucracy.

Patrimonial rulership is an inherent aspect of Leninist states. This is what Andrew Walder has in mind when he labels the Chinese system "neo-traditional." Walder is particularly concerned with what he calls "principled particularism," in which the state offers material rewards for ideological conformity and political cooperation, and with the activist system, in which an "official clientelist network" is established to maintain order in factories.[88] Kenneth Jowitt also offers a systematic understanding of the role of patrimonial rulership in Leninist systems. He argues that Leninist parties combine impersonal

86. Kenedi, *Do It Yourself.* Kenedi's essay is genuinely entertaining and full of insights into the functioning of market socialist economies. It deserves a wide readership.
87. Pye, "On Chinese Pragmatism in the 1980's."
88. Walder, *Communist Neo-Traditionalism;* see esp. 1–27, 186–87. Michael Urban makes a similar argument about the structure of power and legitimacy in the Soviet Union. See Urban, "Conceptualizing Political Power."

and traditional features and are thus able to transform traditional society without being incomprehensible to that society. Leninist parties resemble traditional society because they create a caste-like group of Party members with special privileges and because they emphasize the personal role of powerful cadres. At the same time, Leninist parties have the bureaucratic traits of holding individual members responsible for the execution of tasks and of considering achievement a central criterion for mobility. He argues that Leninist parties end up in a circular pattern in which leaders generate rational-legal reforms that are absorbed or negated by charismatic and traditional aspects of the party. This places Leninist parties in an endless cycle of rational-legal reforms, which never quite succeed.[89]

What then is a Leninist state? The central institution in a Leninist state is a political party with a broad and formalized ideological agenda that penetrates most aspects of society. Leninist states are dominated not by a ruling class but by a ruling institution.[90] The party may or may not directly control all forms of communication, but in all cases it places limits on what Michael Urban calls metacommunication, or the ability to comment on communication itself, thus preventing discussion of fundamental questions or the basic legitimacy of the system.[91] The party, through the government, also has a preponderant role in economic affairs, whether through a Stalinist, market socialist, or other economic system. The party also maintains extensive organization, including supervision of economic, political, and social organization, and even residential units. The party's organization is buttressed by an extensive police network. The party's organization brings society under the party's aegis and preempts autonomous social or political organization.

In a state like this, the kind of authority relationships that Walder speaks of are not just expedient but are structurally determined. Patrimonial rulership is in part an extension of a traditional culture, and

89. Jowitt, "An Organizational Approach to the Study of Political Culture in Marxist-Leninist Systems"; *The Leninist Response to National Dependency*, 48–50; and "Soviet Neo-Traditionalism: The Political Corruption of a Leninist Regime."

90. Maria Hirszowicz writes: "The difference between ruling institutions and ruling classes may seem of purely academic interest, but in fact is extremely important. A ruling institution—be it the church in theocracies, the army in military societies, or the party in one-party states—identifies not with an economic but with a political order which gives it a dominant position in society. In contrast with economic classes which see politics in the reinforcement of their economic privileges, the ruling institutions treat economic systems as instrumental in the maintenance of the position of power" (*Coercion and Control in Communist Society*, 19).

91. Michael Urban, "Conceptualizing Political Power."

corruption is in part a calculated response to an authoritarian bureaucracy, but it is also part of the bureaucracy. Leninist states are not wholly patrimonial. The leadership, as well as other elements within the state, makes use of rational-legal and charismatic rulership, not least to constrain the use of patrimonial rulership. Nonetheless, the most significant source of patrimonial rulership is the state itself, and this has a deep influence on what the state can and cannot accomplish.

CONCLUSION

To return to an examination of the specific strengths and weaknesses of China's Leninist state: Why is it that Leninist states are relatively effective at mobilizing and constraining society and yet far less able to promote economic efficiency? How will this affect the implementation of reforms?

Although the emphasis in this chapter has been on the importance of patrimonial rulership, it is not my intent to argue that China or other Leninist states lack charismatic or rational-legal rulership. Leninist states, like all states, are an amalgam of different types of rulership. In Leninist states pervasive formal state organization, which is at least in part bureaucratic, is intertwined with patrimonial networks. This foundation gives patrimonial rulership in Leninist states a different character from patrimonial rulership in other states. Clients in Leninist states are less able to choose their patrons and are more dependent on single patrons for a wider range of benefits. This is, again, what Walder calls "organized dependency."

This form of state organization has proven a formidable means of controlling and manipulating society; though it has not been able to eliminate conflicts of interest, it has been able to create structures within which most people will choose to conform to the Party's expectations. Those few who do not are denied access to the organizational, ideological, and financial resources that make opposition meaningful.[92] The result is that, on the one hand, social interests and public opinion exist, but they are not organized or clearly articulated and consequently have only a limited impact on the political process. On the other hand, the state has the means to structure powerful incentives to mobilize society.

92. For a vivid fictional account of how individuals make choices, see Shen Rong, "Snakes and Ladders."

This kind of organization is technically very inefficient. By nearly all accounts, official Chinese organizations are inefficient and difficult to deal with. In a typical example, after receiving reports of excessive mortality of ducks being shipped from Beijing to Hong Kong in converted pig transporters, the Ministry of Railways and the Beijing Cereals and Oil Import and Export Company were instructed to develop a new type of duck transporter. They successfully tested a model, but it then sat unused on a railway siding for some months. A newspaper reporter from *Jingji Ribao* disclosed a dispute between the two parties regarding who should cover the development costs. Following the exposé, they agreed to share costs, and the car was loaded. Unfortunately, it sat still for some days—during which the ducks died—held up by the Beijing Railway Veterinary Quarantine Station. It would seem the shipper, a consortium of farms, had not paid fees of less than a cent per duck to exchange the quarantine certificate from the Ministry of Agriculture quarantine station in the area where the ducks were raised for a new certificate issued by the Railway Veterinary Quarantine Station. This dispute had theoretically been resolved months before when the Railway Ministry agreed to accept the Agriculture Ministry's certificates, but the Railway Veterinary Quarantine Station, acting under the authority of the Municipal Animal Husbandry Bureau, had not been informed. Only after protracted negotiations did the ducks leave the station.[93]

93. Robert Delfs, "Bureaucracy Gone Quackers," *Far Eastern Economic Review*, 28 April 1983, p. 42. Another episode from the early stage of reform began when the Xian Brewery received a letter from a foreign collector of beer bottle labels requesting a sample label from their brewery. The brewery had difficulty deciding what to do. At the time they received the letter, Party policy allowed for contact with foreigners, but the head of the brewery Party committee and the assistant head of the factory had "lingering fears" based on the stigma attached to contact with foreigners during the Cultural Revolution. They turned the letter over to the Xian City Number One Light Industry Bureau Technical Section. The engineer in the Technical Section decided to pass the letter on to an assistant head of the Number One Light Industry Bureau, who in turn requested advice from the Provincial Foreign Office. They declined to offer an opinion, and the letter was sent back down the hierarchy to the factory without resolution. For several months the factory leadership refused to post a letter overseas, even though subordinates pointed out the changes in Party policy and Party circulars criticizing this very problem were discussed in factory political meetings. The collector wrote several more times, and the secretary from the factory eventually made a formal application to send a label to the Light Industry Bureau with the general approval of the factory leadership. An assistant head of the Bureau gave his approval, but he was countermanded by the head of the Light Industry Bureau at the last minute. Fortunately, in the meantime, the application had crossed the desk of the head of the Light Industry Bureau's Supply and Marketing Department, who called the cadre at City Commerce Department responsible for trademarks, who telephoned the factory to in-

The price of extensive patrimonial networks is the loss of the various technical advantages of rational-legal organization, such as hiring and promotion based on merit, the ability to coordinate the efforts of diverse specialists, and above all, the ability to subordinate officials' private interests to organizational imperatives. Moreover, this is a structural problem, not just a matter of personnel. Policies to lower the age or increase the technical qualification of cadres will have at most a marginal effect on organizational efficiency. Consequently, the state will have difficulty in promoting the growth of an efficient, internationally competitive economy.

Leninist states also have difficulties in maintaining the boundaries between patrimonialism that serves official purposes and the use of patrimonial networks to serve private interests. With only a very limited ability to make use of rational-legal tools, such as formally defined and delimited spheres of competence and an open appeals procedure, Leninist states have only limited control over their officials. Corruption is an endemic problem, and more important, the center has only a limited ability to implement policies at lower levels. In the past, the Party was able to turn to charismatic appeals to revolutionary virtue to inspire its cadres, but with the death of Mao and other heroes of the revolution, the growth in the percentage of the population that did not experience the revolution, and the unfortunate results of many such campaigns in the past, this option is becoming less and less viable.

What is the relationship between patrimonial rulership and reform? First, it is dialectical. The problems generated by patrimonial rulership motivate the reformers, reform takes place in an environment that is significantly patrimonial, and reform restructures patrimonial networks. The reformers' emphasis on legality and institutionalization, for example, is a response to their perception that corruption and patrimonial rulership had diminished the Party's administrative capacity. Moreover, and more important, reforms are being implemented from above and within the bounds of the existing

---

form them that the label could be mailed. The factory leadership decided that this was not a sufficiently formal authorization and still declined to post the labels. The labels were finally mailed a year after receiving the first request and only following the intervention of the local newspaper. *Xian Ribao* commented that Xian beer was of export quality, but expressed concern that if mailing a label overseas was this difficult, exporting beer would be nearly impossible. "What Was Caused By a Letter from Overseas" (Yifeng guowai lai xin suo yinqide), *Renmin Ribao,* 7 Aug. 1980, p. 3.

system, and therefore the process of implementation is also shaped by the existing pattern of rulership.

Second, patrimonial aspects of Party organization insure that there will be uneven progress in implementing reforms in different localities and continual discrepancies between announced Party policies and the practical state of affairs anywhere. Patrimonial politics means that resistance to policy occurs during the process of implementation rather than during the stage of policy formation. In part, this is because this is the only time at which there is a real chance for local power holders to voice their concerns. It is also a reflection of vertical factions within the Party, with higher-level factional leaders protecting lower-level clients from policies they object to. Finally, it reflects the ability of local leaders to dominate channels of communication between their locality and higher levels, and hence to make it appear as if they were implementing policies that in fact they are not implementing. While the Party dominates society, the Party center's control of the Party has decided limits.

Third, these problems are particularly apparent when any set of reforms aims at strengthening rational-legal authority. Cadres and Party members at any level below the highest level correctly understand that legalization, instituted either as a means of strengthening control from the top down or as a means of building a market-oriented contractual society, means less discretionary authority for individual Party members. Therefore, however much individual units or localities may publicly welcome the promulgation of new laws, actual compliance is bound to fall short of the center's expectations. Moreover, patrimonial authority is particularly adept at taking on the forms of rational-legal authority while reserving a patrimonial substance. New laws can be the source of new delays, which can only be circumvented by courting favor with the right people in the right position, which can be the occasion for still more laws to regulate this very kind of diversion, which in turn becomes opportunities for still more delays.

For a look at how reforms affect patrimonial rulership, I will broadly summarize a few of the accomplishments of reform to date and briefly indicate their consequences. First, one of the most important changes in the Party line since 1976 has been the change in the main focus of Party work from leading class struggle to promoting economic growth. This has helped to control certain classes of political abuses. In particular, as long as the Party was charged with locat-

ing and defeating class enemies, there was a tremendous potential for
Party members to assign labels, or "hats," in a manner that would
serve personal ends. Similarly, the obverse, of assigning a favorable
class status, could also be used to reward relatives, friends, and
followers.[94] Moreover, this change in line has a moderating influence
on the scale of sanctions that can be applied and on the methods of
investigation. Of course, there are important limitations to these
changes. Justice is still dispensed for demonstration effects, there are
still campaign-style crackdowns, and those with power or powerful
relations still enjoy substantially less jeopardy to legal sanctions.[95]
On the whole, however, this form of patronage has been substantially
limited.

A second major achievement of the post-Mao era has been a complex of policies designed to decentralize various aspects of life in
China. In theory, this has been initiated with the goal of improving
economic efficiency. In various ways, more opportunities have been
created for firms to respond to market pressures rather than planned
targets. This has included reducing controls over the allocation of raw
materials and the distribution of finished goods, as well as shifting
toward a financial system based on taxes and bank loans rather than
on returning net revenues to the state and receiving grants. To some
extent, decentralization has created new opportunities for mobility
that are not dependent on the direct approval of individual cadres and
have thus reduced dependence on cadres and lessened some forms of
corruption.

As the focus of the Party's work shifted to economics, there were
many lucrative new opportunities for economic corruption. Economic
crime is not a new phenomenon in China, but nonetheless, following
the Third Plenum of the Twelfth Party Congress, which announced a
policy of economic reform in October 1984, the Party center began to
issue a large number of speeches, communiqués, and regulations concerning economic crime. A new term was coined—"new unhealthy
trends"—which referred to taking advantage of economic reform for
personal or local gain. This surely reflected a real increase in the level
of economic corruption since 1978. Among the most common and

94. Gu Hua's excellent novel *Hibiscus* is one of many accounts of the Cultural Revolution that portray this kind of political abuse.
95. For example, according to *Agence France Press* (9 Nov. 1986), in three years of
a crackdown on crime beginning in November 1983, ten to thirty thousand people
were executed and another six hundred thousand received long prison sentences. See
FBIS-CHI-86-217, 10 Nov. 1986, pp. K1–2.

most deplored "new unhealthy trends" were companies chartered by cadres or their friends or relatives for the purpose of taking advantage of their connections to obtain scarce commodities for resale, to gain lucrative contracts through such connections, or to facilitate the dealings of others.[96]

Also, what has outwardly been decentralization based on an evolving rational-legal framework can also be seen as a devolution of authority to lower levels of a patrimonial hierarchy. Cadres and party members have had the best access to these opportunities. They have also been able to regulate the access of others. Jean Oi, for example, describes how rural cadres have been able to control access to low-priced agricultural inputs, to scarce commodities, to services, and even to markets.[97] Barry Naughton has described how lower levels have gained control of materials and financial resources and used them for local purposes that contradict the intentions of the center.[98]

In conclusion, patrimonial rulership is deeply rooted in the structure of China's Leninist state. While the reforms are motivated by a desire to limit the scope of this rulership, patrimonial rulership also has an impact on the course of reform. Economic decentralization and political relaxation are extremely significant but do not alter the foundations of Leninist state power. Patrimonial rulership is therefore likely to persist.

96. Zafanolli, "China's Second Economy," presents examples of this phenomenon as well as many other kinds of economic corruption.
97. Oi, "Peasant Households Between Plan and Market," and "Commercializing China's Rural Cadres."
98. See, for example, Naughton, "False Starts and the Second Wind."

CHAPTER THREE

Strengthening Socialist Law

Since Mao's death, "strengthening the socialist legal system" has been a prominent reform strategy of the Chinese Communist Party. In December 1978 the Third Plenum of the Eleventh Party Congress established the direction of reform. Six months later the Second Session of the Fifth National People's Congress passed seven laws, including a Criminal Code, a Criminal Procedures Code, and laws detailing the organization and functions of people's procuratorates and people's courts.[1] These laws reestablished and strengthened legal institutions that had not been effective since the 1950s. A second new constitution, promulgated in 1982, broke new ground by declaring that "everyone is equal before the law." This flurry of activity continued, with thirty-seven more laws enacted from 1983 to 1988 and a huge increase in the volume of litigation, including civil suits over economic contracts.[2] This is truly a monumental change from the destructive lawlessness of the previous decade.

Western scholars have used a variety of perspectives to interpret these events. Some have adopted a legal perspective that pays close attention to the content and practice of new laws.[3] This perspective is useful from a human rights perspective, as it facilitates consideration

---

1. For the texts of these laws, see *A Full Translation of the Criminal Law Code, Criminal Procedures Code*, etc., trans. and annotated by Yu Man-king (Hong Kong: Great Earth Book Company, 1980). The Criminal and Criminal Procedures Codes appear also in the *Journal of Criminal Law and Criminology* 73, no. 1 (1982): 138–203.
2. "Progress Made in Legal System," *Beijing Review* 31, no. 6 (18 Apr. 1988): 10.
3. For an excellent example of this perspective, see Shao-Chuan Leng and Hungdah Chiu, *Criminal Justice in Post-Mao China*.

of what legal guarantees are available to Chinese citizens. It finds the obstacles to building a stronger legal system in vaguely formulated laws, the absence of various procedural guarantees in legal codes, and the shortage of trained personnel. Another useful perspective is modernization. This approach is more concerned with the functioning of the legal system in the overall system. It argues that the development of an autonomous legal system, especially a system of civil law that is relatively accessible to society, is a requirement for the development of an advanced economy.[4] This approach also raises important questions about the viability of China's Leninist state and argues that decentralization and eventually democratization are likely results of modernization. In this perspective the most significant obstacle to the development of China's legal system is the persistence of traditional concepts of law. Finally, some scholars have called attention to positive aspects of China's traditional legal system, especially the avoidance of excessive litigation and legal formality and the use of informal mediation.[5]

In reviewing the development of law in China in the context of China's Leninist state, I will attempt to build a comparative approach that is systematic but does not assume that any particular form of modernization is inevitable. In America's liberal-capitalist state, law guarantees some rights against the state, is used by a wide range of relatively autonomous actors, and to some extent constrains even the most powerful actors, including state power holders. Law is an important means of protecting the interests of the dominant class but, for just this reason, restricts the autonomy of the state. In other words, the American legal system is an integral aspect of a state that is based on a relatively autonomous civil society and a market economy. In contrast, Chinese law primarily strengthens the state, and society enjoys only limited access. Traditional Chinese law lacked a distinct civil law and was principally a system of punishments for ordering

4. See David Zweig, Kathy Hartford, James Feinerman, and Deng Jianxu, "Law, Contracts, and Economic Modernization: Lessons from Recent Chinese Rural Reforms"; and Richard Baum, "Modernization and Legal Reform in Post-Mao China: The Rebirth of Socialist Legality." Other scholars have also accepted the dichotomy of revolution and modernization but have bemoaned the decline of revolution rather than hailing the advent of modernization. See, for example, James Brady, *Justice and Politics in People's China.*

5. Victor H. Li, *Law Without Lawyers: A Comparative View of Law in China and the United States;* and Stanley Lubman, "Mao and Mediation: Politics and Dispute Resolution in Communist China."

society.[6] Nonetheless, the limited administrative capacities of imperial and republican governments restricted the ability of the state to apply this tool. Grants of quasi-official judicial authority to clans, guilds, gentry, and other similar groups created social spheres relatively autonomous from the state. Since the revolution China's Leninist state has maintained a system of "law from above," but with an increased administrative capacity that enabled the state to reduce the autonomy of society. Mao eventually found even this legal system too restrictive and attempted to abolish all legal institutions. This proved destructive to the state, let alone to society. Post-Mao leaders have attempted to re-create and strengthen the legal system as one means of revitalizing the state but have found themselves in a dilemma. On the one hand, "law from above" has patrimonial implications and therefore fails to adequately order society or steer the state. On the other hand, an accessible, autonomous legal system would threaten the autonomy of the state and the Party's leading role. Consequently, reforms to date are incomplete and contradictory.

According to Max Weber, the driving force behind the expansion of rational-legal authority in Western society was the market, not the state. He argues that "modern law" resulted from the diffusion of the right to use the legal system—for example, by granting all citizens the theoretical right to form corporations, to establish contracts, and to settle civil disputes, and eventually even by regarding the state (under certain circumstances) as a juridic person that could sue and be sued.[7] He points out that the formal expansion of legal rights and the growth of the market in practice left broad social sectors, particularly workers, fundamentally disadvantaged and subject to coercive market forces.[8] However, this enabled the formation of large organizations that could harness diverse technologies for production and the accumulation of capital and facilitated society's relative autonomy from the state.

In Chinese history, law was both rejected as immoral and used as a tool of state power. On the one hand, Confucian thinking favored the use of moral exhortation over the application of legal penalties. On the other, Legalists who advocated the use of law and rational-legal

6. For a comparison of the development of civil law in China, the West, and the USSR, see Yu Youzhi, "The Evolution of Contract Law in China: Comparisons with the West and the Soviet Union."

7. Weber, *Economy and Society*, 666–752.

8. Ibid., esp. 729–31.

authority aimed to strengthen state power vis-à-vis society.[9] Derk
Bodde and Clarence Morris state:

> After more than two millennia of a highly developed legal tradition, the
> Chinese continued to view law primarily as a governmental instrument
> applied from above to punish infractions of the social and political order,
> rather than as a means, theoretically, at least, within reach of anyone wish-
> ing to assert a claim against someone else or against the government
> itself.[10]

Together, these two traditions produced a legal system that was not
based on a market system, was not very accessible to society, and pos-
sessed only limited autonomy.

Traditionally, Chinese Marxists have not recognized the possibility
for any other sort of legal system. They have argued that in bourgeois
systems law is also only a tool of state power.[11] For Cultural Revolution theorists, this was reason enough to reject any form of law, but
current reformers argue that in socialist China, law is still an appropriate means of strengthening state power. For example, Pitman Potter argues that for Peng Zhen, a leading advocate of "strengthening
socialist law" until 1957 and after Mao's death, "law served first as a
statement of policy and then to provide an organizational framework
for the enforcement of policy."[12] An authoritative book explaining the
efforts to "strengthen socialist law" states:

9. Benjamin Schwartz states: "Beyond their addiction to harsh penal law, the legalists thus became the advocates of what Max Weber would call the 'rationalization'
(within the limits of the period) of the social order from the point of view of enhancing
the power of the state. They were advocates of the bureaucratic principle, of something
like a conscript army, of sweeping economic reforms, etc. Thus, *fa* (law) became with
them not only penal law but all forms of state-initiated institutional change." See
Schwartz, "On Attitudes Toward Law in China," cited in Jerome A. Cohen, *The Criminal Process in the People's Republic of China 1949–1963*, 62–70.

10. Bodde and Morris, *Law in Imperial China*, 413.

11. For example, Cao Zudan (Ts'ao Tzu-tan) writes: "The brutal means of suppression employed by the exploiting class against the laboring people [in bourgeois sys-
tems] is the combination of military suppression and penal suppression. Military suppression is used generally in emergencies; in normal circumstances, when the political
power of the ruling class is comparatively stable, the means of penal suppression are
primarily and massively employed. By so doing, it is possible, on the one hand, to take
advantage of the absolute superiority of political rule to suppress in time any act of
resistance that may endanger its conditions of existence; on the other hand, this may
also serve the function of deceiving the masses as well as reducing the resistance and
animosity of the masses against the incumbent regime. The fact that penal suppression
is usually undertaken through the promulgation of laws and court trials facilitates their
covering up the nature of their class dictatorship under the cloak of 'justice' and 'legality.'" See Cao Zudan, "On the Relationship Between Crime and Class Struggle,"
82–83.

12. Potter, "Peng Zhen: Evolving Views on Party Organization and Law."

Therefore, a state led by the proletariat must establish and perfect a legal system and bring into play the full effects of law in order to more effectively perform the functions of the state and protect the rights of the people. From the law, each state organ, each state cadre, and the masses can learn doing what in what way is permitted by the state, and doing what in what way is not permitted by the state.[13]

In this perspective socialist law is a scientific truth and the Party is the agent of its inevitable triumph. The Party argues that the eventual victory of the proletariat is a scientific fact, and since the new laws are the will of the proletariat and a tool of the proletariat's state, they are also an inevitable result of history. This equates the development of legal systems by rising classes with the discovery of laws of nature. The Party proposes that only by discovering and manipulating the laws governing historical progress can classes make rapid historical progress.[14] For example, Li Honglin compares social law to the laws of hydraulics, and the promotion of social development to the irrigation of a field. Just as the laws of hydraulics must be observed to get water to the crops, social laws must be observed to advance the people.[15]

In practice, as long as law primarily serves purposes of state, and ordinary members of society have only limited access to law, patrimonial norms will dominate social interaction. When ordinary citizens cannot use law to probe and limit official acts, state officials will be continually tempted to use law for their private purposes, and ordinary citizens will seek informal understandings and private mediation rather than formal legal adjudication.

In both contemporary and traditional China, the privileged status of officials was protected by the legal system.[16] Traditional Chinese

13. Chen Chunlong et al., *Questions and Answers on Legal Knowledge,* 21–22.

14. In general the ideology of the Chinese Communist Party since the Third Plenum has emphasized "historical inevitability" and "scientific necessity." For example, Hu Qiaomu argues that socialist planners must observe economic laws to promote rapid economic progress. This argument assumes that with a proper Marxist foundation, economics can be understood as a natural science, and that by manipulating allegedly known scientific principles, or laws of nature, desired goals can be more speedily attained. See Hu Qiaomu, "Observe Economic Laws, Speed Up the Four Modernizations." This understanding of law stands in particularly sharp contrast to that of conservative Western philosophers such as Burke and Oakeshott, who argue that law can function as law only if it is woven into the social fabric over the reaches of history and that it will be destroyed in any attempt to bend it to serve "rational" functions. Edmund Burke, *Reflections on the Revolution in France;* and Michael Oakeshott, "Rationalism in Politics."

15. Li Honglin, *Socialism and Freedom,* 1–2.

16. Weber notes that rational-legal law replaced the traditional "particularistic mode of creating law which was based upon the private power or the granted privileges of monopolistically closed organizations" (*Economy and Society,* 698).

law created a system of "ranks and privileges." Offenders of different social statuses were accorded different sentences for committing the same crime, and the seriousness of crimes was judged in terms of the relative status of the offender and the victim. While the Party is now formally bound by the constitution and legal codes, Party members are often judged according to Party statutes rather than state law and may utilize informal ties to protect themselves from official justice. Chinese commentators frequently complain that "some cadres" believe that law applies only to the masses and not to officials.

Ezra Vogel's concept of a "public security" orientation outlines the logic of this system of law.[17] Vogel argues that traditional Chinese governments lacked the capacity to administer justice in a rational-legal style. Instead, Chinese thought and acted in terms of "preserving order." To preserve order, Chinese officials look for problems before they occur, maintaining a degree of social surveillance that would be considered a violation of the right to privacy in the West. They intervene and detain potential troublemakers before they have actually violated laws. When violations do occur, the response is calculated, not by standards of law, but in terms of the relevance of the violation to the preservation of order. When significant threats to public order do occur, the authorities will feel obliged to respond quickly and forcefully. To use Vogel's example, a black marketeer who is apprehended at a time when the black market is a severe problem will receive a severe sentence accompanied with considerable publicity, whereas another person committing the same crime at a time when the black market is not an urgent problem will quietly receive a lesser sentence. If the authorities discover later that they have arrested an innocent party, they may release him, but quietly and with some face-saving excuse. If an important figure is caught violating the law, authorities may choose to deal with the problem quietly and privately to avoid antagonizing his followers, who, if antagonized, may present a more serious threat to order. Only if the person in question insists on exhibiting a public spirit of defiance will the authorities intervene publicly, and then they must do so forcefully.

Why has this type of law persisted? Part of the answer is that traditional culture persists. But why has traditional culture persisted? In the context of a Leninist state, this judicial logic is inevitable. As long as the state as a whole remains relatively autonomous, it will be difficult for law to gain autonomy from the immediate interests of offi-

17. Ezra Vogel, "Preserving Order in the Cities."

cials, society will find extralegal means of representing itself vis-à-vis the state, and those with disputes will seek to avoid calling in arbitrary and unpredictable state officials and will instead search for informal mediation. Such a legal system is unlikely to provide a means of guaranteeing individual rights, a foundation for a relatively autonomous civil society, or a source of rational-legal norms leading the way to success in the Four Modernizations. But as long as the state seeks to maintain its autonomy and the Party its "leading role," this is the likely outcome.

DISSENSION OVER LAW

In the People's Republic, law has not provided a least common denominator or "rules of the game," but has been an object of conflict, and winners of the moment have altered the constitution, changed laws, and restructured institutions.[18] Besides the "law from above" orientation outlined above, the two most important concepts of law in the People's Republic are the charismatic Cultural Revolution perspective and a less well defined quasi-liberal line. The former was dominant for the decade prior to the reforms and had a tremendous impact. The latter, while seldom articulated from a position of power, has been repetitively restated during periods of relative freedom, such as the Hundred Flowers campaign and on Democracy Wall, and the current reformers have seen fit to respond to it at length.

During the Cultural Revolution Mao and other Cultural Revolution theorists favored the transforming of human consciousness and attacked laws and institutions.[19] They argued that law is innately bourgeois and would corrupt socialists.[20] For example, in "On Exercising All-Round Dictatorship Over the Bourgeoisie," Zhang Chun-

18. The legal history of the People's Republic has been detailed by several authors. See, for example, Jerome A. Cohen, *The Criminal Process in the People's Republic of China 1949–1963;* Philip Chen, *Law and Justice: The Legal System in China 2400 B.C. to 1960 A.D.;* Victor H. Li, "The Evolution and Development of the Chinese Legal System"; and James Brady, *Justice and Politics in People's China.*

19. "Criticism of Selected Passages of 'Certain Questions on Accelerating the Development of Industry,' " trans. in *And Mao Makes Five,* ed. R. Lotta (Chicago: Banner, 1978), 287–300, esp. 293.

20. They cited Marx, evoking the imagery of the Paris Commune and his famous dictum "But the working class cannot simply lay hold of the ready-made state machinery and wield it for its own purposes." See Karl Marx, "The Civil War in France," 347.

qiao argued that any vestige of "bourgeois right" could be the basis of a "bourgeois restoration."[21] This critique first had a serious effect on institutions during the Anti-Rightist campaign in 1957. Law schools were closed and prosecutors were told not to pay attention to "trivial legal procedures" or the "rights and status of the defendant."[22] During the Great Leap Forward courts were expected to process large numbers of cases very quickly. According to one estimate, judges in Beijing averaged ten minutes per case.[23] During the Cultural Revolution there were attempts to abolish all judicial organs. In 1967 in Changsha, a group of three, including Hua Guofeng, emerged from an interview with Mao to report that he had said: "It seems as if (some people think that) it wouldn't do if there were no public security organs, procuracy and courts; (on the contrary), if they should collapse, I would be happy."[24] In 1967 Mao also castigated the "commune" established by Zhang Chunqiao in Shanghai and specifically criticized the laxity of the public security departments.[25]

The dismantling of institutions actually increased the obligations of citizens. As Max Weber argues, charismatic movements like the Cultural Revolution create weighty new obligations even as they discredit prior obligations.[26] The cult of Mao transformed trivial acts into se-

21. Zhang Chunqiao, "On Exercising All-Round Dictatorship Over the Bourgeoisie," 209–20.

22. Cohen, *Criminal Process,* 15.

23. Victor Li, "Chinese Legal System," 234.

24. Tao-tai Hsia, "Legal Developments in the PRC since the Purge of the Gang of Four." Hsia also reports that at one Cultural Revolution rally, Mao stood alongside Xie Fuzhi while the latter repetitively claimed that Mao called for smashing the public security bureaus, procuratorates, and courts. Jiang Qing also called for revolutionary action against the judicial organs: "The public order units, the Investigation Department [a special political police section] and the Supreme People's Court were all introduced from bourgeois countries. They were all above the Party, and the government and the Investigation Department investigates over our heads and censors our material. These are all bureaucratic organs which have opposed the Thought of Mao Tse-tung for several years. I suggest that the Public Order Units be taken over [by the revolutionaries] except for the fire department" (Brady, *Justice and Politics,* 200).

25. See Mao, "Talks with Chang Ch'un-ch'iao and Yao Wen-yuan," in *Chairman Mao Talks to the People,* ed. Stuart Schram, 278.

26. Weber writes: "From a substantive point of view, every charismatic authority would have to subscribe to the proposition, 'It is written . . . but I say unto you. . . .' The genuine prophet, like the genuine military leaders and every true leader in this sense, preaches, creates, or demands *new* obligations—most typically, by virtue of revelation, oracle, inspiration, or of his own will, which are recognized by the members of the religious, military, or party group because they come from such a source. Recognition is a duty" (*Economy and Society,* 243–44). James Brady compares the degree of self-scrutiny demanded by Chinese thought reform with charismatic Christianity, point-

rious crimes. *Nanjing Bao* reported one case where an elementary school physical education teacher was leading students in the cheer "Turn to the left, long live Chairman Mao; turn to the right, smash Liu Shaoqi" and unfortunately got one word wrong, which led to a ten-year sentence during which he died.[27] Revolutionary vigilantism put pressure on all citizens to demonstrate their own vigilance by aiding in "ferreting out" those less vigilant. Under these circumstances, those tainted by any accusation could hardly expect a fair trial.[28] Moreover, punishments were often harsh and included torture.[29] In retrospect, these attacks on the legal system were meant to remove minimal existing procedural guarantees that might hinder the struggle against alleged "class enemies," not to create a Paris Commune style of democracy.

The results were catastrophic. Neither Mao nor other activists were bound by the standards of virtue that they proclaimed. Large numbers of innocent people were murdered or otherwise persecuted. Attacks on institutions severely diminished the state's administrative capacity and eventually threatened to dismantle the state itself. Widespread hypocrisy and lawlessness led to a general decline in social order. Many Chinese perceived the result of the Cultural Revolution to be a general breakdown of society, ranging from mundane aspects of

---

ing out passages from the Sermon on the Mount, such as: "Ye have heard that it was said by them of old time, thou shalt not commit adultery. But I say unto you, that whosoever looketh on a woman to lust after her hath committed adultery with her already in his heart," and "And if thy right eye offend thee pluck it out and cast it from thee, for it is profitable that one of thy members should perish and not that thy whole body should be cast into hell." See Brady, *Justice and Politics*, 22.

27. "City Culture and Education and Health Systems Hold Large Rehabilitation and Exoneration Meeting" (Shi wenjiao weisheng xitong zhaokai pingfan zhaoxue dahui), *Nanjing Bao*, 4 Dec. 1978, p. 1.

28. Western observers of a Cultural Revolution mass meeting wrote: "Basically, these meetings are only peripherally about the offenses committed: they are aimed at everyone else. Criminality is useful and in some ways necessary to them in this. The function of justice in China becomes clear: the laws do not pretend to protect society, ordinary people, so much as the regime, the authorities, and them alone—against anyone and everyone else. They aren't meetings of accusation by the masses which the authorities invite us to attend, but meetings of *accusation of the masses* which we are compelled to witness" (Claudie and Jacques Broyelle and Evelyne Tschirhart, *China: A Second Look*, 167–68; emphasis in original).

29. The relative frequency in the post-Mao press of articles condemning torture is some indication that torture was a common practice. See, for example, Wang Shunhua, "Why Should Extracting a Confession by Torture Be Strictly Forbidden?" (Weishenma yao yanjin xingxun bigong), *Guangming Ribao*, 19 Mar. 1980, p. 3. Amnesty International reports that while torture is officially deplored, it remains a problem. See Amnesty International, *China: Torture and Ill-Treatment of Prisoners*.

daily life to basic personal security. As an example of the kind of un-fortunate incident that many Chinese found sadly typical, *Beijing Wanbao* reported the case of a railroad worker shopping for vegeta-bles who took it upon himself to go behind the vegetable stall to pick and choose his own tomatoes. When the salesperson told him to stop, he "not only did not stop, but struck and injured the salesperson."[30] After Mao died, newspapers reported many spectacular cases of mur-der, rape, gang fighting, and other violent crimes, indicating that China was far from the crime-free society that Cultural Revolution propaganda had portrayed.[31] Many urban Chinese women felt unsafe in side streets after dark, and many Chinese felt that the government was concerned only with counterrevolutionaries and not with ordi-nary criminals, who had a much greater impact on ordinary lives.

Post-Mao reformers who favored a revitalized system of "law from above" saw it as necessary to remedy all of these problems, not just to promote economic modernization. They believed that laws of all kinds were being routinely violated, including scientific laws, eco-nomic laws, criminal laws, administrative procedures, and even prin-ciples of civility. They sought law as a means of restoring order in a fundamental sense.

Other people in China also favored a strong legal system, but emphasized making law accessible to society as a means of restrain-ing the abuse of power instead of imposing order. This quasi-liberal perspective was not new. During the Hundred Flowers campaign many jurists and intellectuals sharply criticized the pace of progress toward stronger legal institutions, even following the Eighth Party Congress's endorsement of building legal institutions.[32] After Mao died, the need for legal institutions was again a prevalent theme at Democracy Wall.[33] During the relaxed atmosphere of 1978 and 1979,

30. "Playing Rough and Rude Destroys Goods and Injures People" (Shua manheng hui-wu shang-ren), *Beijing Wanbao*, 16 Aug. 1980, p. 1.

31. One of the crimes that aroused the most public attention in Nanjing involved a rape and an attempted murder on top of the city wall. The top of the wall is popular with young couples because it affords some privacy. One such couple was approached by a young man claiming to be from the Public Security Bureau. He proceeded to push the young man off one side of the wall and then beat the young woman, bashed her head with a rock, raped her, and then pushed her off the other side of the wall. See "Murder Case on City Wall at Wuding Gate" (Wuding men chengqiang shang de can'an) *Nanjing Ribao*, 25 Oct. 1979, p. 4.

32. A brief selection of such comments is reprinted in *The Hundred Flowers*, ed. Roderick MacFarquhar (London: Stevens & Sons, 1960), 114–16.

33. Wei Jingsheng, though not representative of the mainstream of Democracy Wall, even went so far as to argue that the legal reforms announced so far might un-

articles advocating legal reform as a means of guaranteeing Western-style human rights were published in official journals as well. Chen Liang asks:

> How can people have faith that when they make use of the democratic right of freedom of speech they will not fall into the pitfalls of the 1950s or the abysses of the Cultural Revolution period? This is a problem until today. . . . Only if there is a law guaranteeing freedom of speech, giving speakers and listeners equality before the law, a law possessing greatest authority, can citizens dispel dread that speech will result in incrimination.[34]

Spokesmen are still intermittently silenced, but each time they return to speak again.

Authoritative explanations of the reforms have been constrained to take account of such views. For example, after stating that law is a means of prosecuting class struggle, an authoritative guide to the new line stated: "Protecting the people's democratic rights and using democratic methods to deal with disputes and problems among the people are important motives of our country's law."[35] These were not just words, as some reforms, such as creating a code of civil law, indicate a respect for these views within the Party leadership. However, as would be demonstrated by closing Democracy Wall, proclaiming the Four Cardinal Principles, and attempting to eliminate "bourgeois liberalization" and "spiritual pollution," this perspective on law remains far from gaining a dominant position.

In sum, the new laws were very controversial and faced a long uphill struggle before they could become an accepted part of everyday society. The Cultural Revolution left a legacy of disorder, weakened institutions, and many cadres who believed that laws and legality would "fetter them hand and foot." Many Chinese agreed on the need for change but were unable to find a consensus on what kind of reform. Not only were the laws imposed from above, but even the idea of "law from above" was also imposed from above.

CAMPAIGNING FOR LAW

The new laws were implemented in a thoroughly Leninist fashion. Before they were on the books, the Party initiated a series of campaigns,

---

fortunately serve only the interests of dictatorship, but that law should ideally serve the interests of democracy. See Wei Jingsheng, "The Fifth Modernization," 67.

34. Chen Liang, "Freedom of Speech and Law that Guarantees Freedom of Speech," 18–20.

35. Chen Chunlong et al., *Questions and Answers on Legal Knowledge,* 9.

each of which was carefully controlled from above. The word "campaign" should be understood in a limited sense, as these were not campaigns like those of the Cultural Revolution, and Chinese did not refer to them with terms like *yundong* that were used for Cultural Revolution campaigns. They did not involve the "spontaneous" participation of the masses or a violent search for "class enemies." Nonetheless, they were coordinated national movements originating at the highest levels of the state and reaching down to villages and neighborhoods throughout China. At one level the state's ability to mobilize these campaigns demonstrates the power of China's post-Mao Leninist state, but at another level the results of these campaigns, like those of prior campaigns, fell short of official expectations.

The most important theme in this series of campaigns has been the promotion of "public security," which is often stated in terms of "everyone obeying the law." The first such campaign began in 1978 with a general crackdown on all those the state defined as disrupters of public security, including both common criminals and Democracy Wall activists. I will focus on this campaign, as it set the pattern for future campaigns, but it was only the first of a series that has persisted until the present. A second important theme has been the promotion of the new standards of justice, especially the rectifying of previous injustices. This theme was more readily consonant with the quasi-liberal perspective on law. As an example of this sort of campaign I will discuss briefly the rehabilitation of those unjustly persecuted during the Cultural Revolution and Anti-Rightist campaigns.

The first post-Mao campaign for public security began in 1979 and was closely associated with the repression of Democracy Wall. In late 1978 and early 1979 many young people participated in wide-open discussions at democracy walls in Beijing and other large cities. They talked, put up big-character posters, and distributed unofficial publications. Deng Xiaoping gave Democracy Wall a qualified endorsement.[36] However, in late January 1979 a few of the most outspoken Democracy Wall activists were arrested. On March 30 Deng Xiaoping gave a speech demanding adherence to the Four Cardinal Principles.[37] These four principles, "keeping to the socialist road,"

---

36. There are several good accounts of Democracy Wall; Chen Ruoxi, *Democracy Wall and the Unofficial Journals*, and James D. Seymour, *The Fifth Modernization: China's Human Rights Movement, 1978–1979*, deserve special mention. For an eyewitness account of Deng's endorsement, see John Fraser, *The Chinese: Portrait of a People*.

37. "Uphold the Four Cardinal Principles," *Selected Works of Deng Xiaoping*, 166–91.

"upholding the dictatorship of the proletariat," "upholding the leadership of the Communist Party," and "upholding Marxism-Leninism and Mao Zedong Thought," have from that time to the present served as the most authoritative limits on political activity, and in this speech were specifically delivered in criticism of Democracy Wall activists.

At about this time, the Beijing, Nanjing, and other city revolutionary committees issued "notices" announcing stricter enforcement of regulations in a range of areas relevant to urban order, including banning meetings not authorized by the police, regulating big-character posters, banning speculation, building without permits, and boarding public transport without buying tickets.[38] In Nanjing, public security substations (*paichusuo*) immediately organized meetings for security committee backbone elements, neighborhood residents, and juvenile delinquents.[39] The range of activities selected for attention is indicated by a report from an inspection group, including some of the city's leading cadres, who toured the city in May and complained of the city's unfortunate appearance, including chamber pots, coal dust, and industrial parts stored in the streets, and excrement and urine in the city train station.[40]

Soon after the Second Session of the Fifth National People's Congress passed the new laws, the Party initiated programs to educate legal specialists. In late July the Central Political and Judicial Group announced that it had "entrusted the Central Cadre School of Political Science and Law with the specific responsibility of conducting the national training class for political and judicial cadres," and estimated that it would graduate two thousand cadres in the remainder of 1979.[41] Local initiatives followed. In Nanjing in July the public security bureaus, procuratorates, and courts pledged to become models in upholding the law. In September city authorities announced a year-long training course for fifty-six cadres in city and district legal depart-

38. Some of the research for this paper was conducted in Nanjing in 1979–80, and therefore I had access to newspapers such as *Nanjing Bao* and have used Nanjing as an example in this chapter. See "Beijing City Revolutionary Committee Notice" (Beijing shi geming weiyuanhui tonggao), *Beijing Ribao*, 31 Mar. 1979, p. 3; and "Develop Peace and Unity, Protect Favorable Order" (Fazhan anding tuanjie xingshi weihu lianghao zhixu), *Nanjing Bao*, 20 Mar. 1979, p. 1.

39. "Baixia District Doggedly Attacks Criminal Activities" (Baixia qu henhen daji fanzui huodong), *Nanjing Bao*, 22 Mar. 1979, p. 1.

40. "Many Problems Discovered, Prompt Resolution Requested" (Faxian wenti duo yaoqiu xian qi jiejue), *Nanjing Bao*, 20 May 1979, p. 1.

41. Beijing Xinhua Domestic Service, 28 July 1979, trans. in FBIS-CHI-79-147, 30 July 1979, p. L4.

ments.[42] At the same time, law departments at major universities and political-legal institutes throughout China dramatically increased enrollments.[43] At a more mundane level, as will be discussed later, efforts were taken to revitalize grass-roots Party committees, neighborhood committees, public security committees, and mediation committees.

The implementation campaign assumed major proportions late in 1979.[44] On December 6 the Beijing city revolutionary committee issued the notice that closed the Xidan Democracy Wall. On December 8 a national meeting on urban security was convened under the theme of attacking criminal elements and guaranteeing normal social order.[45] These events were echoed and amplified in Nanjing and throughout the country.[46] In Nanjing intensive public discussion of "propaganda month" began in November. This involved mobilizing cadres at the city, district, and neighborhood levels and convening many meetings at all levels. At the highest level, the city revolutionary committee met to convey the spirit of national and provincial directives on urban public order and to cite model units in security work. Mass organizations, schools, and the army all followed suit. At the grass-roots level, "backbone elements" worked among urban residents, using blackboards and propaganda walls and going door to door to explain and publicize the new legal codes. Juvenile delinquents were singled out for special attention. One estimate claimed that 90 percent of the population had been reached. At a citywide meeting in early January, convened to mark the end of the first stage of the process of rectifying social order, a secretary from the city committee claimed that the campaign had already reduced crime significantly.[47]

42. "Those Who Implement the Law Should Take the Lead in Understanding and Obeying the Law" (Zhi fa ren yao daitou dong fa shou fa), *Nanjing Ribao*, 11 July 1979, p. 1; and "Conduct Political-Legal Basics Courses, Train Legal Cadres" (Juban zheng-fa jichu ban peixun sifa ganbu), *Nanjing Ribao*, 18 Sept. 1980, p. 4.

43. Interviews by author at various law departments and political-legal institutes in Shanghai and Beijing in 1980.

44. The laws were scheduled to come into effect on January 1, 1980.

45. Beijing Domestic Service, 6 Dec. 1979, trans. in FBIS-CHI-79-237, 7 Dec. 1979, p. L1; and "National Meeting on Urban Security Begins in Beijing" (Quan guo chengshi zhi'an huiyi zai jing juxing), *Guangming Ribao*, 9 Dec. 1979, p. 1.

46. FBIS translations indicate that provincial-level meetings on law and order were held in early December 1979 in several provinces, including Hubei, Jiangxi, Guangxi, and Sichuan. See FBIS-CHI-79-238, 10 Dec. 1979, p. P2; FBIS-CHI-79-239, 11 Dec. 1979, pp. O3–4; FBIS-CHI-79-242, 14 Dec. 1979, p. P7; and FBIS-CHI-79-243, 17 Dec. 1979, p. Q2.

47. This account of Nanjing's "propaganda month" is compiled from extensive coverage in *Nanjing Ribao*, including the following articles: "Jiangning County Takes

While propaganda emphasized the publicizing of the content of the new laws and the imperative of obeying the laws, the campaigns assumed a public security orientation. For example, a Central Committee document stated:

> In overhauling public order, it is necessary to carry out the Party's consistent policy of "attacking the few, winning over, dividing, and reforming the majority" and implement the basic policy of associating punishment with leniency . . . those whose cases are especially abominable and damaging should resolutely be given the death sentence according to the law. It is not necessary to kill many; the point of killing is to frighten the enemy and punish the criminals.[48]

Subsequent campaigns adopted a similar form. For example, in August 1983 the Party initiated another crackdown, which began with a police sweep of suspected criminals and led in three years' time to 10,000 to 30,000 executions and 600,000 long prison sentences.[49] To facilitate this crackdown the new legal codes were amended to eliminate the right to appeal a death sentence to the Supreme People's Court, to increase significantly the types of crime that received a

---

Firm Grasp of Training Security Cadres" (Jiangning xian zhua hao zhi bao ganbu de peixun), 18 Nov. 1979; "Leaders Should Strictly Implement Law, Should Not Substitute Affection for Law" (Lingdao yao yange zhi fa buneng yi qing dai fa), 20 Nov. 1979, p. 1; "Energetic Legal Propaganda Is 100% Necessary" (Dali xuanchuan fazhi shi fen biyao), p. 1; "Develop Legal Education" (Kaizhan fazhi jiaoyu), 24 Nov. 1979, p. 4; "Broadly Develop Legal Propaganda" (Guangfan kaizhan fazhi xuanchuan), 5 Dec. 1979, p. 1; "City Committee Yesterday Convened a Large Meeting of Party Members and Responsible Cadres" (Shi wei zuo zhaokai dangyuan fuze ganbu dahui), 8 Dec. 1979, pp. 1 and 4; "City Committee Deploys All the City's Responsible Cadres" (Shi Wei zuo xiang quan shi fuze ganbu zuo bushu), 10 Jan. 1980, p. 1. The magazine *Democracy and Legal System* reported a pattern of legal propaganda activities in Shanghai similar to those in Nanjing. A cadre from a relevant department in Shanghai told the magazine that throughout the city lecture courses had been organized by propaganda departments to train ten thousand people to form "a backbone contingent for legal propaganda." County and district propaganda departments trained another large contingent of legal-propaganda workers. Systems and units conducted their own legal-propaganda work, and the experimental and highly successful experience of units was shared at special meetings. Units lagging behind were prodded to join the movement. Electronic and print media disseminated information on the new legal system in a "question-and-answer" format. Theaters ran relevant plays, cinemas played slide shows developed by the legal departments, television stations broadcast special programs, and publishers printed explanatory books. See "What Preparatory Work Is Being Done While Shanghai Implements the New Laws?" (Shanghai zai shishi xin falu zhong zuo le naxie zhunbei gongzuo), *Democracy and Legal System* (Minzhu yu fazhi), no. 1 (1980): 17. The similarity between this and the campaign in Nanjing, in addition to reports of campaigns elsewhere at the same time, is strong evidence of detailed central planning.
    48. "The CCP Central Committee's Instructions Concerning the Improvement of Political and Judicial Work," *Issues and Studies* 20, no. 4 (Oct. 1984): 97.
    49. "Anti-Crime Drive Jails 624,000 Since 1983," *Agence France Press*, Hong Kong, 9 Nov. 1986, trans. in FBIS-CHI-86-217, 10 Nov. 1986, p. K1.

death sentence, and "for those persons accused of murder, rape, armed robbery, and other violent crimes, the NPC Standing Committee suspended practically all guarantees of due process."[50] Even while higher authorities violated the spirit of the laws, further mass campaigns were mounted to promote legal education. For example, a leading official claimed that within a year's time, a five-year campaign mounted in 1985 had reached 360,000 people.[51]

Despite the scale and drama of these campaigns, society does not necessarily receive the message that leaders are trying to broadcast. For example, in the case of a murder widely discussed in Nanjing, two youths, Zhao and Ying, became romantically inclined while employed at a snack bar. Ms. Ying was unexpectedly reassigned to a better job in a more prestigious unit. In China it is extremely difficult to change units, and the snack bar at that time promised a bleak future, so this was a significant improvement in her life prospects. Ying capitalized on her improved prospects by taking up with another young man, Xia, who also had better prospects than Zhao, who had remained at the snack bar. Ying returned Zhao's letters, declared her intent to break off their relationship, and married Xia. Zhao refused to give up. He wrote Xia in an attempt to break up the newlyweds, and when this failed, stole a vegetable knife from the snack bar, went to the newlyweds' apartment, and finding Ying alone, stabbed her horribly to death.[52]

State and society perceived this crime in quite different terms. Many people in Nanjing raised questions about Ying's infidelity for the sake of material gain, as well as about what she might have done to secure the job transfer. Zhao was considered a romantic hero. The authorities took pains to attack Zhao's prestige by denying rumors that he had intended to commit suicide with a poisoned cigarette but

50. Shao-Chuan Leng and Hungdah Chiu, *Criminal Justice in Post-Mao China*, 110. The new provisions in the legal code were applied retroactively to those who had committed crimes before the changes. See Amnesty International, *China: Violations of Human Rights*.

51. "Qiao Shi Urges Efforts to Publicize Law," *Xinhua*, Beijing, 20 Dec. 1986, trans. in FBIS-CHI-86-245, 22 Dec. 1986, p. K4. See also Zhang Yanping and Xiao Du, "Strive to Disseminate Basic Legal Knowledge Among All People in Five Years" (Zhengqu wu nian shijian quan min jiben puji falu zhishi), *Renmin Ribao*, 16 June 1985, p. 1; and "Strive to Disseminate Basic Legal Knowledge Among All Citizens in About Five Years" (Zhengqu wu nian zuo you shijian zai quanti gongmin zhong jiben puji falu zhishi), *Renmin Ribao*, 17 June 1985, p. 4.

52. See "Clarify the True Facts of the Zhonghua Street Murder" (Chengqing zhonghua lu xiongsha de shishi zhenxiang) and "Murderer Zhao Lenan Receives Death Sentence" (Sharen fan Zhao Lenan bei pan sixing), *Nanjing Ribao* 10 and 16 July 1980.

was foiled by the prompt arrival of the public security forces. Even Zhao's defense attorney explained his actions as the result of feudal attitudes (toward women) and excessive (bourgeois) individualism.[53] The authorities argued that while Ying's actions were unethical, Zhao's were illegal.

In this case, social perceptions of the crime appear to have been based on a set of categories completely different from those used by officials. In a society used to far more dramatic campaigns than this, the immediate effect of propaganda on law may well have been minimal. Society may perceive the nature of the public security orientation—from the top down—as more relevant than the substantive content of propaganda at any given moment.

An example of a campaign more closely oriented to the theme of promoting justice and more closely in accord with the quasi-liberal orientation toward law was the campaign to rehabilitate those unjustly persecuted during the Cultural Revolution and Anti-Rightist campaign. The first and most important point about this campaign is that it brought some relief to the 326,000 people who were rehabilitated.[54] These rehabilitations were a necessary aspect of "strengthening socialist law," just as investigations into the fate of those who disappeared in Argentina are a crucial aspect of building democracy in that country. Public sentiment forced the Party leadership to take some action on behalf of these victims.

Rehabilitation faced complex obstacles. The Party was embarrassed by publicly admitting it had perpetrated so much injustice. Many of the cadres responsible for injustice remained in office and would not happily accept the return of those they had wronged. Moreover, Party leaders undoubtedly knew that in Czechoslovakia in 1968 and Hungary in 1956, groups of rehabilitated former political prisoners were among the most militant critics of the old regime, and they feared that a similar situation could arise in China.

The solution was to mount another organized campaign within the confines of the existing Leninist political structure. Higher levels pressured lower levels to make progress on rehabilitation, and ordinary citizens were allowed only minimal input. *Nanjing Bao* states that

53. In this particular case bourgeois or feudal remnants are no more important than the socialist system of allocating jobs. One of Zhao's alleged faults, excessive individualism, was frequently cited as the failing of Democracy Wall activists.

54. Wu Jiafan, "The Building of China's Democracy and Legal System," *Renmin Ribao*, 16 July 1985, p. 2, trans. in FBIS-CHI-85-143, 25 July 1985, p. K1.

work on unjust cases in Nanjing began in the spring of 1978 under
the direction of the city Party committee, which was in turn acting on
instructions from the highest levels of the Party. The city Party committee in turn mobilized lower levels.[55] In general, rehabilitation
work was organized and accounted for by systems and units rather
than counties or districts and neighborhoods.[56] Cases of cadres at
higher levels were reinvestigated before lower-level cadres, and the
higher the level of the victim, the higher the level of organization assigned to reinvestigate.[57] For example, at the City Candy, Liquor and
Tobacco Company, cases of middle level and higher cadres, difficult
or significant cases, and cases involving irregular deaths were handled
at the company level, while economic and lifestyle cases were handled
by basic-level Party branches.[58] In other words, higher levels supervised lower levels at all times.

As a result, rehabilitation work encountered a patrimonial pattern
of resistance.[59] "Rightists" were usually given their "hats" within
their unit, and very often the leaders who had given them a "hat"
remained in office at the time of reexamination. The cadres directly
responsible for investigating potential wrongful judgments were likely
to be subordinates of those who had originally approved the sentences, or at least to be vulnerable to attacks from them, and consequently experienced "lingering fears" of being tainted by even the

55. "Strengthen Leadership to Move Reexamination of Cadres a Step Forward"
(Jiaqiang lingdao jin yi bu zhua hao shengan fucha gongzuo), *Nanjing Bao*, 12 Sept.
1978, p. 1.

56. A "unit" (*danwei*) is the factory, commune, school, etc., that provides each Chinese with his basic social identity and many social services, and "systems" (*xitong*) are
hierarchical organizations of units. For example, progress on rehabilitation work was
typically announced at meetings convened by systems and reported in terms of systems,
not localities. See, for example, "Our City's Industry and Transport System Convenes a
Mass Meeting for Rehabilitations" (Wo shi gongjiao xitong zhaokai pingfan zhaoxue
dahui), *Nanjing Bao*, 24 Nov. 1978, pp. 1–2.

57. "Strengthen Leadership."

58. "Integrated Division of Labor from Top to Bottom" (Shang-xia jiehe fengong
fuze), *Nanjing Bao*, 10 Oct. 1978, p. 3.

59. In the words of a spokesman for the Political Department of the Nanjing City
Industrial and Transport System, four problems faced in rehabilitation work were,
first, cadres who lacked class solidarity with those who had suffered from the persecu-
tion of the Gang of Four and lacked understanding of the urgency of implementing this
policy; second, cadres who viewed the issue in factional perspective and were especially
unwilling to reverse verdicts where they made mistakes; third, cadres who had fears
that while at present the "rightists" were criminals, after this policy had been implemented those who exonerated rightists could become the criminals; and fourth, lack of
attention to the quality of the rehabilitation. See Hu Jingui, "Where Are the Obstacles
to Righting Wrong Cases?" (Pingfan yuan an de zuli hezai), *Nanjing Ribao*, 4 Dec.
1978, p. 3.

appearance of aiding even alleged "rightists." Real reinvestigation often required personal courage on the part of the reinvestigator. In a
short story Wang Yaping portrays these problems in dramatic form.
The protagonist, Policeman Wang Gongbo, observes that Bai Shun
has been given an unusually severe sentence for an alleged attempted
rape. His investigation determines that Bai had chanced upon evidence that a cadre from the Long March had been framed in a murder case to promote the fortunes of the rebel faction during the
Cultural Revolution. The real murderer had in turn framed Bai for the
rape. As Wang closes in, the villains, now powerful cadres, manipulate policy directives from Beijing to stall Wang, declare that he has
an "ulterior counterrevolutionary motive," and then attempt to murder the crucial witness, whom Wang saves at the cost of his own
life.[60] While a willingness to murder to prevent rehabilitation probably overdramatizes the usual risks, lesser threats could still impede
justice. Obstacles like these explain why commentators frequently
state that strengthening leadership was necessary for successful rehabilitation work and note that that kind of leadership was difficult to
develop.[61] Even if an individual were formally exonerated, there was
no guarantee that his trials were over. Former rightists often found
that they had a "tail" they could not easily shake off.[62] For example,
when a former rightist bank worker dared to criticize a county Party
secretary's corruption, his boss announced that regardless of his exoneration, "a rightist after all is a rightist" and proceeded to perse-
cute him to death.[63]

In both the campaign to publicize the new laws and the campaign
to rehabilitate victims of previous political campaigns, the Party mobilized its extensive organization to reach a vast audience. In each
case the initiative came from the state center and proceeded outward

60. Wang Yaping, "Sacred Duty," in *Prize-Winning Stories from China, 1978–79*.
Although this story is set before the fall of the Gang of Four, this is a frequent literary
device employed to protect authors from the charge of criticizing the current regime.

61. In reports from various locations, the percentages of reexamined cases that resulted in rehabilitations were approximately equivalent, suggesting the possibility that
one means of exerting pressure on lower levels was to establish quotas. That reinvestigation work was usually reported in terms of numbers of cases reinvestigated and the
percentage of those charged during the Cultural Revolution also suggests higher-level
attention to quotas.

62. See "Grasp Reinvestigation of Cases, Implement Party Policy" (Zhua hao anjian
fucha luoshi dang de zhengce), *Nanjing Bao*, 10 Nov. 1978, p. 1.

63. "Hebei Provincial Committee of Chinese Communist Party Sternly Handles a
Case of Persecuting a Cadre" (Zhonggong Hebei shengwei yansu chuli yi qi pohai
ganbu anjian), *Renmin Ribao*, 21 Sept. 1981, p. 3. See also *Renmin Ribao*, 27 Oct.
1981, p. 4, trans. in FBIS-CHI-81-211, 2 Nov. 1981, p. 19.

along the lines of formal authority and allowed for only minimal grass-roots initiative. Local power holders and lower-level cadres had the ability to delay and deflect the costs of the campaigns. While welcoming the direction of the reforms, society probably experienced the form of these campaigns more than the content.

AUTONOMOUS LAW OR MORE VIGOROUS PUBLIC SECURITY?

In comparison with previous standards, the reforms strengthened institutions and procedures. Even after the reforms, however, Chinese law still granted substantial authority to lower-level officials to administer justice according to ad hoc standards and informal procedures. Even in the sphere of justice under the jurisdiction of formal judicial officials, once involved in the system, Chinese law still has a public security orientation. This suggests that Chinese law still has only limited autonomy and remains primarily a tool of state power. In the following survey of institutional reforms I will discuss briefly the nature of the reforms and then discuss each level in China's hierarchy of justice from informal neighborhood committees to the courts.

Various aspects of the reform laws do strengthen institutions and promote universalistic standards of justice. First, as China lacked a criminal code before 1978, the mere promulgation and publication of the new codes promised some greater regularity in judicial practice.[64] Second, the new laws declare that the official judicial organs—the public security forces, the procuratorates, and the courts—have the sole right to their respective judicial functions.[65] Following decades of political campaigns where ad hoc tribunals administered their own justice, this was a significant reform. Third, the new laws declare that the courts and procuratorates will exercise their "authority indepen-

---

64. The criminal legal code contains provisions that can be manipulated to serve immediate interests. Article 79 of the new code states that acts not expressly defined as crimes can be punished as crimes under provisions defining similar crimes, thus reviving the practice of "crime by analogy" from traditional Chinese law. This procedure was invoked in the trial of Wei Jingsheng. For a discussion of this provision, see Hung-dah Chiu, *Socialist Legalism*, 16–17. An explanation of the criminal code edited by the Beijing Political-Legal Institute Criminal Law Teaching and Research Section states that because of China's large size and population, the many nationalities, and the different levels of political, economic, and cultural development, such a clause is practically necessary. See *Criminal Law Questions and Answers* (Xingfa wen-da), Beijing: Qunzhong Chubanshe, 1980, 96.

65. See Section 3 of the Criminal Proceedings Code.

dently according to the law."[66] These provisions repeal the system of "deciding a case by secretary," whereby all verdicts passed by the people's courts were to be approved by a Party secretary. Party secretaries were often ignorant of the law, allowed Party policies of the moment to take precedence, and at times allowed personal considerations to interfere with the course of justice.[67] These new laws also promise fairer trials, including the defendant's right to a public trial and legal counsel. Finally, the new laws promise some degree of mutual supervision among the three judicial organs to guarantee that each obeys the law. A national radio broadcast, which was later widely distributed, explained:

> Because of the different tasks assigned to the public security forces, procuratorates, and courts, sometimes while handling cases differing opinions will occur. Having differing opinions is normal and beneficial. Through the discussion of different opinions, correct decisions can be made, and while the three organizations handle cases, correct execution of state law can be better guaranteed. Therefore, on the foundation of fulfilling their common task, the relations of these three organizations are mutually cooperative and conditioning.[68]

Despite these steps toward institutionalization, in practice the judicial system retains significant elements of a public security orientation. First, the system as implemented leaves the greater portion of justice outside of the formal judicial system. Most justice is still dispensed by informal authorities, such as the committees at the grassroots level of the urban political hierarchy, or by the public security bureaus without consulting the courts or the procuratorate. Second, while in theory the public security bureaus, procuratorates, and courts offer a system of checks and balances, in practice they form a hierarchy, with each level increasingly likely to approve decisions made at lower levels. Finally, procedural guarantees considered important in Anglo-Saxon law are missing, which allows for a very high rate of guilty verdicts and the use of trials for public propaganda.

The campaign to "strengthen socialist law" included strengthening subofficial organizations such as mediation committees and security committees. Liu Enqi states that the Third Plenum of the Eleventh

66. Section 9 of the "Organizations of the People's Public Prosecutions Departments Code" and Section 4 of the "Organizations of the People's Courts Code."
67. See Hungdah Chiu, *Socialist Legalism*, 9–11.
68. *Talking About Strengthening the Socialist Legal System* (Jiaqiang shehuizhuyi fazhi jianghua), Beijing: Qunzhong Chubanshe, 1979, 98–99.

Party Congress announced a policy of "comprehensive administration" of public security, which means:

> Public security organs should cooperate with all units and mass organizations to mobilize social power to fully utilize political, economic, cultural, educational, administrative, and all other legal means to attack and reform criminals, and to rescue those who have taken a wrong step in life to basically prevent and reduce crime.[69]

The reformers claim that the "ten years of turmoil" weakened the mediation committees.[70] Shortly after the Third Plenum, the Eighth National People's Judiciary Workers' Convention announced the reactivation of the mediation committees and other grass-roots political organizations.[71] At about the same time that the new laws came into effect, the 1954 regulations that established the people's mediation committees were republished.[72] In August 1981 a national conference on mediation was convened in Beijing.[73] According to one report, over five thousand mediation committees were revived or established in Shanghai alone between 1977 and 1979.[74]

The social effect of subofficial forms of justice is complex. In part, as Victor Li has pointed out, the emphasis on formal procedures in American justice often leads to cases of substantive injustice, and an informal and accessible system of justice seems preferable.[75] The members of neighborhood mediation committees are not specialists but typically retired neighborhood residents who may or may not have had a few hours of training. They administer what James Brady

69. Liu Enqi, "Fully Understand and Properly Implement the Policy of Comprehensive Administration" (Quanmian lijie he zhengque zhixing zonghe zhili de fangzhen), *Renmin Ribao*, 4 Nov. 1983, p. 4.

70. Luo Fu, "City Dwellers and the Neighborhood Committee," *Beijing Review*, no. 44 (3 Nov. 1980): 19–25.

71. "Communes and Lanes in This City Extensively Set Up Judicial Assistants and Found People's Mediation Committees" (Benshi gongshe jiedao guangfan shezhi sifa zhuli yuan jianli renmin tiaojie weiyuanhui), *Beijing Ribao*, 26 Feb. 1979, p. 2.

72. This was done on the orders of the Standing Committee of the National People's Congress. See *Xinhua*, 19 Jan. 1980, trans. in FBIS-CHI-80-017, 24 Jan. 1980, pp. L2–9.

73. "Wan Li Addresses National Conference on Mediation," *Xinhua Radio*, 26 Aug. 1981, trans. in FBIS-CHI-81-166, 27 Aug. 1981, p. K12.

74. Duan Chunsheng, Huang Shuangchuang, and Wu Zhangfa, "Report of an Investigation Into People's Mediation Committees in the Shanghai Region" (Shanghai diqu renmin tiaojie weiyuanhui diaocha baogao), *Shehui Kexue* (Shanghai), no. 3 (1981): 101–3, 148. A later report indicates a total of over 8,000 mediation committees in Shanghai in 1983. See "Mediators Handle Civil Cases in Shanghai," trans. in FBIS-CHI-83-050, 14 Mar. 1983, p. O2.

75. Li, *Law Without Lawyers*.

calls "popular justice" or what Max Weber calls "Khadi-justice."[76] This style of justice is based in part on the traditions and values of the relevant community but is not restricted by the complexities of formal judicial procedures or precedents. A case from *Beijing Review* points out the advantage of folk wisdom over formal judicial procedures. In this case, Messrs. Liu and Li each claimed that the other had stolen his chicken. The resourceful mediator had the disputants place their chicken coops some distance apart in the middle of the street and then placed the chicken in question midway between them. For three trials in succession the chicken promptly joined the other chickens in the Liu family coop, forcing Li to renounce his claim.[77] In cases like this, there is a clear advantage in resolving a dispute in a manner acceptable to those directly involved and without the cost in time and money of formal judicial procedures.

Subofficial justice also represents the Leninist state's penetration of the grass roots of Chinese society. Both mediation and security committees create intrusive networks that can easily be abused and can potentially be seen by local residents as informers. Mediation committees are expected to maintain close surveillance of their neighborhoods and to "resolve disputes before they occur"—that is, actively intervene in community affairs before any legal violation occurs and without the prior approval of any higher organ.[78] As Stanley Lubman pointed out nearly twenty years ago, since the Communist Party began to promote community mediation it has promoted "principled" mediation.[79] This means that the community mediators are expected not only to base decisions on community standards but also to act as the Party's agents.

76. Brady, *Justice and Politics,* 165–66; Weber, *Economy and Society,* esp. 976–78.
77. Zhou Zheng, "China's System of Community Mediation."
78. Duan Chunsheng et al., "Report." An example from *Nanjing Ribao* illustrates the ideal type of how mediators resolve problems before criminal violations occur. In this case, four neighbors feuded, to the detriment of community sanitation. The Guan family maintained a chicken coop beneath the Yan family's windows, creating awful odors for the Yans on hot days. The Yans could not complain, because they had left the remnants of a fish in the communal kitchen for a prolonged period, creating another awful odor. The Zhu and Guan families, who lived adjacent to the kitchen, resented the smelly fish, and the Guans took action by placing their commode under the Yans' window. The street committee reasoned with all, organized retired people and unemployed youths to clean the kitchen, and eventually found a more suitable location for the chickens. All parties were satisfied and relieved at the resolution of the dispute. See "Neighborhood Cadres Find and Promote Early Resolution of Disputes" (Jumin ganbu xianchang yang faxian jiufen zao jiejue), *Nanjing Ribao,* 29 Jan. 1980, p. 4.
79. Lubman, "Mao and Mediation."

Like the mediation committees, security committees are composed of local residents who work under the dual leadership of neighborhood offices and the local public security substation.[80] Security committees maintain watch on their neighborhoods, keep tabs on potential criminals, "educate" previous and potential offenders, including those charged with political crimes, educate residents in crime prevention, and occasionally assist public security forces in tracking down or apprehending criminals. While this work can be as innocuous as keeping an eye out for unlocked doors, it also constitutes a surveillance system rooted in the neighborhood and reporting to the official public security organization.[81]

Local residents probably prefer neighborhood committees to public security bureaus or the courts. In large part this follows Victor Li's reasoning—the neighborhood organizations are more flexible and comprehensible and less threatening. In this regard, much as in traditional China, subofficial justice acts as a buffer between state and society.[82] But security and mediation committees must be put in the context of the larger order they fit into—that is, they should be viewed as an informal extension of the "forces of order." Since a very high percentage of those who become involved with "higher" judicial organs receive some form of sanction, mediation committees are the last stage of the process at which an ordinary citizen has an effective appeal. Consequently, the attraction of subofficial justice may depend more on fear of what comes next than on its intrinsic appeal.

The reforms sought to institutionalize the public security bureaus and strengthen their struggle against crime and disorder. There are many indications that the Cultural Revolution led to a decline in the

80. See "Provisional Regulations Adopted Governing the Organization of Public Security Committees," trans. in FBIS-CHI-80-017, 24 Jan. 1980, pp. L7–9. These regulations, originally adopted in 1952, were republished in 1980. In addition to neighborhood organizations, plants, enterprises, schools, and administrative villages were authorized to form security committees.

81. Although mediation committees have been the focus of much more scholarship than security committees, security committees are at least as prevalent, if not more so, than mediation committees. *Beijing Review* states that in Beijing in 1980 there were 1,378 mediation committees and 1,672 security committees under 1,794 neighborhood offices. For accounts of security committee activities, see *Nanjing Ribao*, 7 Dec. 1979, "Masses' Participation in Security Work Produces Very Good Results" (Qunzhong gao zhi bao xiaoguo dique hao); *Nanjing Ribao*, 27 June 1980, "Jianye District Assembles Security Committee Leaders for Training" (Jianye qu jixun jiedao zhi bao zhuren).

82. This view of the mediation committees, in particular their ambiguous role as an extension of state organization and as a buffer between local society and the state, is similar to Victor Nee's portrayal of rural militias in "Between Center and Locality: State, Militia, and Village."

ability of public security bureaus to maintain order. Some commentaries suggested that public security bureaus were lax in the struggle against criminals because they had previously devoted themselves only to the struggle against "class enemies." Other reports indicate popular disrespect for public security organs and doubts about their effectiveness in serving citizen needs such as recovering stolen property.[83] Other reports indicate at least a limited number of instances of serious police abuses, including the extortion of protection money.[84] There are also indications that many Chinese believe that police may grant "special favors" if supplied with appropriate gifts and that police are reluctant to arrest children of members of the public security organs or high cadres.[85]

In response to these problems, the public security organs undertook various "legalizing" reforms. In August 1979 the Nanjing City Public Security Bureau Political Department announced that the first class of over forty public security bureau cadres had graduated from a course on the new laws.[86] At the same time, one of the city's districts

83. Some reports from *Nanjing Ribao* indicate overt popular antipathy for the public security bureaus. One report complained about a cadre who had not only refused to cooperate when public security officers came to his door seeking help in apprehending a rapist, but had snatched their gun away from them. See "Appeal to All Social Circles to Support Public Security Bureau's Attack on Criminal Elements" (Huyu shehui ge jie zhichi gong'an jingcha daji weifa fanzui fenzi), *Nanjing Bao*, 22 Apr. 1979, pp. 1, 3. In another incident the public security forces had detained and fined a worker who had knocked over and broken a public trash can and then manifested a "bad attitude" toward the public security officers. When the officers arrived at the worker's factory to do education work, coworkers obstructed their efforts, and four left their posts to file a complaint. See "Obstructing the Police from Carrying Out Their Duty Is Against the Law" (Zunao minjing zhixing renwu shi weifade), *Nanjing Ribao*, 27 June 1980. Other reports note citizen skepticism of the possibility of regaining stolen property. See, for example, Zhang Xu and Wu Zhenying, "More Than Ten Thousand Yuan Returned in the Last Six Months" (Shang ban nian fahuan xiankuan wan yu yuan), *Beijing Wanbao*, 15 July 1980, p. 2.

84. *Nanjing Ribao* reported that one member of the public security forces had abused his authority, to rape women and distribute pornographic materials. See Si Ming, Chen Li, and Lai Qing, "Gong Nongjun Breaks the Law While Enforcing the Law; Receives Stern Punishment" (Gong Nongjun zhifa weifa shoudao yan cheng), *Nanjing Ribao*, 30 Aug. 1980, p. 1. *Beijing Wanbao* reported that a public security officer extorted cash and goods as protection money from gamblers. See Tan Fengping, "Li Zhangsheng Given Two-Year Criminal Sentence" (Li Zhangsheng bei pan xing liang nian), *Beijing Wanbao*, 7 Oct. 1980.

85. See, for example, Sun Yunlong, "Xiaolingwei Police Station Sternly Deals with Beating Incident" (Xiaolingwei paichusuo yansu chuli dou ou shijian), *Nanjing Ribao*, 15 Aug. 1979, p. 4; "Head of Police Station Refuses Gift; Manages Affairs According to the Rules and Does Not Open the Back Door" (Paichusuo zhang jue shou liwu an Zhang ban shi bukai houmen), *Nanjing Bao*, 14 Mar. 1979, p. 3; "Impartially Enforcing the Law" (Binggong zhifa), *Nanjing Ribao*, 23 Nov. 1979, p. 4.

86. "City Public Security Bureau's First Class on Legal System Completed" (Shi gong'an ju di yi qi xunlian ban jieye), *Nanjing Ribao*, 9 Aug. 1979, p. 1.

announced that classes on the new laws were being held in each public security substation (*paichusuo*), regardless of the hot weather then
afflicting the city.[87] Nanjing public security forces also took steps to
strengthen their fight against crime. They added night patrols, and
Nanjing Ribao reported that women working the night shift were
much reassured.[88] Newspapers reported model policemen, who were
models not because they had broken up political conspiracies or rings
of saboteurs but because of their bravery, diligence, and skillful detec-
tive work.[89]

The new model retains the public security orientation. It encourages maintaining close contact with the community and dealing with
potential problems before they become legal problems. For example,
one public security substation in Beijing was commended for assisting
old folks by carrying water to their apartments from the public water
taps, especially on rainy days, and on one occasion for helping an
elderly widow arrange her deceased husband's funeral.[90] Viewed in
other terms, this degree of community involvement is extremely intrusive. Another police station, commended for solving 95.6 percent of
its cases, draws four principles from its experience: (1) carefully
watch residents and be especially informed on the activities of potential criminals; (2) rely on the masses to supply clues and coordinate
work with lane cadres and security committee cadres; (3) rely on security committee activists and organize retired workers and "waiting-
for-employment" youths to keep watch on intersections, lanes, and
out-of-the-way places; and (4) educate youths who exhibit criminal

87. Wang Zhengxi, "Many Xiaguan District Public Security Branch Organizations
Take Turns Training Police" (Xiaguan qu gong'an fen ju pubian xun lian ganjing),
Nanjing Ribao, 9 Aug. 1979, p. 1.

88. "City Public Security Bureau Dispatches Patrols for Night Patrol" (Shi gong'an
ju paichu zhi'an xunluodui yejian xunluo), *Nanjing Ribao*, 25 Nov. 1979, p. 4.

89. See, for example, "Heroes on the Security Battle Front Come Forth in Large
Numbers" (Zhi'an zhanxian yingxiong beichu), *Nanjing Ribao*, 30 Apr. 1980, p. 4.
This article featured pictures and brief accounts of various "heroes'" deeds. Other articles featured detailed accounts of particular cases that were solved by doughty and
clever police work. One article told how, following the discovery of a body alongside
railroad tracks in the countryside, the railroad branch of the public security organs
worked six days round the clock to identify the victim, who had hopped a freight, and
to identify and arrest the alleged perpetrators, escapees from a local prison camp who
had hopped the same train. See Sun Yunlong and Liu Laibao, "Public Security Railroad
Branch Six-Day Investigation Breaks a Major Case of Murder and Robbery" (Tielu
gong'an fen chu liu tian zhen po yi zhongda qiangjie sharen an), *Nanjing Ribao*,
25 May 1980.

90. "Chaoyangmen Police Station Does a Lot of Good Things for the Masses"
(Chaoyangmen paichusuo wei qunzhong daban hao shi), *Beijing Wanbao*, 24 Apr.
1980, p. 1.

behavior.[91] The counterpoint to close relations between police and community is a network of informers.

In addition, the public security organs enjoy substantial judicial autonomy. The Security Administration Punishment Act, a 1957 law that was republished in 1980, authorizes public security organs to administer "noncriminal" sanctions for any act that "disrupts public order, interferes with public safety, infringes citizens' rights of the person, or damages public or private property."[92] "Administrative punishments" include warnings, fines of up to 30 yuan, "administrative detention" for up to fifteen days (*xingzheng juliu*),[93] and "labor reeducation" (*laodong jiaoyang*) for one to three years.[94] In practice,

91. Yan Jiugou, "High Clearance Rate" (Po'an lu gao), *Nanjing Ribao*, 6 Dec. 1979, p. 4.
92. Jerome Cohen, *The Criminal Process in the People's Republic of China 1949–1963*, 205; pp. 200–37 provide the best available discussion of this act.
93. Newspaper articles reported instances of "administrative detention" for the following: fighting after a bicycle accident brought on by drunkenness; smoking in a theater and punching the protesting usher in the ear; failure by construction company officials to properly mark a ditch across a road, leading to injuries of nighttime bicycle riders; joyriding; the organization of gambling by a Party member at an agricultural brigade; cutting down a roadside tree; playing a "ghetto-blaster" at high volume while strolling at night, and failing to respond to the subsequent summons from the police station; smoking at a gas station, leading to a fire and injuries; and throwing rocks from a truck at a young woman by the side of the road. See Qin Zhong, "Cai Jilin Bullies People, Liu Shifu Stands Up to Him" (Cai Jilin xujiu qi ren Liu Shifu zhichi), *Nanjing Ribao*, 9 Sept. 1979; Zhu Zhentang, "Punishment Received for Creating Disturbance in Theater" (Daoluan yingyuan zhixu shoufa), *Nanjing Ribao*, 15 Sept. 1979, p. 4; Wang Wenyi and Tong Zepu, "Those Directly Responsible Suffer Detention" (Zhijie zerenzhe shou juliu chufen), *Beijing Wanbao*, 31 July 1980, p. 2; "Zhang Shanghai Detained for Driving Without a License" (Zhang Shanghai wu zhao xing che bei juliu), *Nanjing Ribao*, 15 Aug. 1980; Zhang Jiafu and Wu Yuzhi, "Gambling Party Member Dealt With" (Dangyuan dubo shou chuli), *Nanjing Ribao*, 24 May 1980; He Yajiang, "Sun Faquan Receives Fine for Felling and Stealing Roadside Trees" (Sun Faquan dao fa gonglu shumu bei fa kuan), *Nanjing Ribao*, 3 Apr. 1980, p. 4; "Pan Yihu Detained for Obstructing Police from Fulfilling Their Duties" (Zu'ai minjing zhi qin), *Nanjing Ribao*, 28 Aug. 1980, p. 4; "Smoking Against Regulation" (Wei zhang xiyan), *Beijing Wanbao*, 1 Sept. 1980, p. 1; Zhu Qunqi, "Detention for Throwing Stones at People; Just Deserts Obtained" (Tou shi zhen ren shou juliu zui you ying de), *Beijing Wanbao*, 25 Aug. 1980, p. 1.
94. Additional time can be added to labor reeducation sentences. Labor reeducation camps are administered by provincial-level governments and by large and medium cities by committees, including members from labor departments, civil affairs departments, and public security departments. See *Legal Studies Dictionary* (Faxue cidian), ed. Legal Studies Dictionary Editing Committee (Shanghai: Shanghai Dictionary Press, 1979), 325. According to regulations issued in 1957, "application" for labor reeducation can be made by a civil affairs or public security department, by an individual's unit, or by a parent or guardian. Cohen, *Criminal Process*, 249–51. One observer reported that labor reeducation camps are very similar to labor reform (*laodong gaizao*) camps where those officially subjected to criminal sanctions are sent. Bao Ruo-wang reports that in 1960 a warder stated, in responding to complaints from some inmates undergoing labor reeducation, that their conditions were just as bad as those undergoing labor re-

these provisions provide public security organs with a wide range of discretion beyond the scrutiny of other organs. According to a judge interviewed in Nanjing, those awarded administrative punishments have the right to appeal to higher levels of the public security organs and to the courts, but I am not aware of any cases of appeal of administrative punishments.

Under the reform laws the procuratorate should act as a check on the abuse of power by the public security organs, at least in those cases considered "criminal." The procuratorate must issue a warrant before public security forces can formally arrest a suspect (although detention may occur prior to arrest), and only the procuratorate can bring suit in criminal cases. In addition, the procuratorates are directed to investigate abuses of power by state cadres, such as economic crimes or the violations of the rights of suspects by public security officers.[95]

Chief procurators' reports to the national people's congresses do portray an increasingly large and active national cadre of procurators. In September 1980, the then chief procurator, Huang Huoqing, reported to the Third Session of the Fifth National People's Congress that following the adoption of the new laws in 1979, the procuratorates had convened a national meeting and commenced organizational and educational work, followed by the resumption of full-scale procuratorial work in January 1980.[96] In his report to the First Session of the Sixth National People's Congress in 1983, he stated that the nation had developed a contingent of 116,000 procurators and had annually approved the arrest of an average of 197,000 individuals and been involved in the prosecution of nearly 100 percent of those going on to trial.[97] In 1987 his successor, Yang Yichen, reported to the

---

form: "We have received complaints from some of you. You have a right to complain because you are still citizens, but you seem to forget that Lao Jiao [labor reeducation] people have committed serious mistakes, otherwise you wouldn't be here. Lao Jiao people are here to expiate their mistakes by hard work. As far as the farm administration is concerned, there can be only two kinds of treatment meted out here—one for people who have never made any mistakes and another for those who have. Well, all of you here have made mistakes, so as far as we are concerned Lao Jiao and Lao Gai are the same" (Bao Ruo-Wang, *Prisoner of Mao*, 212).

95. In their annual reports to the National People's Congress, chief procurators have taken pains to demonstrate growing attention to those problems. See, for example, Huang Huoqing, "Report on the Work of the Supreme People's Procuratorate."

96. Ibid., 130–42.

97. "Report on People's Procuratorates at Sixth NPC," trans. from *Xinhua* Beijing, 25 June 1983, in FBIS-CHI-83-125, 28 June 1983, pp. K1–7.

Sixth Session of the Sixth National People's Congress that the procuratorates had approved 315,000 arrests and prosecuted 319,000 cases.[98] The chief procurators also reported a growing number of prosecutions against officials for violating citizens' rights, from 14,000 in 1983 to 32,000 in 1987.[99]

A very high percentage of those detained by the public security forces are approved for arrest, charged, and convicted. Huang also told the National People's Congress that "the pressing task in enforcement of the laws is to punish criminal offenders and ensure stability and unity."[100] He stated that in 1982 the procuratorates approved 89.4 percent of public security bureau applications for arrest warrants and prosecuted 91 percent of the cases transferred from the public security bureaus to the procuratorates.[101] In 1987 the president of the Supreme People's Court, Zhen Tianxiang, stated that of all those tried from the beginning of the August 1983 crackdown to the end of 1987, only 0.7 percent were acquitted. In other words, about eight out of ten of those detained by the public security organs are convicted and sentenced by the procuratorates.[102] The small percentage of those detained but not prosecuted may encourage the public security to pay more attention to procedures, but clearly those who fail to resolve their problems before becoming involved with the public security organs stand a very good chance of suffering criminal sanctions.

While the procuratorates prosecute eight out of ten of those detained by the public security organs, the courts convict an even higher percentage of those prosecuted by the procuratorates. Questioned on the frequency of guilty verdicts, a judge of the Nanjing City Court replied that before any case reached the court, it had first been investigated by the public security organs, then reinvestigated by the procuratorates, and consequently the people's court only rarely found errors.[103] In fact, various aspects of the trial system create an institutional bias that favors guilty verdicts.

98. "Procuratorates Work Report," *Xinhua* Beijing, 6 Apr. 1987, trans. in FBIS-CHI-87-066, 7 Apr. 1987, pp. K8–9.

99. "Report on People's Procuratorates at Sixth NPC."

100. Huang, "Report," 1980, p. 132.

101. Huang, "Report," 1983, pp. K3–4. It is possible that some of those not prosecuted or not approved for arrest are nonetheless given administrative sanctions.

102. "Report by Zheng Tianxiang, president of the Supreme People's Court, on the Work of the Supreme People's Court, Delivered at the First Session of the Seventh NPC on 1 April 1988," *Renmin Ribao*, 18 Apr. 1988, 2, 3, trans. in FBIS-CHI-88-081, 27 Apr. 1988, 19–29. The remainder may also be subject to noncriminal sanctions.

103. Interview in Nanjing, November 1980.

First, Chinese law does not formally presume that the accused is innocent until proven guilty.[104] In theory, Chinese courts assume neither innocence nor guilt, but "take facts as the basis and law as the yardstick." However, as Gelatt observes, "the primary standard for the arrest of an 'offender' is that 'the principal facts of [his] *crime* have already been clarified,'"[105] which implies, in accordance with the judge's statement above, that anyone formally certified for arrest and prosecution has already been judged guilty. Defendants may also be compelled to offer evidence against themselves.

Second, defendants are allowed only limited legal representation. Gelatt also notes that the Criminal Procedures Code denies the "offender" the right of counsel at pretrial hearings (such as during the procuratorate's investigation).[106] Even after the accused gains legal representation, lawyers are officially instructed to place the truth and socialism before the interests of their client. As a result, "[lawyers] generally play a passive role in court proceedings. They tend to confine their defense to pleading for leniency and are reluctant to challenge the prosecution or to exercise such rights as cross-examining government witnesses and calling witnesses of their own."[107]

Third, Chinese law pressures the accused to confess. Section 71 of the Criminal Code specifies that those who manifest repentance for their crimes can have their sentences reduced up to half the otherwise specified penalty.[108] Section 63 specifies that those who turn themselves in will receive a lighter sentence. In practice those who protest their innocence or appeal guilty verdicts are perceived as unrepentant and are liable to be dealt stricter sentences.[109] This also discourages

104. The best available discussion of the presumption of innocence in Chinese law is Timothy A. Gelatt, "The People's Republic of China and the Presumption of Innocence."

105. Ibid., p. 286, quoting from article 40 of the Criminal Procedures Code.

106. Gelatt points out in addition that relevant passages of the Criminal Procedures Code refer not to the "accused" but to the "offender" (which practice is replicated in the Chinese press), that provisions allow for indefinite extension of pretrial detention under certain circumstances, do not mandate fresh consideration of the evidence at the trial, and do not specify which side bears the burden of proof (300). He concludes that the Chinese Criminal Procedures Code is less consistent with the presumption of innocence than other continental or procuratorial systems, including the French and Soviet codes.

107. Leng and Chiu, *Criminal Justice in Post-Mao China*, 95.

108. This applies to sentences of supervision, penal servitude, limited-term imprisonment, and life imprisonment. In the case of a life sentence, the minimum sentence after reduction is ten years. The reduction can be made in more than one increment and can be allotted either at the time of judgment or during incarceration.

109. For examples of cases where confession and repentance or their omission had an effect on the sentence, see "A Group of Criminal Elements Turn Themselves In" (Yi

the appeal of a verdict, as those who appeal are perceived as unrepentant.[110] The prejudice against the defendant is symbolically expressed by the common practice of shaving the head of the accused prior to the trial. Standing before the dock with a downcast and shaved head, he is undoubtedly guilty.[111]

The high percentage of guilty verdicts suggests that public trials are more a source of propaganda than an impartial consideration of the evidence. Explanations of the constitution's provision requiring open trials state that they are both a means of guaranteeing popular supervision of the courts and a means of disseminating propaganda for socialist law.[112] A former president of the Supreme People's Court stated that "heavily and swiftly punishing a small number of active criminals in cases . . . which seriously disrupt social order [is] within the scope of the law."[113] Trials and sentencing are often held in sports stadia or large auditoria before large audiences, who may loudly cheer prosecutors and jeer defendants.[114] Several offenders' sentences may be handed down at once. On such occasions the judge, the prosecutor, the defense lawyer, and sometimes other public officials make lengthy speeches regarding the lessons that ought to be drawn from the cases at hand and the problem of disorder in general. At the conclusion of such meetings, if death sentences have been handed down—which seems inevitable if thousands of people have been gathered to witness the sentencing—the condemned are immediately escorted to the execution ground in a noisy cavalcade and publicly executed.

---

pi fanzui fenzi tou'an zishou), *Beijing Wanbao*, 8 June 1980, p. 2; Zhao Zhijian and Wu Anping, "Thief Han Lianqi Receives Additional Two-Year Sentence" (Daoqie fan Han Lianqi bei jia zhong pan xing liang nian), *Beijing Wanbao*, 10 June 1980.

110. In the interview cited in n. 103 above, the judge estimated that courts of appeal altered the original verdict in less than 5 percent of cases. In theory an appellate court cannot increase the sentence. It can remand the case to the original court for retrial, however, and this procedure occasionally leads to a heavier sentence for the defendant, even when he, not the procuratorate, lodged the appeal. See, for example, Zhang Mingfei, "Criminal Wang's Sentence Changed to Suspended Death Sentence, Criminal Meng's to 12 Years' Imprisonment" (Gai pan Wang fan si huan Meng fan tuxing shi er nian), *Beijing Wanbao*, 30 May 1980, p. 1.

111. Shaving an offender's head was a light punishment in imperial China. See Wang Yu, "A Short Discussion of Shaving Heads" (Ti guangtou xiao yi), *Democracy and Legal System*, no. 1. (1980): 35–36.

112. See, for example, Chen Chuchang et al., *Questions and Answers on the Socialist Legal System*, 162.

113. Beijing Xinhua Domestic Service, 15 Dec. 1981, trans. in "Jiang Hua Report to NPC on Judicial Work," FBIS-CHI-81-244, 21 Dec. 1981, p. K2.

114. In some trials tickets are distributed in advance and are not publicly available.

Despite the reforms, the public security orientation is still the central logic of Chinese justice. The reforms have not weakened but rather have strengthened the extensive network of mediation and security committees. While these committees constitute an enormous surveillance system, Chinese are far more able to negotiate with these grass-roots organizations than with higher-level organizations. Although in theory the procuratorates and courts exercise a check against the abuse of powers by the public security organs, in practice public security organs have a wide range of sanctions at their discretion that the other judicial organs do not supervise. Also in practice a very high percentage of those detained by the public security organs are convicted. By the time a defendant reaches trial and is legally entitled to counsel, his case has been judged. Trials are often used as a means of calling public attention to problems of public security and of deterring potential offenders.

CONCLUSION

China's post-Mao legal reforms have not brought an end to the public security orientation toward law. Chinese law remains a tool of state power. Both the content and the form of China's legal system were imposed from above. Power holders have dealt with the legal system with a series of campaigns and crackdowns and have readily changed statutes and eliminated procedural guarantees to serve their goals of the moment. A pervasive subofficial justice system keeps tabs on all society. Public security forces can impose sanctions without judicial review. Once involved in the formal justice system, defendants have limited rights and are highly likely to be found guilty. Trials are often treated as a message to society rather than as an end in themselves.

In one important respect, modernization theory is misleading. China's legal reformers have not seen legal traditions like mediation committees as an obstacle to legal reform. To the contrary, in keeping with the logic of the public security orientation, reformers have sought to rebuild informal grass-roots organization, including both mediation committees and public security committees. Even in the most "modern" sphere of legal reform, the growing system of civil law, mediation precedes nearly all litigation.

The most widely cited evidence that China is developing a modern, Western approach to law—even creating an autonomous legal system—is the growth of civil law. The number of civil suits has increased at a rapid rate. Zhen Tianxiang, president of the Supreme People's Court, reports that in 1987 China's courts tried nearly 1,200,000 civil cases, an increase of over 20 percent from 1986.[115] First, nearly half of these are divorce cases. Second, in almost mandatory pretrial mediation either party may be forced to give up contractual rights, which indicates that laws and contracts are still soft. Third, and more important, this is still not very many civil cases. The record number of civil cases in one year in the People's Republic is 1,800,000.[116] That was in 1953; since then the population has more than doubled and the economy has become several times larger. Finally, in 30 percent of economic disputes court decisions are not enforced.[117] Thus, while civil law is clearly increasingly important, it does not yet indicate the growth of an autonomous legal system.

One might also argue that the contrast between Chinese and Western legal systems is overdrawn. Many aspects of Chinese justice have American counterparts. For example, American police exercise considerable discretion, plea bargaining raises questions about the presumption of innocence in practice, and judges with crowded calendars are inclined to rely on presentencing reports, and so forth. Nonetheless, when the whole of the Chinese legal system is considered, including the networks of neighborhood committees, the public security bureau's authority to sentence alleged offenders for up to two years without a trial, the lack of a presumption of innocence, the high rate of convictions, and the manipulation of trials for propaganda, it is clear that the Chinese legal system follows a different logic from the American system.

The fundamental difference between the two legal systems is that whereas Chinese law is primarily a tool of state power, American law protects a margin of relative social autonomy. This distinction reflects the difference between the two states: whereas the United States has a liberal-capitalist state based on a market that requires autonomous social activity, China's Leninist state is based on the leading role of the Party. In each case, law is an aspect of the relationship between state and society and works in concert with a wide spectrum of state, social, and economic institutions.

115. "Supreme People's Court Work Report to NPC," p. 21.
116. "Civil Courts Seen Handling Increasing Case Loads," *Xinhua* Beijing, 4 Mar. 1985, trans. in FBIS-CHI-85-043, 5 Mar. 1985, p. K11.
117. "Anti-Crime Drive Brings Results," *Beijing Review* 31, no. 6 (18 Apr. 1988): 11.

Why has the public security orientation to law persisted? Of course, the present always begins with the past, but any statement that traditional attitudes persist because they are congruent with traditional culture is incomplete. Contemporary Chinese law in some ways resembles traditional Chinese law because the contemporary state in some ways resembles the traditional state and because both use law for similar purposes. The most important similarity is that both are relatively autonomous states that avoid granting society rights that could be used to restrict their autonomy. The most important difference is that the contemporary state has the administrative capacity to build grass-roots organization throughout society and can thereby avoid granting autonomy to clans, guilds, or other social groups.

The persistence of the public security orientation has positive aspects. As Victor Li and others have pointed out, the emphasis on formal procedural justice makes the American legal system absurdly complex and expensive and not infrequently results in substantive injustice.[118] China's informal system of justice depends on a pervasive network of subofficials who keep watch on society and often results in the denial of rights by either American or Chinese definitions of that term.

All of this is important primarily because it means that the Chinese legal system may not accomplish the goals intended by reformers. First, "law from above" is unlikely to provide a foundation for a social consensus. Chinese officials have repeatedly claimed that the crime rate is falling, and the more vigorous public security system seems likely to strengthen law and order. Society did not agree, however, to "law from above," and campaign-style education and enforcement seems unlikely to send clear signals about what is and is not legal. Therefore, this kind of legal system seems unlikely to communicate clearly to society the official "will of the proletariat."

Second, "law from above" is unlikely to provide an effective means of ordering the state or binding officials to official purposes. Without an effectively autonomous legal system, whistle-blowers are likely to be discouraged by the lack of legal protection. For example, Xing Yixun's popular but controversial play "Power Versus Law" portrays the complications that result when an accountant attempts to reveal

118. Victor Li, *Law Without Lawyers.*

the corruption of a deputy secretary of a municipal Party committee. The deputy secretary orders the chief of public security to arrest her on trumped-up charges. The newly appointed secretary of the municipal Party committee calls off the arrest in the nick of time. The public security chief immediately switches loyalties, but to the new secretary, not to the law. Though the chief is immediately chided for failing to heed the law, Xing obviously means to ask whether or not (personal) power can be defeated by law.[119] In a Leninist state, law is all too likely to become a means of protecting the privileges of state power holders. Anticorruption campaigns have been dogged by the limited ability of enforcement agencies to arrest and prosecute powerful leaders. When the misdeeds of powerful leaders are exposed, the leaders all too often receive lighter punishments based on Party regulations instead of on criminal law.[120] Without effective supervision, the privileged elite of state power holders can only be expected to use their power for personal ends.

Third, the relationship between this kind of law and economic modernization is complex. The post-Mao legal reforms have created a far more propitious environment for economic growth than did the Cultural Revolution. This is as much a matter of eliminating negatives as of providing positives. The economic success of other East Asian nations demonstrates that an Anglo-Saxon legal system is not an absolute prerequisite for rapid economic growth or technological advance. That does not mean that the reformed Chinese legal system will promote economic growth. In China, courts and contracts will not be as important as they are in the Western world. Other channels will have to be found for communication between consumers and producers.

In sum, "law from above" is unlikely to have the consequences the leadership hopes for. Exactly what kind of legal system China should have is, as was noted above, a controversial issue. Many powerful leaders have rejected Western-style law or do not recognize the existence of a real alternative to "law from above." Nor does China ap-

119. This play is translated in *Chinese Literature*, no. 6 (June 1980): 31–97.
120. For example, a delegate to the Second Session of the Sixth People's Political Consultative Conference compared the case of a thief who was executed for stealing 3,500 yuan and that of an assistant mayor who had illegally purchased land, forged documents, and illegally built himself a villa, but was merely relieved of his duties. "Law Should Be Strengthened, Implementation of the Law Should Be Just" (Fazhi yao jianquan zhifa yao gongzheng), *Renmin Ribao*, 22 May 1984, p. 4.

pear to be developing a Western-style legal system. Reformers still hope that the legal system will have results akin to those attributed to Western-style law—that is, that the new legal system will provide a basis for social order, guide and limit the activities of officials, and provide a foundation for economic modernization. Unfortunately, in terms of these goals, "law from above" will have ambiguous results at best.

CHAPTER FOUR

Elections to Local People's Congresses

In June 1979 the National People's Congress passed the Election Law for the National People's Congress and the Local People's Congresses of the People's Republic of China (the Election Law) and the Organic Law of the Local People's Congresses and the Local People's Governments (the Organic Law), which altered the structure of local government and election procedures. They abolished the revolutionary committees formed during the Cultural Revolution and reinstituted the system of people's congresses and people's governments. They guaranteed various democratic procedures, such as a choice of candidates on ballots, the use of secret ballots, and the right of deputies to submit motions and query state administrators. For the next eighteen months the Party led a campaign to implement the new laws. The Ministry of Civil Affairs organized and mobilized provincial governments, which mobilized county governments, which mobilized grassroots units. Despite many reports of delays and malfeasance by lower-level cadres, each of the nation's 2,757 county-level jurisdictions eventually held direct elections for deputies to local people's congresses and reconstituted people's governments. These elections established the pattern for subsequent direct elections to local people's congresses held in 1984 and again in 1987. By examining this "implementation campaign," the kind of resistance it engendered, and the context in which it occurred, in this chapter I will reach conclusions about implementation in Leninist states and about the potential for democratic reform in China.

A study of how the state organized the implementation of "law from above" and of the results that can be expected was made in the preceding chapter; this chapter is a study of "democracy" from above and its likely consequences. In each case, the state is seeking to remedy problems associated with excessive state autonomy by developing institutions—a legal system and parliaments—associated with "bourgeois" democracy. In both cases, however, dominant groups in the leadership have rejected crucial aspects of the Western model, such as the relative autonomy of civil society associated with Western law, and the relatively free competition associated with Western elections. This raises serious questions in both cases about whether the reforms will successfully remedy the problems.

One of the most important problems faced by post-Mao reformers is to construct the Party's legitimacy. As was noted in chapter 1, the violent campaigns of the Cultural Revolution exposed a wide gap between state and society, and the reformers sought to remedy this problem by establishing more inclusive political institutions and increasing popular participation in politics. Furthermore, like the legal system, people's congresses are supposed to make government more effective. Leninist states can adopt far more draconian policies than other authoritarian states and can mount impressive campaigns to implement these policies. This autonomy is gained at a high price, however.

First, when access to policy formulation is limited, as Merilee Grindle writes, "the process of implementing public policies is a focus of political participation and competition."[1] This kind of political activity consists mainly of bargaining between the center and localities. This is not equivalent to American-style pluralism, it is patrimonial. Success or failure depends on personal relationships between officials at various levels in the hierarchy, and as often as not, localities must exchange something of personal benefit to a higher official in exchange for "special treatment." Leninist state organization encloses bargaining within narrow vertical hierarchies, and potential interest groups are less able to form autonomous organization than in other types of authoritarian states. While this strengthens the bargaining position and the autonomy of the center,[2] it still results in a frag-

---

1. Grindle, "Policy Content and Context in Implementation."
2. Ghita Ionescu, in "Patronage Under Communism," refers to this as a "sellers' market for patronage."

mented and uncertain process of implementation. Patrimonialism constitutes a passive but powerful and pervasive form of resistance to the state.

Second, Leninist states are often unable to evaluate policies. Peter Cleaves states:

> In closed systems, on the other hand, the state concentrates enormous relative power within its boundaries, but it tends to become blind to the society of which it is a part. . . . A frequent occurrence is that leadership, exhilarated by the reflection of its own power, sponsors highly problematic policies that fail spectacularly.[3]

Indeed, China's leaders and many other Chinese have argued that in China the abuse of state power is a greater problem than the lack of state power.

Leninist states have tried to solve this problem with more campaigns from above, only to re-create the sources of the problem. For much of its history the CCP has been locked in a cycle of fighting corruption by mounting campaigns that generate more corruption. The Yan'an rectification, the Sanfan-Wufan campaign, the Siqing campaign, the Cultural Revolution, the Yida-Sanfan campaign, and since the death of Mao, struggles against "bourgeois liberalism," "spiritual pollution," and the recent campaign for Party rectification have all had the fighting of corruption as a central theme, but patrimonialism remains a pressing problem. "Open" rectification campaigns, like the Cultural Revolution, have aroused popular energies but severely weakened institutions, leaving little alternative to personalistic politics. "Closed" campaigns, conducted within the bounds of formal organization and with the goal of strengthening that organization, have resulted in temporary gains, but leave the structure of organization unchanged. Their future can only be more of the past.

The reforms discussed in this chapter were an attempt to break out of this dilemma and solve these problems. They aimed to replace the despotic "feudal" government of the Cultural Revolution with democratic institutions. The Election and Organic Laws defined institutions and procedures to strengthen popular supervision of government through the system of people's congresses.[4] China currently has people's congresses at the county, provincial, and national levels, and in

---

3. Cleaves, "Implementation Amidst Scarcity and Apathy."
4. For a general discussion of the new laws, see Liu Zhuanchen, Pan Bowen, and Cheng Jiyou, *Questions and Answers on Election Law Knowledge*.

some cases, at intermediate levels, such as cities under the jurisdiction of a province. At each level of government, people's congresses are theoretically the highest authority, subject only to higher levels of government, except the National People's Congress, which is "the highest organ of state power."[5] The most important provisions of the new laws stipulated that all deputies to county-level congresses should be elected directly by voters. Previously, deputies to rural county-level congresses were elected by commune-level congresses.[6] Other important reforms follow: (1) The new laws guarantee the use of secret ballots. Previously, secret ballots were used in urban areas, but elections in rural areas were often conducted at mass meetings by a show of hands. (2) The Election Law mandates that ballots should always have more candidates than positions. Previously, the number of candidates on the ballot usually equaled the number of positions available.[7] (3) The new law reaffirms the right of citizens to nominate candidates for deputy positions at the county level. During the previous decade candidates were usually nominated by the Party.[8] (4) The new laws reaffirm the right of deputies to query state administrators and to submit motions to the congresses.[9] (5) The Organic Law empowers people's congresses at the county level to establish standing committees, a privilege previously restricted to higher-level congresses. As full sessions of county-level congresses usually occur only

5. *The Constitution of the People's Republic of China* (Beijing: Foreign Languages Press, 1982), 45.

6. Cheng Zihua, minister of civil affairs, stated that in the future direct election will be extended to higher levels. See Brantly Womack, "The 1980 County-Level Elections in China: Experiment in Democratic Modernization," 263. However, as of 1989, direct election has been extended to only a few municipalities.

7. Under the 1979 law the number of candidates for county-level deputies was to exceed the number of positions by 50–100%. In the 1986 revisions to the Election Law, the ratio was reduced to 33–100%. See Tong Ming, "Election with the Same Number of Candidates as Positions and Election with More Candidates Than Positions," *Renmin Ribao*, 21. Feb. 1980, p. 5, trans. in FBIS-CHI-80-50, 12 Mar. 1980, p. L16; "Wang Hanbin Explains NPC Electoral Law Revision," *Xinhua* Beijing, 15 Nov. 1986, trans. in FBIS-CHI-86-225, 21. Nov. 1986, pp. K6–10; and "Text of People's Congress Law Revision," *Xinhua*, 4. Dec. 1986, trans. in FBIS-CHI-86-235, 8. Dec. 1986, pp. K2–10.

8. Actually, nominating is not equivalent to putting a candidate on the ballot. Voters submit nominations to election committees, which, in consultation with voters, establish the actual lists. As Zhang Qingfu and Pi Chunxie argue, the new laws revitalize "democratic consultation" and "integrate the higher with the lower level." See "Revise the Electoral Laws to Institutionalize Democracy," *Renmin Ribao*, 22 May 1979, p. 3, trans. in FBIS-CHI-79-103, 25 May 1979, p. L5.

9. The right to submit motions is not unprecedented. Townsend states that in the 1950s deputies submitted "fantastic" numbers of motions, just as they do now. See James R. Townsend, *Political Participation in Communist China*, 109.

once a year for a few days, theoretically this will allow for more continuous supervision of local administration.

While reformers denied any intention of creating a "bourgeois" democracy, they claimed that the reforms would provide many benefits
associated with "bourgeois" democracy. In introducing the new laws
to the Second Session of the Fifth National People's Congress, Peng
Zhen declared:

> Local revolutionary committees are to be replaced by local people's gov-
> ernments. . . . Local people's governments are responsible and accountable
> to the people's congresses at the corresponding levels and to their standing
> committees. As a result of these changes, in localities at or above the
> county level, the people's control and supervision over the local people's
> governments will be substantially strengthened.[10]

Nonetheless, the reformers rejected many aspects of "bourgeois democracy" and instead retained key features of the existing Leninist
state. As I have argued in preceding chapters, following a period of
debate over the definition of democracy, Deng Xiaoping asserted the
need to uphold the Four Cardinal Principles of adherence to the socialist road, insistence on the dictatorship of the proletariat, upholding the leadership of the Party, and sticking rigidly to Marxism-
Leninism Mao Zedong Thought.[11] At the same time that the reform
laws were passed, Democracy Wall activists were arrested, democracy
walls were closed, unofficial publications were suppressed, and intellectuals who had taken part in the wide-ranging debates were
silenced.

The people's congresses are to uphold the Four Cardinal Principles.
Xu Chongde and Pi Chunxie argue that in capitalist parliaments opposing cliques of monopoly capitalists fight and struggle, but in the
people's congresses deputies represent the common interests of the
people and are able to work with "one heart and one mind" to
achieve unanimity.[12] Many Chinese support this quest for peace and
unanimity. Mao and revolutionary vigilantism extolled the virtues of
conflict, but as Edward Friedman writes, Mao carried a lighted
match, looking for the "forces that would explode and advance egalitarian and communitarian goals."[13] Given the turbulence of the Cul-

10. Peng Zhen, "Explanation of the Seven Draft Laws," 197.
11. Deng Xiaoping, "Uphold the Four Cardinal Principles."
12. Xu Chongde and Pi Chunxie, *Questions and Answers on the Election System*, 158.
13. Friedman, "The Innovator," 313.

tural Revolution and other political campaigns, and the very vivid turmoil of Chinese society throughout the first half of the twentieth century, most Chinese would like to avoid any more explosions. The Western proposition that social conflict strengthens democracy seems absurd in this context. Confining the reforms within the strictures of a Leninist state raises doubts, however, about the degree to which the people's congresses would provide for popular supervision of government, let alone provide an adequate check on practice.

Moreover, the reforms themselves amounted to a limited political campaign. In contrast to former political campaigns, post-Mao political and administrative reforms are relatively cautious attempts to restrain the use of state power and aim to prevent further dramatic failures. And yet these reforms still occur on a grand scale that would daunt most governments. The Election and Organic Laws sought to alter fundamentally the structure and process of government in China's 2,757 county-level governments. The campaign to implement the Election and Organic Laws involved building still more organization that stretched from central offices in Beijing to the grass roots of all China and involved massive amounts of propaganda. However reduced in scale or intensity from previous political campaigns, these reforms are still testimony to the autonomy of China's Leninist state.

Opposition naturally took the same form it took during previous state initiatives. Lower-level cadres opposed the reforms for a variety of reasons, but above all because these threatened their personal authority. Any reform that attempts to institutionalize authority threatens the ability of cadres to use power for personal purposes. Cadres naturally used their patrimonial authority to delay and deflect the implementation of the new laws. The Party leadership could only turn to the Party's Leninist organization to impose the reforms—having closed the door on broader definitions of democracy, it had no alternative—and thereby reasserted the elite and exclusive nature of Chinese politics that provides the foundation of Leninist politics in the first place.

The election campaign was intended to solve fundamental dilemmas in Leninist politics, but actually re-created the classic cycle of Leninist politics. The reforms were intended to open new, inclusive channels of communication that would break up stifling patrimonial networks. But they were implemented by ordinary Leninist means. As Brantly Womack states: "However popular these democratizing measures are, it was the support of central leadership rather than popular pressure that led to their adoption."[14] As a result lower-level cadres who did not want reform were able to resist reform through patrimonial channels. The elections did open some new channels of communication, but they fell far short of the promises made at the outset of the election campaign.

IMPLEMENTING THE REFORMS

The reformers issued authoritative instructions regarding the content of the reforms and the procedures to be used in adopting them. These statements were publicized in the media and in official state and Party documents. Preexisting government and Party organization were adapted to implement the reforms. This organization enabled higher levels to mobilize lower levels, culminating in door-to-door canvassing of most of the Chinese citizenry. During the actual process of nominating and voting, grass-roots election committees, in cooperation with other grass-roots organizations, closely monitored all proceedings. This Leninist campaign of implementation proved very effective. Besides managing a reform of local government in a reasonably short time, it produced an enormous voter turnout and, with a few exceptions, elected what the regime could consider "responsible" deputies.

Through their organization the central authorities were able to establish and impose an official definition of the reforms despite the general lack of consensus. By Chinese standards the instructions issued to lower levels were precise and public. First and foremost, the reforms were announced and defined in laws publicly promulgated and widely discussed. By Western standards the new laws were imprecisely worded, but in a Chinese context, where there are few laws and where most administrative directives have been and remain "internal" (*neibu*) or secret, these laws were a bold and forceful means of proclaiming commitment to the reforms. Second, various reports indicate that the state and Party issued other, more detailed "internal" instructions to lower levels.[15] Third, the Ministry of Civil Affairs and the General Office for National Direct Election at the County Level produced other, less formal documents explaining the reforms,

14. Womack, "County-Level Elections," 162.
15. See, for example, Hefei, Anhui Provincial Service, 13 Feb. 1980, trans. in FBIS-CHI-80-032, 14 Feb. 1980, pp. O3–4.

including at least one widely distributed manual that contains 120 straightforward questions and answers on the elections.[16] While there were various means of resisting implementation, the organizational force behind these announcements made public criticism difficult.

The implementation campaign began at the national level. Although Party activities relevant to election work were not widely discussed in the press, they were of crucial importance. At a Central Party Conference on Election Work it was stated: "The fundamental guarantee for successful elections is to strengthen Party leadership."[17] Election work was formally launched and monitored by the National People's Congress and its Standing Committee. Peng Zhen associated himself with the reforms. As a prominent victim of the Cultural Revolution, Peng's visible presence highlighted the regime's commitment to change, but his long-standing commitments to organization, order, and the Party also suggested limits to "democratization." Election work at the national level was conducted by the Ministry of Civil Affairs and the General Office for National Direct Election at the County Level (the General Office). Cheng Zihua served both as minister of civil affairs and director of the General Office. The Ministry of Civil Affairs began by conducting experimental elections in five selected county-level jurisdictions.[18] These experiments established the sequence of procedures used to conduct elections throughout the country: preparation, propaganda, voter registration, nomination of candidates, balloting, and the convening of congresses.

Election work at the provincial level officially began following a resolution adopted by the Standing Committee of the Fifth National People's Congress in February 1980.[19] This resolution was something of a formality, however, as the central authorities had begun to mobilize provincial authorities in December 1979. First, they held a conference attended by provincial leaders at which the experimental elections were discussed. The ministry also sent work teams staffed by cadres from the General Office to twenty-one provinces to supervise

16. Xu Chongde and Pi Chunxie, *Questions and Answers*.
17. Beijing Xinhua Service, 11 Feb. 1980, trans. in FBIS-CHI-80-031, 13 Feb. 1980, p. L6.
18. Beijing Xinhua Domestic Service, 11 Feb. 1980, trans. in FBIS-CHI-80-031, 13 Feb. 1980, pp. L4–6. See also Shenyang, Liaoning Service, 25 Oct. 1979, trans. in FBIS-CHI-79-210, 29 Oct. 1979, pp. S2–3.
19. Beijing Domestic Service, 12 Feb. 1980, trans. in FBIS-CHI-80-31, 13 Feb. 1980, pp. L1–3.

experimental election work.[20] Provincial authorities later supervised further experimental elections.[21] Just as election work was monitored at the national level by the National People's Congress and conducted by the General Office, election work at the provincial level was monitored by provincial people's congresses and conducted by provincial election committees. Provincial election committees generally included approximately twenty leading provincial figures and had a staff to conduct day-to-day business.[22] With the weight of state and Party organizations bearing down from above, provincial cadres were under tremendous pressure to promote implementation of the reforms and to follow Beijing's guidelines. Accordingly, county-level officials were soon mobilized at work conferences convened by provincial authorities.[23]

To follow the process of implementation from the provincial to the grass-roots level, I will focus on two districts in the city of Nanjing. Nanjing is the capital of Jiangsu province and has a population of about three and one-half million. Administratively, Nanjing resembles a prefecture (*diqu*), being an intermediate level between the province and counties and having jurisdiction over several county-level units. At the time of the elections (1980) Nanjing was subdivided into three suburban counties (*xian*) and nine urban districts (*qu*). This portion of this chapter will focus on election work in two of those districts, Baixia and Gulou. Gulou district, with a population of about 300,000, is Nanjing's largest district and is located in the center of the city. Baixia, with a population of about 200,000, is also predominantly urban.

The election campaign reached Nanjing in early June 1980 when Jiangsu province launched a second wave of trial elections.[24] At that time the Standing Committee and the leading Party group of the city revolutionary committee convened one or more meetings of leading comrades from county and district revolutionary committees and civil

20. Cheng Zihua, "Cheng Zihua's Report," Beijing Xinhua Domestic Service, 11 Sept. 1981, trans. in FBIS-CHI-81-177, 14 Sept. 1981, pp. K2–10.

21. See, for example, Nanchang, Jiangxi Provincial Service, 25 Feb. 1980, trans. in FBIS-CHI-80-041, 28 Feb. 1980, p. O2.

22. See, for example, Changsha, Hunan Provincial Service, 25 Mar. 1980, trans. in FBIS-CHI-80-066, 3 Apr. 1980, p. P6.

23. See, for example, Hefei, Anhui Provincial Service, 11 Mar. 1980, trans. in FBIS-CHI-80-055, 19 Mar. 1980, p. O9.

24. Nanjing, Jiangsu Provincial Service, 28 Dec. 1980, trans. in FBIS-CHI-80-252, 30 Dec. 1980, pp. O1–3.

affairs departments to begin work.[25] Zhou Bopan, an assistant secretary of the city revolutionary committee explained the goals of election work, announced the formation of a municipal election committee, and outlined procedures to be followed. In organizational and procedural matters Zhou closely followed guidelines from above. The municipal election committee was chaired by Zhou Bopan, had approximately twenty members, and was supported by an office staff. Election work was to proceed in four stages: preparation, propaganda and voter registration, nomination of candidates and consultation to determine the official candidates, and voting and convening the congresses. The city's leaders also announced the schedule for subsequent election work in Nanjing. Work on experimental elections in Jiangning county and Baixia district was scheduled to begin immediately, with the goal of convening people's congresses in the first third of September.[26] Other districts and counties were to begin election work on July 1 and to convene congresses by the end of September.

The first stage of election work, preparation, called for extending election organization from the city level down to the grass roots. First, election committees were established at the district level. In both Gulou and Baixia districts the district election committee was formally under the direct supervision of the district revolutionary committee. The Gulou district election committee had nineteen members and an office with twenty-seven staff members.[27] According to the higher level's guidelines, election committees were to be composed of people from as many different circles as possible. In both Gulou and Baixia, district election committees were reported to include leading members of the district Party organization, representatives from other democratic parties, and representatives from the mass organizations for workers, women, and youth. In addition, the Gulou committee, and probably the Baixia committee, included representatives from the district public security, civil affairs, and propaganda departments.[28]

25. For a general account of this meeting, see Ling Xuan, "City Committee Plans District and County Direct Election Work" (Shi wei bushu xian qu xuanju gongzuo), *Nanjing Ribao*, 15 June 1980, p. 1.

26. "Our City Makes Concrete Plans for County and District Direct Election Work" (Wo shi juti bushu xian qu zhijie xuanju gongzuo), *Nanjing Ribao*, 3 June 1980, p. 1.

27. Interview with election officials at Gulou District Office, 23 Sept. 1980.

28. Interview at Gulou District Office, and Jun Ji and Jia Hu, "Baixia District Direct Election Work Fully Launched" (Baixia qu zhijie xuanju gongzuo quanmian zhankai), *Nanjing Ribao*, 21 June 1980, p. 4.

Second, election work was organized from the district level down to the grass roots. The district election committees divided their districts into election districts (*xuanju qu*) and established an election committee in each.[29] Election districts could consist of a single unit, an amalgamation of two or more smaller units, or a residential neighborhood. The Baixia district election committee convened a meeting of all election-district election committee members to plan further work in early June 1980.[30] Still another layer of election committees was formed at the unit level. All units (except those affiliated with the PLA), including lane offices, soon formed election work groups.[31]

The second stage of election work, propaganda, called for a general mobilization. By any standards except those of the Cultural Revolution, this was a major effort in social mobilization. Throughout the city, approximately 74,000 "backbone elements" explained to voters both the procedures and the "significance" of the elections. They used blackboards, materials published by the districts, the network of loudspeakers in Chinese residential areas, and meetings. Throughout Nanjing there were approximately 12,700 meetings held in conjunction with this propaganda effort. The municipal election committee estimated that 80 percent of the city's three and one-half million people received education regarding the elections.[32] Gulou district officials claimed to have reached everyone in the district at least once and to have reached many people several times.[33]

Voter registration, conducted by election-district election committees, was also a form of mobilization.[34] Voter registration, like previ-

29. In Gulou district, a population of approximately 300,000 was divided into 173 election districts, each district having from 500 to 8,000 voters and electing from 1 to 12 representatives. Each representative represented from 500 to 1,500 voters, with an average of about 800. The national average was about 1,250 voters per representative (Cheng Zihua, "Cheng Zihua's Report"). Larger units, such as Nanjing University, were intentionally underrepresented, as their problems and interests were considered distinct from those of the district as a whole (interview at Gulou District Office).

30. Jun Ji and Jia Hu, "Election Work."

31. "On the County (District) Direct Election Question" (Guanyu xian (qu) zhijie xuanju wenti), *Nanjing Ribao*, 27 June 1980, p. 4.

32. Ling Xuan, "Our City's Election Propaganda Fully Launched: Vast Numbers of Voters' Political Zeal Runs High" (Wo shi xuanju xuanchuan quanmian zhankai guangda xuanmin zhengzhi reqing gaozhang), *Nanjing Ribao*, 25 July 1980, p. 4.

33. Interview at Gulou District Office, 23 Sept. 1980.

34. In 1986 the National People's Congress approved changes to the Election Law that eliminated the time-consuming procedure of scrutinizing each voter prior to each election. Now, once registered, a voter may vote in all subsequent elections, barring formal deprivation of political rights. Hence, this stage of election work was not part

ous campaigns, involved assessing the political standing of each citizen. Whereas in past campaigns the emphasis was usually on "ferreting out" counterrevolutionaries, in this campaign the emphasis was on rehabilitating those unjustly accused. In Gulou district, nine people were deprived of political rights.[35] Cheng Zihua reported to the Standing Committee of the National People's Congress that political rehabilitations occasioned by the process of voter registration were one of the campaign's major achievements.[36]

The third stage, the nominating process, is supposed to be a cycle of democratic consultation between voters and cadres. According to the 1979 election laws, any voter, seconded by three other voters, can nominate the candidate of his choice.[37] In practice, however, the final list of candidates is established by the election-district election committee "in consultation" with small groups of voters. The process used in Nanjing (and in most other places) is known as the "three ups and three downs" (*san shang san xia*). In the first round, voters meeting in small groups based on their work group or their residence, depending on the type of election district they vote in, are encouraged to make nominations. The election manual urges the selection of candidates who support the Party and its policies, who are "progressive," who are enthusiastic workers, and who enjoy close relations with the masses.[38] A member of the election work group of Nanjing University set forth similar criteria for prospective candidates.[39]

The initial round of nominations usually produces a surfeit of nominees. In Baixia district, the Nanjing Aviation Institute election district produced 511 nominations for 3 positions.[40] These initial lists are forwarded to the election-district election committee, which narrows the field according to its own dictates. At the Aviation Institute,

---

of the 1987 round of elections. See "Wang Hanbin Explains NPC Electoral Law Revision" (n. 7 above) and "Text of Electoral Law Revision," *Xinhua*, 4 Dec. 1986, trans. in FBIS-CHI-86-235, 8 Dec. 1986, pp. K2–10.

35. Interview at Gulou District Office, 23 Sept. 1980. Another 218 people were denied the right to vote on the basis of mental incompetency.

36. Cheng Zihua, "Cheng Zihua's Report" (n. 20 above).

37. In 1986 this provision was amended to require ten voters to sponsor a nomination. See "Wang Hanbin Explains NPC Electoral Law Revision" and "Text of Electoral Law Revision."

38. Xu and Pi, *Questions and Answers*, 12.

39. Interview with staffer of Nanjing University election work group, 25 Sept. 1980.

40. Tan Jiahu, "Masses Satisfied with Deputies Selected in Nanjing Aviation Election District" (Nanhang xuanqu xuanchu de daibiao qunzhong manyi), *Nanjing Ribao*, 18 July 1980.

which was cited as a model, the entire list, reduced to 269 names by eliminating duplications, was returned to each small group. The small groups were asked to select the best 5 or 6 candidates from the entire list and to return the short list to the election-district election committee. The committee in turn narrowed the field to 23 candidates and then held a meeting of representatives from the Party, the school administration, the union, the youth league, and "all sections of the masses" to choose the final 5 or 6 candidates.[41] While the 1979 law allowed for primary elections, officials in Gulou district were aware of only one election district that had held a primary election, and this was regarded as an unfortunate breakdown of the "three ups and three downs" process. In 1986 the Election Law was amended to delete the clause allowing for primary elections.[42] Even in theory, the nominating process is closely supervised by lower-level cadres and they can easily exert more influence than is formally permitted.[43]

The fourth stage of the election campaign is voting. The new law is supposed to guarantee voters a choice by putting more candidates on the ballot than there are positions to be filled. The choices are limited, however: the nominating procedure largely prevents political independents from appearing on the ballot; and despite clauses in the electoral law allowing candidates to "campaign," in practice candidates are restricted from making direct overtures to voters. Cheng Zihua has criticized Western-style election campaigns: "In their election campaigns bourgeois candidates often give an extravagant account of what they are going to do and make promises of one kind or another, but after they are elected they often refuse to do what they promised."[44]

Other provisions in the Election Law, stipulating that the list of official candidates is to be posted twenty days before the election along with "background data" on the candidates for "repeated discussions and democratic consultations," more closely approximate

41. Ibid. The exact number of candidates is determined during the "three ups and three downs" process by the election committee. The laws only stipulate that the number of candidates appearing on the ballot for county-level deputies should outnumber the number of positions by 33–100%. Gulou district officials had a preference for keeping the list as short as possible.

42. See "Wang Hanbin Explains NPC Electoral Law Revision" and "Text of Electoral Law Revision."

43. Barnabas Racz states that in multiple-candidate elections held in Hungary in 1983, "The weakest and most manipulated part of the electoral process is precisely the nomination phase" ("Political Participation and Developed Socialism: The Hungarian Elections of 1985").

44. Cheng Zihua, "Cheng Zihua's Report."

practice.[45] In their officially endorsed election manual, Xu and Pi state that it is better for election committees to publish materials on behalf of all candidates than for candidates to conduct individual propaganda. In the Nanjing University election district, campaign literature consisted of a single sheet of paper briefly outlining candidates' biographies and displaying their pictures. The few instances where candidates have conducted their own election campaigns have proven extremely controversial.

All these procedures result in the election of deputies already endorsed by the Party, such as model workers, Party members, activists, and "backbone elements." In Gulou district, of 339 deputies elected, 164 were model workers and about the same number were Party members.[46] In the press, some commentators have deplored this problem, arguing that while model workers are good people, they may not be the best qualified individuals to actively represent the masses in the congresses.[47] Even official guidelines and ranking leaders have urged election workers to work against the tendency to nominate and elect too many Party members.[48]

The manner in which results of elections are reported indicates that the opinions or platforms of candidates are noncontroversial or are taken for granted. In a few isolated instances the names of successful candidates are reported, but usually election results are reported only in an aggregate form. For example, cadres in the Gulou District Office reported that in Gulou district, of 339 deputies elected, there were 213 men and 126 women and that there were 47 cadres, 37 workers, 18 scientists or technical workers, 53 educators, 38 from the commercial sector, 13 doctors, 46 from organs of the government and Party, 11 from the public security department, 56

45. For the relevant codes, see "People's Republic of China Electoral Law for the National People's Congress and Local People's Congresses at All Levels, Article 28," reprinted in *Chinese Law and Government* 15, nos. 3 and 4 (Fall and Winter 1982–83): 201–2. The NPC Standing Committee Work Report to the First Session of the Seventh National People's Congress states that in the 1987 round of elections to local people's congresses, "Some localities have also organized candidates to meet or hold dialogues with voters or their representatives and to answer their questions and suggestions so that the voters or their representatives can gain a full understanding of the candidates." I interpret this statement to indicate that the chances for real communication between candidates and voters remain quite limited. See "NPC Standing Committee Work Report Published," *Renmin Ribao*, 19 Apr. 1988, trans. in FBIS-CHI-88-081, 27 Apr. 1988, pp. 11–19.

46. Interview at Gulou District Office, 23 Sept. 1980.

47. Li Yuan, "Bring into Full Play the Role of NPC Deputies," *Guangming Ribao*, 14 Apr. 1981, p. 3, trans. in FBIS-CHI-81-082, p. K2.

48. See, for example, Cheng Zihua, "Cheng Zihua's Report," p. K8.

neighborhood activists, 6 national minorities, and 4 from Taiwan.[49] Exclusive use of this form of reportage implicitly admits the irrelevance of the deputies' own viewpoints. The only reports describing the attitudes of successful candidates emphasize that they are the kind of candidates that the guidelines favor nominating: individuals who support the Party, who are enthusiastic workers, and who enjoy "close relations with the masses." The Party's ability to insure the election of such candidates is strong evidence of its ability to suppress social conflict and gain at least formal popular legitimation for its activities.[50]

The high rate of participation in the elections reveals both the symbolic quality of the elections and the regime's mobilizational capacity. Juan Linz writes that elections in "totalitarian" systems are characterized by "an extraordinary emphasis on participation and involvement of the voter, very often in the preelectoral process as well as in the election."[51] Cheng Zihua, minister of civil affairs and director of the General Office for National Direct Election, emphasized precisely the high rate of participation:

> Those who actually cast their votes [in 1,925 county-level units holding elections to date] . . . account for 96.56 percent of the registered voters. Never before had there been such a high rate of participation in voting. In this regard, the broad masses said contentedly: "The flowers we grew ourselves are beautiful; the fruit trees we planted ourselves give us sweet fruits."[52]

The most important message conveyed by the electoral process is, not which candidates won, but that society participated and thereby, willingly or not, legitimated the Leninist state's practice of "democracy."[53] Linz goes on to state: "Perhaps outside observers are too often tempted to consider the 99.9 percent figure endorsing totalitarian

49. Interview at Gulou District Office, 23 Sept. 1980.
50. Jacobs reports that in the Soviet Union, the demographic composition of local Soviets is carefully considered and carefully engineered. See Everett M. Jacobs, "Norms of Representation and the Composition of Local Soviets."
51. Juan Linz, "Non-Competitive Elections in Europe," 44.
52. Cheng Zihua, "Cheng Zihua's Report," p. K6.
53. Writing of Soviet elections in the 1960s, in which there was only one candidate, Jerome M. Gilison states: "The regime attempts to make each election a plebiscite, in which the sole issue, as George Barr Carson puts it, is 'support or non-support on a question which no one publicly dares reject—do you favor the soviet system?' " Given multiple candidates, this formulation is too strong, but still captures an essential point. See Gilison, "Soviet Elections As a Measure of Dissent: The Missing One Percent."

elections as delegitimizing the regime's authority, but for many citizens living under such regimes its total authority can be terribly real."[54]

RATIONAL-LEGALISM AND PATRIMONIALISM

The Party center's strategy of using rational-legal authority to mobilize lower-level cadres to implement the Organic and Election Laws—the leaders of the Chinese state made official statements of policy and then made use of extensive formal organization—has proven a powerful means of implementing state policy, a means more powerful than those available to the leaders of most other kinds of states. Rational-legal authority is only one aspect, however, of authority in Leninist states and must be understood in relation to patrimonial authority. Even though the new laws aimed to strengthen rational-legal authority at the expense of patrimonial authority, they were co-opted by the existing system, and their effect was limited.

Higher-level cadres responsible for implementing the election reforms left no doubt that many subordinate cadres resisted their implementation. Peng Zhen reported:

> At present, quite a number of cadres and other people are not yet familiar with these procedures of socialist democracy [i.e., the reform laws]. This is especially true because the lingering influence of the fascist dictatorship instituted by Lin Biao, Jiang Qing, and their ilk still exists, *and the vestiges of feudalism are still quite strong.* As a result, some of our cadres, including leading cadres, lacked understanding of socialist democracy and are not accustomed to democratic practices. They are averse to democracy and elections, thinking that they cause too much trouble. "Elections? What's the point?" they grumble.[55]

Many lower-level cadres failed to follow the provisions of the Election Law. They procrastinated in organizing elections, gerrymandered election districts to increase representation of government and Party offices, arbitrarily intervened in the nomination process, failed to place on the ballot more candidates than there were positions to be

54. Linz, "Non-Competitive Elections," 51.
55. See, for example, Peng Zhen, "Report on the Work of the Standing Committee," in *Main Documents of the Third Session of the Fifth National People's Congress* (Beijing: Foreign Languages Press, 1980), esp. 90–91. A slightly different translation is available in FBIS-CHI-80-186 Supplement 076, 23 Sept. 1980, pp. 29–31. Emphasis added.

filled, revoked the credentials of individual deputies lawfully elected but not supported by the local leadership, invalidated entire elections when the results did not please the local leadership, and halted entire county election campaigns in mid-course.[56]

Cadres were *not* resisting the reforms because they threatened to reduce the authority of the Party. Guidelines from higher levels specifically adjured local cadres to "correctly make use of the methods of democratic centralism, concentrate the correct views of the majority of the masses in a timely way, and guard against letting things drift."[57] In other words, the reformists at the Center remain Leninists. They have no intention of abandoning the leading role of the Party and have made this amply clear to lower-level cadres.

In fact, the center claimed that implementation of the Organic Law would increase the legal authority of local governments. Xu Chongde argued that this would give local authorities more control over local administration:

> In the past, work departments (offices, bureaus, sections, divisions, and so forth) were under so-called dual leadership. However, in actual practice they were more often under the control of the department at the next higher level, so that the people's government at the same level could not give full play to its enthusiasm. Now the organic law stipulates that all work departments should be under the unified leadership of the local government at the same level.[58]

Strengthening rational-legal authority threatened individual cadres if not the Party as a whole. Rational-legal authority creates difficulties for those accustomed to patrimonial or patron-client politics by restricting opportunities to use official position for personal profit and by enforcing the use of cumbersome procedures. When the leaders of the state acted to strengthen rational-legal authority, lower-level cadres resisted, not because the reforms threatened to diminish their formal authority or the Party's, but because they threatened to change the basis of authority from patrimonial authority to rational-legal authority.

56. See, for examples, Shijiazhuang, Hebei Provincial Service, in FBIS-CHI-81-099, 22 May 1981, p. R5; Beijing Xinhua Domestic Service, 3 Sept. 1980 in FBIS-PRC-80-173, 4 Sept. 1980, pp. L12–13; Changchun, Jilin Provincial Service, 4 Sept. 1980, trans. in FBIS-PRC-80-176, 9 Sept. 1980, p. S5; and Peng Zhen, "Report on the Work of the Standing Committee."

57. *Renmin Ribao*, 10 Aug. 1980, p. 1, trans. in FBIS-PRC-80-167, 26 Aug. 1980, pp. L12–14.

58. Xu Chongde, "Give Full Scope to the Functions of Local Organs of Power," *Renmin Ribao*, 17 July 1979, trans. in FBIS-CHI-79-146, 27 July 1979, pp. L2–7.

Renmin Ribao reported a case of "sabotaging democratic elections" that provides a glimpse of the struggle between the rational-legal authority of the state and the patrimonial authority of lower-level cadres. According to this account, Neiqiu county of Hebei province has a long history of factional politics, centering around the issues of central versus local control and corruption versus reform. Before the Siqing (Four Cleans) campaign of 1964, a faction of local cadres dominated Neiqiu county. During Siqing, the local faction was supplanted by "outsiders." During the Cultural Revolution, the Rebel Faction, led by Li Qingquan, demanded that Neiqiu county be governed by Neiqiu people and "rolled" the outsiders out of the county. Li became a leading figure in the county, paving the way for the pre-Siqing county secretary to return.

Li was removed from office in 1980 but was replaced by Han Jintang, who had been an official in the pre-Siqing administration. Han removed some of Li's Rebel Faction followers but protected others, who were subsequently accused of various Cultural Revolution brutalities. Han engineered a shake-up of leading cadres throughout the county and down to the commune level. According to *Renmin Ribao,* Han used the shake-up to place "trusted followers" (*qinxin*) in positions of power. Han and his associates were eventually accused of gross corruption. When the county Party committee established thirteen serious cases of economic crimes to be investigated, Han and his cronies blocked investigation of all but two. Some of his associates stood accused of embezzlement, and his own family received preferential treatment in obtaining urban residence permits and finding good jobs. It is clear from this account that any reform that would institutionalize elections would have been a threat to this style of politics.[59]

By making the nominations procedure public, the reform laws create problems for grass-roots cadres. As was discussed in chapter 2, the power of local cadres is derived in large part from their ability to distribute patronage. The ability of superiors to reward employees flexibly, according to subjective evaluations, has provided fertile ground for the growth of pervasive networks of informal social ties based on *personal* loyalties."[60] A position as deputy is a bit of patronage used

59. "Local Factionalism Problem in Neiqiu County Receives Strict Handling" (Neiqiu xian difang zongpaizhuyi wenti shoudao yansu chuli), *Renmin Ribao,* 8 Nov. 1983, p. 5. Many cases of counties run like Neiqiu have been "exposed" in the media. One of the most famous cases is described in Liu Binyan, "People or Monsters."

60. Andrew Walder, "Dependence and Authority in Chinese Industry" (emphasis in original).

by leaders to reward activists who have demonstrated personal and political support.[61] Under the prereform nominating procedures, the leader had broad discretion to offer the position to the candidate of his choice. Under the reform rules, ordinary unit members, though unlikely to risk antagonizing their leaders by nominating or voting for "inappropriate" candidates, are witness to a greater portion of the proceedings. The leader now must manage the election process in a public forum presumably subject to the new laws. Moreover, the leader will be put in an unfavorable light with his superiors if problems are conspicuous. The "three ups and three downs" nominations procedures require far more time and effort and expose lower-level cadres to greater risks, regardless of how democratic they are.

To regard patrimonial authority as a basis of resistance helps put into context the kinds of problems encountered in implementing the reforms. The main form of resistance available to lower-level cadres is delay. While outright opposition is risky, they can plead for individual exemptions from established schedules. If county-level officials fail to keep up the pressure, then entire county election campaigns could halt in mid-course. Higher-level cadres can overcome this problem with enough attention to organization and mobilization, but there are limits to the number of such campaigns that the center can manage during any given period.

In other cases, cadres formally implement the policy but covertly subvert its intent. This line of resistance is more feasible if the tacit approval of immediate superiors can be obtained. Instances of this kind of resistance range from the use of strong-arm tactics during the "three ups and three downs" to violations of major provisions in the new laws. For example, *Nanjing Ribao* reported the case of one cadre who informed voters prior to balloting that while there were five names on the ballot, it would be best if the middle three were elected.[62] Election organizers have been tempted to "gerrymander" on behalf of their own units to maximize their personal influence.[63]

61. Explaining why the Soviet Union prefers single-candidate elections, Victor Zaslavsky and Robert Brym write: "Single-candidate elections function to reinforce virtual monopoly control by ruling cadres over such determinants of power as material resources (for instance jobs)" ("The Structure of Power and the Functions of Soviet Local Elections").

62. "Elections Cannot Be 'Escorted' with Strong Commentary" (Xuanju bu neng ying 'baojia' shuping), *Nanjing Ribao*, 24 Aug. 1980, p. 4.

63. Shijiazhuang, Hebei Provincial Service, in FBIS-CHI-81-099, 22 May 1981, p. R5.

On a grander scale, in April 1983 the Standing Committee of the Jiangxi Provincial People's Congress declared that county-level people's congresses in twenty-two jurisdictions in two prefectures (about one-fifth of all jurisdictions electing representatives to the Jiangxi congress) had failed to have more candidates than positions on the ballot. The credentials of 196 deputies to the provincial people's congress were rejected, and the 22 lower-level congresses were ordered to conduct new elections.[64]

Cadres objecting to a policy may implement it in a manner that discredits it. Evidence for the use of this tactic is circumstantial but compelling. For example, in Changsha, at the Hunan Teachers' Training College, faced with the candidacy of a self-proclaimed non-Marxist, the normal nominating process broke down. Unable to secure what they considered an appropriate list of candidates by normal means, the authorities organized a series of primary elections and, still failing to obtain a "suitable" list, arbitrarily placed candidates of their own choosing on the list. This instigated student marches and a fast. The students succeeded in opening a channel of protest to Beijing but were nonetheless suppressed, as higher-level authorities were evidently more willing to accept rigged elections than marches or fasts.[65] Even Cheng Zihua condemned the students.[66]

The patrimonial environment captured the people's congresses as well as the elections. In theory, deputies to people's congresses are vested with the authority to raise universalistic demands and to represent broad interests. According to official proclamations, the people's congresses are the final authority at each level of government. Deputies are organized to inspect various aspects of local administration, they have the formal right to query local cadres, they can submit motions in the congresses and elect deputies to the next higher congress and leading officials at their level of government. In practice, however, deputies are primarily concerned with narrow particularistic problems of a type that in an American legislature would be considered constituency casework. These problems are usually resolved at the discretion of administrators case by case and rarely are incorporated into formal legislation.

64. Nanchang, Jiangxi Provincial Service, 21 Apr. 1983, trans. in FBIS-CHI-83-082, 27 Apr. 1983, pp. O4–5.
65. See Shan Zi, "Election in Changsha," SPEAHRhead 12 and 13 (Winter and Spring 1982): 20–22.
66. Beijing Xinhua Service, trans. in FBIS-CHI-81-172, 4 Sept. 1981, p. K2.

The most significant channel of communication opened by the reforms is the deputies' right to bring their constituents' concerns to the attention of administrators by submitting motions to the people's congress sessions. At most of these sessions very large numbers of motions are received. The Second Session of the Fifth National People's Congress received 1,890 motions, and the Third Session received 2,300.[67] At the Baixia District People's Congress, deputies put forward 565 motions.[68] Motions usually consist of individual problems or vague policy recommendations. For example, one deputy complained that a construction company building a new building failed to finish sidewalks and left residents with muddy walkways. Other deputies at the Baixia congress submitted motions regarding the failure of night-soil collectors to regularly service public rest rooms, and the failure of garbage collectors to enter certain lanes or to allow residents enough time to get their garbage to curbside before departing.[69] In Beijing a Moslem deputy succeeded in reopening a Moslem restaurant for his Moslem constituents.[70] Other motions, especially those submitted at the National People's Congress, may involve grander problems but still cannot attain the force of law. Instead, motions are submitted to a motions committee or to the congress presidium. If these bodies find merit in the motion, they forward it to the relevant department. For example, in the case of the complaints related to construction projects, the motion would be forwarded through the hierarchy of local government to the construction company. In this regard, the processing of deputies' motions resembles the handling of letters to the editors of newspapers. Deputies are less vulnerable to reprisals than are letter writers, but they still have limited influence.[71] The only time the congress as a whole reviews the handling of motions occurs when the leadership of the congress makes a general report to the deputies at the succeeding congress session regarding the handling of all the motions submitted at the prior session.

67. Beijing Xinhua Service, 1 July 1979, trans. in FBIS-CHI-80-190, 29 Sept. 1980, pp. L5–6.
68. "People's Deputy for the People" (Renmin daibiao wei renmin), Nanjing Ribao, 3 Sept. 1980, p. 4.
69. Ibid.
70. Sun Guiben, "Dongcheng District Chunxia Moslem Restaurant Back in Business" (Dongcheng qu chunxia fanguan huifu yingye), Beijing Wanbao, 6 June 1980, p. 2.
71. For an account of one reasonable motion that encountered unreasonable delays, see "Ordeal of a Deputy's Motion," Renmin Ribao, 7 May 1981, p. 4, trans. in Chinese Law and Government 15, nos. 3 and 4 (Fall and Winter 1982–83): 191–92.

Inspection tours provide another limited opportunity for deputies to offer suggestions to administrators. While on tour, deputies have far greater freedom of information than is usual in China, but the tours nonetheless are guided, organized by administrators or leaders of a congress.[72] Prior to convening the Nanjing Municipal People's Congress, two hundred deputies were organized into ten small groups to inspect various aspects of city administration. Accompanied by responsible cadres from the relevant bureaus, deputies inspected the city bus system, city schools, drainage channels and public rest rooms, and various enterprises. Some of the inspection groups effected on-the-spot solutions to problems. For example, one group discovered that a pricing dispute between producers and marketers of padded jackets had left a batch of scarce jackets languishing in a warehouse. The deputies negotiated a compromise that brought the jackets into the stores in time to serve seasonal demand.[73] After the inspection tour in Nanjing, deputies spent a day and a half in conference with the city Party committee, the city revolutionary committee, and responsible cadres from all of the city's departments and bureaus.[74] This produced some informal commitments from the city leadership. For example, as a result of one inspection group's findings, the city announced a plan to remodel forty-three public rest rooms and their intention to search for means to keep others in more sanitary conditions.[75] Because these tours are organized by higher levels and because the resulting commitments are informal, the inspection tours at best are vehicles for particularistic, not universalistic, demands, and at worst can be an opportunity for wining and dining.

Deputies have the formal right to query officials at their level of government while their congress is in session. At the National People's Congress, deputies' queries have been used to bring up controversial issues and to criticize government boondoggles and tragedies such as the Bohai oil-rig disaster (an incident where owing to gross

72. See, for example, Beijing Xinhua Service, 21 May 1981, trans. in FBIS-CHI-81-099, 22 May 1981, pp. K1–2.

73. Ning Fang, "Padded Jackets One After the Other Supply the Market" (Yipi mianyi luxu ying shi), *Nanjing Ribao*, 9 Dec. 1980, p. 1.

74. Tan Jiahu, "People's Deputies and Political Consultative Conference Members Inspection Activities Conclude" (Renmin daibiao zhengxie weiyuan shicha huodong jieshu), *Nanjing Ribao*, 5 Dec. 1980.

75. Chen Shungeng, "43 Public Rest-Rooms to Be Built or Rebuilt" (Xin jian gaijian gong ce 43 cuo), *Nanjing Ribao*, 9 Dec. 1980, p. 1.

negligence lives and property were lost at sea).[76] *Nanjing Ribao* urged local deputies to make good use of their right to question authorities and encouraged authorities to provide forthright answers and especially not to blame all problems on the " 'evil gang of four.' "[77] It is unclear how freely deputies are able to use their right to query officials. Each National People's Congress session has been touted as more democratic than its predecessors.[78] In one widely publicized scandal, a county Party secretary was criticized for investigating a deputy who publicized the shortage of oil in that county.[79]

Deputies also have formal authority to elect various local leaders and deputies to the people's congress at the next higher level.[80] While the tendency has been toward more choice at higher levels, these elections appear to be more closely supervised than lower-level elections. In Beijing and Shanghai, municipal people's congresses have elected leading cadres recently transferred from leadership positions in other provinces. In Shanghai, Hu Lijiao, former chair of the Henan Provincial People's Congress Standing Committee, was elected chair of the Shanghai Municipal People's Congress Standing Committee within a few months of his transfer from Henan to Shanghai.[81] In Beijing, Jiao Ruoyu was elected mayor of Beijing three months after he arrived in the capital.[82]

Though limited by the environment in which they occurred, the reforms are significant. First, the elections had a significant impact on local leadership. In his "Summing Up Report" to the Standing Committee of the National People's Congress, Cheng Zihua listed the election of "fairly good leading bodies" as a main achievement of

76. Beijing Xinhua Service, 5 Sept. 1980, trans. in FBIS-CHI-80-175, 8 Sept. 1980, p. L26.

77. "How Did You Respond to Inquiries?" (Ni zenyang huida zhixun), *Nanjing Ribao*, 25 Sept. 1980.

78. Although one delegate to a Chinese People's Political Consultative Conference in 1988 stated: "I have realized that a CPPCC member is indeed an 'ornamental vase.' I really doubt my role." See "Members Critical of CPPCC Functions," *Zhongguo Tongxun She*, Hong Kong, 1 Apr. 1988, trans. in FBIS-CHI-88-064, 4 Apr. 1988, p. 47.

79. "An Incident of Wantonly Interfering in the Work of the People's Congress Occurs in Shaoyang County, Hunan," *Renmin Ribao*, 7 Nov. 1986, trans. in "Renmin Ribao Reports Local Abuse of Power," FBIS-CHI-86-218, 12 Nov. 1986, pp. K1–3.

80. The new laws specify that county-level people's congresses will elect their county's representatives to higher-level people's congresses, members of the standing committee of their congress, leading comrades of the district or county people's government, and the leading cadre of the people's procuracy and leading judges of the district court.

81. *Beijing Review,* no. 18 (4 May 1981): 5.

82. Beijing City Service, 28 Apr. 1981, trans. in FBIS-CHI-81-091, 12 May 1981, pp. R1–3.

the elections, noting that the age of the county-level leadership elected by the congresses was 3.4 years younger than the previous group. In Nanjing, elections of county and district leadership by county-level congresses resulted in a 30 percent turnover of county and district magistrates and assistant magistrates. This turnover decreased the average age of this group by four years (with the average age becoming 49.8) and increased the proportion with high school or higher degrees to one-third.[83] This turnover of lower-level cadres aroused great resentment. *Nanjing Ribao* reported that some cadres (erroneously) equated losing elections with being purged in a campaign and argued that they had to accept that the people were the masters of the country.[84]

Second, deputies previously were not allowed to speak out on even particularistic issues. One member of the Jiangsu delegation to the Fourth National People's Congress (which was convened during the ascendancy of the Jiang Qing group) reported that his departure to congress sessions had to be kept secret even from his family and that at the session, deputies were only permitted to vote yes.[85] The right to speak out, even if not equivalent to the right to shape policy, is very important. In the National People's Congress the right to speak out is the right to bring up issues like the Bohai oil-rig disaster. In Baixia district it is the right to complain about filthy toilets and muddy walkways. These may seem small matters, but they mark a significant step toward more open and humane government. In evaluating the significance of these reforms, it is important to keep in mind that Western local politics are also particularistic. However, because of the relative autonomy of Western civil society, even at the local level, politics are relatively open and competitive.

In China's local people's congresses, it is not just that the issues are particularistic, but that the vertical hierarchies of the Leninist state structure the entire process. Patronage is still closely rationed and distributed by state officials and not by deputies or ordinary citizens. It is not just that the channels through which voters or deputies can speak are relatively restricted, but that these channels are a relatively

83. "Our City's County and District People's Congresses Each Select New Leadership" (Wo shi xian qu rendaihui fenbie xuanchu xin de lingdao), *Nanjing Ribao*, 1 Nov. 1980, p. 1.

84. Jin Zhong, "Refute Defeated Candidates' 'Bitter Disappointment' Theory" (Bo luox uan 'hanxin' lun), *Nanjing Ribao*, 5 Oct. 1980, p. 1.

85. "Transform the Style of Leadership to Work for the Well-Being of the Masses" (Gaibian lingdao zuofeng wei qunzhong mo fuli), *Nanjing Ribao*, 27 Sept. 1980, p. 2.

small portion of the people's-congress system, which is in turn a relatively small part of Chinese politics. The greater part of congress sessions are taken up by lengthy reports delivered by local administrators. Despite the reforms, the primary role of the people's-congress system remains the mobilization of lower levels to implement decisions made at higher levels.

CONCLUSION

Two contradictory themes have been explored here. First, the Leninist mode of implementation—mobilization and organization—is a powerful tool for promoting political change. The campaign to implement the Election and Organic Laws is evidence of the power of this tool. In particular, reforming the structure of local government in more than 2,757 county-level units in two years and mobilizing over 95 percent of voters to vote are impressive achievements. Second, extensive patrimonial networks are powerful impediments to the implementation of any reform in China and particularly to reforms that seek to promote rational-legal authority. In the case of the election campaign, the patrimonial authority of lower-level cadres was used to narrow the scope of already limited reforms.

China's Leninist-style organization facilitates both mobilization to implement policies *and* patrimonial resistance to central initiatives. The hierarchy of election reform offices reaching from ministries in Beijing to the streets of Nanjing could not have been constructed and would not have been effective without the preexisting organizational trellis. Leninist mobilization depends on the ability of cadres at all levels to reward the "correct" participation and to sanction "mistakes." This same organization also generates patrimonial opposition. It grants enormous authority to leaders at nodal points in the system without providing an adequate means of supervision, and constrains political-demand making to particularistic patterns, resulting in widespread use of public office for personal gain.

In this case study, patrimonial rulership blocked the reforms that were implemented from having the full impact that reformers intended. The congresses were not as inclusive as reformers had hoped. Subsequent commentaries indicated that reformers thought too many Party members had been elected to the congresses. The congresses were not able to make local government significantly more accountable or effective. The point is not that local people's congresses did not become Western-style democratic institutions, as this was not what was intended by reformers, but that patrimonial rulership impeded the realization of the Party's publicly declared purposes.

There is little indication that this cycle of vertical implementation and patrimonial resistance is coming to an end. Election campaigns in 1984 and 1987 were also mobilized from above. In these elections the state was again largely able to prevent the emergence of truly independent candidates. In 1987 students in Anhui organized to protest election restrictions, but in general lower-level cadres continued to dampen democracy. The most the Standing Committee of the National People's Congress could claim regarding the 1987 elections was that "most localities actually respected the wishes of the voters in the implementation of the election laws." It also stated:

> In some localities, however, because some cadres are not familiar with or do not understand the relevant laws or because they do not have a strong concept of the legal system, are afraid of trouble, or want to simplify matters, some undemocratic phenomena or cases which do not conform to the law have occurred.[86]

In practice, the limits to Leninist implementation are roughly analogous to the limits Alec Nove finds in the Soviet command economy. He argues that in specific sectors where central authorities focus their attention, such as defense, the Soviet economy is able to achieve impressive results, but that on the whole, command economies cannot be as efficient as market economies. This is because central planners have a limited capacity to process information and to issue instructions and consequently must focus their attention on a limited number of policy spheres.[87] In China it is difficult for local authorities to resist implementation of any policy energetically promoted by the center. Central authorities are limited, however, both in the span of policies they can attend to at any given time and in the length of time they can devote to any single issue. Consequently, they may achieve fine results in some areas while leaving a legacy of chaos in others.

For example, the county-level election reform was more successfully implemented than lower-level election reform primarily because it was a focus of higher-level attention. Attempts to popularize the

---

86. "NPC Standing Committee Work Report Published."
87. Nove, *The Soviet Economic System.*

election of cadres in factories and in people's communes have failed.[88] The county-level campaign "succeeded" because it became a "flagship" policy. The massive campaign organized for implementing the county-level elections required huge amounts of expertise, time, and money that were unavailable for organizing lower-level elections. The amount of organization a Leninist campaign requires increases exponentially for each level down the hierarchy the campaign must reach. In addition, implementation will be most successful where rational-legal authority is strongest and when direct confrontation with patrimonial authority can be avoided. Deputies to county-level congresses are relatively marginal figures and pose little threat to the distribution of power. Conversely, a unit or work-group leader, whether or not the job is pleasant or desirable, has an important role in the further distribution of penalties and rewards and consequently is in a far more controversial position. Ironically, because China is compartmentalized, lower-level jobs can sometimes be more important. The implementation of unit-level elections could be extremely disruptive, whereas county-level elections could occur almost unnoticed.

In sum, the cycle of Leninist implementation and patrimonial resistance severely restricted the attempt to democratize Chinese politics. The limited results of the election campaign were not due to the reformers' unwillingness to experiment with democracy, nor to any open opposition. Nor did the reformers fail to grasp the nature of their dilemma. Instead, the reforms were diluted as they were transmitted through the state's Leninist organization. This cycle appears so firmly in place that even attempts at reform can breed more cynicism. Some students at Nanjing University were so skeptical that any real democracy was possible that they declined to vote for any of the candidates appearing on the ballot and instead wrote in *Man from Atlantis*, the star of a B-grade American TV series then showing on Chinese TV.[89]

88. See, for example, John Burns, "The Implementation of Sub-Village Elections in South China, 1979–82" (paper presented at conference "Implementation in Post-Mao China," Ohio State University, June 1983).
89. Interview at Nanjing University, 25 Sept. 1980.

CHAPTER FIVE

Party Rectification

Party rectification has been the most important attempt to date to reform the Party. In September 1982 the First Plenum of the Twelfth Party Central Committee of the Chinese Communist Party announced a general Party rectification, designed to systematically transform all levels of Party organization. Hu Yaobang, then general secretary, proclaimed: "The Central Committee has decided on an overall rectification of Party style and consolidation of Party organizations, which will proceed by stages and by groups over a period of three years beginning from the latter half of 1983."[1] Hu categorically declared that Party rectification was of the highest importance. He stated: "The style of a political party in power determines its very survival."[2] According to the announced schedule, the Second Plenum of the Twelfth Party Congress released a thirteen-thousand-word "Decision on Party Rectification" (hereafter referred to as the Decision) that more specifically outlined goals, plans, and procedures,[3] and over the next four years, over forty million Party members were mobilized, beginning with central- and provincial-level units in late 1983, followed by prefecture- and county-level units the next year, and by township- and village-level units in 1986 and 1987. In May 1987

---

1. Hu Yaobang, "Create a New Situation in All Fields of Socialist Modernization," 37, 38.
2. Ibid.
3. See "Decision on Party Rectification," trans. in FBIS-CHI-83-199, 13 Oct. 1983, pp. K1–17. The Decision allowed for three to three and a half years to complete Party rectification.

the central leaders proclaimed the successful conclusion of Party rectification.[4]

In China, the Soviet Union, and other Leninist states, the central concern for reformers is to promote economic growth and efficiency. But their Marxist intellectual orientations and their practical experience both lead reformers to conclude that inappropriate political institutions and ideas are the most important obstacle. Western social science also tells us that political systems must adapt to meet economic challenges. World market theory argues that international economic competition forces states to adopt policies that facilitate the efficient use of capital, labor, and technology regardless of the ideological proclivities of the regime. Writing from a political-development perspective, Richard Lowenthal made much the same point when he argued that the leaders of communist countries must eventually abandon the utopian goals of revolutionary Marxism for modernization.[5]

The problem is, as the now large literature on the state argues, that states have a measure of autonomy and pursue their own interests. The autonomy of a state vis-à-vis society might be demonstrated through the ability of state power holders to implement policies that have a heavy social cost, but it is also demonstrated by the ability of state institutions to withstand pressures for change from below *or above*. In other words, ideologies and institutions are not simply costumes that a state or a party might wear or discard, or which leaders might change like a man changing his shoes.

In this regard, Max Weber's discussion of the routinization of charisma supplements Lowenthal's discussion of "utopia vs. modernization."[6] Lowenthal conceptualizes the transformation as a series of policy choices where leaders sequentially discard utopian policies for modernizing policies, such as choosing "Reds" over "experts." Weber's ideal types of rulership unite ideology and organization into a seamless whole. The routinization of a charismatic revolution is not just a series of policy choices, but entails radical transformations of both ideology and organization.

4. "National Party Rectification Work Basically Completed" (Quanguo zhengdang gongzuo jiben jieshu), *Renmin Ribao*, 28 May 1987, p. 1.
5. Lowenthal, "Development vs. Utopia in Communist Policy." See also Lowenthal's more recent work, "The Postrevolutionary Phase in China and the Soviet Union."
6. For Max Weber's discussion of charismatic authority, see Weber, *Economy and Society*, 241–54, 266–70, 1111–57.

The key to political reform in Leninist states is transforming the Party's ideology and organization to facilitate economic development. Party reform is crucial because the Party is at the center of the political system and is the principal means of communication and control. If the Party cannot be reformed, it will be an obstacle to many other reforms.

Because Leninist states were established as a means of politically dominating the economy, it is particularly difficult to transform them so that they will serve the needs of economic development. Marx was justifiably appalled by the uncontrolled business cycles of nineteenth-century laissez-faire capitalism and projected that in the future, society would gain conscious mastery over its economy. Revolutionaries inspired by Marx in less-developed countries have seen in the socialist project the potential to insure rapid economic growth as well as equitable distribution. Accordingly, once in power, they established states with the political and administrative capacity to plan—or dominate—economies. They created states in which economics was no longer the foundation of political superstructure, states in which politics overshadows economics. Ironically, in such a system, economic demands are easily subordinated to political pressures, and the rewards for economic achievements are far less than the rewards for political achievements. As a result, in Leninist states, economies have stagnated while bureaucracies have flourished. The goal for reformers must be to build a state that is more responsive to economic demands.

The reformers must transform both the Party's organization and its ideology. As Weber points out, ideology and organization are deeply entwined. In organizational terms, most observers agree that the Party must promote rational-legal administrative standards for both its internal affairs and its interaction with the rest of the government and society. To do this, patrimonial networks that would distribute power according to criteria and for purposes other than modernization must be overcome. At the same time, to the extent that the Party wants to maintain its leading role, it must also retain an ideological claim to charismatic authority. The Party's claims to charismatic authority must be redefined. Originally, the Party claimed to possess virtues appropriate to a political quest for a communist utopia. Now it must claim virtues suitable for a more rational-legal attempt at economic modernization. As in the reforms discussed in the preceding two chapters, reformers would find this task difficult.

In sum, Party rectification was intended to revitalize and restructure the Party systematically in order to make it possible to implement a broad range of new, economically oriented policies. Using state power to transform a state is a difficult project, however. States are complex entities open to only a limited range of transformations. In this particular case, the attempt to reform the Party, like attempts to reform other institutions, has been limited by the nature of those institutions. In this chapter I will trace the process of Party rectification, examine the goals of the reformers and the obstacles they encountered, assess the results, and consider the implications for the broader reform project in China and other Leninist states.

UNHEALTHY PRACTICES AND PATRIMONIAL RULERSHIP

Party rectification was supposed to turn the tide against "unhealthy practices" (*buzheng zhi feng*). Unhealthy practices include the following: (1) the ignoring of rules and instructions from higher levels; (2) nebulous organization that accomplishes little substantive work; (3) informal networks of personal relationships; (4) graft and corruption; and (5) dissemination of false information. Chinese leaders leave no doubt that unhealthy practices are widespread and seriously impair the workings of the Party. The danger the reformers see in "unhealthy practices" is not just that they discredit the Party in popular eyes (which they do), but also that they impede the Party's ability to achieve its formal goals, not least to implement reforms. Examining these problems will not conclusively establish a quantitative measure of unhealthy practices, but will suggest that they constitute, to use Max Weber's term, patrimonial rulership. The most useful commentaries are case studies presented as negative models. These are found both in official media and in literature, such as the "reportage fiction" of Liu Binyan, an outspoken critic of official corruption who was ejected from the Party in early 1987.[7]

First, Party secretaries are often criticized for arbitrarily ignoring Party rules or policies and managing affairs according to arbitrary or particularistic considerations. Bo Yibo, a leading figure in Party rectification, stated:

7. Two examples of Liu Binyan's reportage fiction are "People or Monsters" and "Let Me Tell You Some Secret."

In some localities and units, the phenomenon of leading bodies and Party-member cadres disregarding Party spirit and discipline is very serious. . . . They have completely ignored the instructions and circulars issued by the Party Central Committee and the State Council, or have decided to comply or not to comply with them, depending on their personal or small-group interests. Those instructions that are in their favor are implemented, while those that are not in their favor are not implemented.[8]

A State Council document noted the negative impact on the national economy:

Blockades against industrial products manufactured in other localities have prevailed in many areas. Despite the fact that certain electrical machinery, farm machines, and other industrial products in these areas are of low quality, poor in performance, and not wanted by users, efforts are being made in these areas to promote the sales of such products by force. At the same time, rigid regulations are enforced, forbidding users to purchase high-quality products of the same category from other localities. Some areas have even set up organizations to screen and approve these kinds of applications. . . . This practice . . . is extremely harmful to the national economy.[9]

Second, Party and state bureaucracies are often criticized for creating a large nebulous organization that accomplishes little. One *Renmin Ribao* commentator called this "putting on a show":

Meetings are held on all matters, whether big or small. They are under a multitude of names, such as commendation meetings, prize-award meetings, commemorative meetings, experience-exchange meetings, and New Year's Day and Spring Festival tea parties, with the scale of meetings becoming larger and larger and the quality of food and drink being better and better. . . . Circulars or documents are issued on all matters, whether big or small. The circulars and documents are more or less the same in wording, such as "it must be pointed out," "we must pay attention to," "1, 2, 3, 4," and "A, B, C, D." Some documents can hardly resolve problems, and just waste paper and readers' time. . . . And so on and so forth. Although people do such things in a lively way, they are but putting on a show. Putting on a show, also known as carrying out mere formalities, is a

8. Xinhua Service, 12 Mar. 1985, trans. in FBIS-CHI-85-050, 14 Mar. 1985, p. 5.
9. "A Document of the State Council *Kuo-fa* (1982), no. 60," *Issues and Studies* 4 (1983): 81. Compare this with Max Weber's discussion of the economic consequences of patrimonialism: "Patrimonialism can resort to monopolistic want satisfaction. . . . In this case, the development of markets is, according to the type of monopolies involved, more or less seriously limited by irrational factors. The important openings for profit are in the hands of the ruler and of his administrative staff" (*Economy and Society*, 238).

game which feudal bureaucrats were good at. . . . Those officials in old societies often played such official games, which were a stepping-stone to promotion.[10]

Third, informal networks of personal relationships displace official organization. Typical exposés chronicle decades of rivalry between local factions. The standard tactics include flattery, bribery, libel, intimidation, violence, and the manipulation of judicial organs.[11] Informal solidarity is established through the exchange of favors and personal relationships. Liu Binyan finds that unofficial networks are often cemented by marriage. He claims that in one city of 400,000 over 200 cadres at the middle level and above are related by marriage.[12] Liu and others have quoted a popular saying that comments on the proclivity of officials to find jobs for friends and relations: "If the dogs of the municipal Party and government leaders could talk, they would be section chiefs."[13] He concludes: "At the bottom all this was an exchange of goods that was effected by trading off power."[14]

Fourth, there are frequent reports of graft and corruption. One rectification commentator writes: "We should realize that the bureaucratic work-style of taking advantage of one's office for personal gain is very common."[15] Cases like the Hainan Island automobile scandal discussed above demonstrate institutionalized, not just individual, corruption.[16] Qiang Xiaochu, secretary of the Central Discipline and Inspection Committee, stated:

> By so-called unhealthy practices of trades and industries, we mean such obnoxious practices as willful blackmail and extortion. . . . They commit such acts by taking advantage of their operational condition or the special

10. "Do Not Put On a Show," *Renmin Ribao,* 3 May 1984, p. 1, trans. in FBIS-CHI-84-089, 7 May 1984, p. K8.

11. See, for example, "Local Factionalism Problem in Neiqiu County Receives Strict Handling" (Neiqiu xian difang zongpaizhuyi wenti shoudao yansu chuli), *Renmin Ribao,* 8 Nov. 1983, p. 5, and "Leader of Work Team of Central Discipline Inspection Commission Answers Questions," *Guangming Ribao,* 15 Jan. 1984, pp. 1, 4, trans. in FBIS-CHI-84-019, 27 Jan. 1984, pp. K7–11.

12. Liu Binyan, "Let Me Tell You Some Secret."

13. Ibid.

14. Liu, "People or Monsters."

15. "We Must Continue to Implement the Principle of Carrying Out Simultaneous Rectification and Correction of Defects," *Zhengzhou, Henan Provincial Service,* 29 Feb. 1984, trans. in FBIS-CHI-84-045, 6 Mar. 1984, p. P3.

16. *Nanfang Ribao,* 4 Aug. 1985, pp. 1, 2, trans. in FBIS-CHI-85-153, 8 Aug. 1985, pp. P1–9, and Niu Zhengwu, "Hainan: The Future Remains Bright," *Liaowang* 33 (19 Aug. 1985): 19–20, trans. in FBIS-CHI-85-172, pp. 6–10.

power of being in charge of personnel, finances, and materials. Different lines of operations have different forms of unhealthy practices. . . . The building trade asks for prices at will, gives false estimates, and subcontracts projects to others for easy profits. The commercial department sells commodities for private gain, hoards commodities in short supply, forces customers to buy unsalable goods along with whatever they buy, passes inferior goods off as quality goods, and demands kickbacks; the railway department loads and unloads cargos extremely carelessly, treats passengers brutally, charges passengers and increases prices illegally, and seeks private gains through "coaches"—whoever gives bigger tips gets cargo coaches; the power department capitalizes on customers' urgent need for power supply and practices extortion, and cuts off the power supply if customers fail to satisfy its demand.[17]

Finally, information is controlled to serve private purposes. *Xinhua* complained: "Reports from various localities show that the phenomenon of practicing fraud, seeking only appearance, and reporting no bad news but only good is not only found in the Army: it is there in the local party and government departments as well."[18] Not only public reports but also official Party communications are subjected to disinformation. A *Renmin Ribao* commentator stated:

"Racking their brains to take a perfunctory attitude toward the higher authorities" is "customary" to some cadres whenever they think about or do something. When doing summarizing and debriefing work, what they first think of is how to please their leaders; they do not attend to the real state of affairs in their work . . . they lay special stress on achievements but pay indifferent attention to some outstanding problems, and they indulge in empty talk and do not present the facts.[19]

When upper levels do mount investigations, they often fail to penetrate through the "web." *Jiefang Jun Bao* urges: "When comrades from the higher level come to make inspections, we should let them see things as they are ordinarily, not arranged just for the inspec-

---

17. Xinhua Service, 28 May 1986, trans. in FBIS-CHI-86-106, 3 June 1986, pp. K8–9.

18. *Xinhua*, 17 Nov. 1984, trans. in FBIS-CHI-84-224, p. K7. An egregious example occurred when *Yunnan Ribao* reported that a military commander's son was a model of implementing new economic policies when in fact he had just been arrested for swindling. See "The Report 'Military Subdistrict Commander Li Guozhong Encourages His Son to Engage in Individual Business' Is Seriously Inconsistent with Facts," *Yunnan Ribao*, 1 Mar. 1984, trans. in FBIS-CHI-84-053, p. Q2.

19. "Taking a Perfunctory Attitude Toward the Higher Authorities Is Also an Unhealthy Trend," *Renmin Ribao*, 29 Dec. 1985, p. 1, trans. in FBIS-CHI-86-001, 2 Jan. 1986, p. K12.

tions. We should let them hear reports reflecting the true rather than the false situation. In reflecting the situation, a report must tell what is true."[20]

Local leaders are often able to block those under their jurisdiction from reporting abuses to higher authorities. *Renmin Ribao* states that some comrades "even see the work of handling people's letters and visits as a matter of coaxing the masses to go home and to give up their complaints so as to 'protect their leaders.' "[21] Whistle-blowers who persist are vulnerable to pressure from above. Liu Binyan details the forms of retaliation available to local power holders seeking to suppress individuals trying to report corruption to higher levels:

> If classified according to the degree of severity, the punishments could be roughly listed as follows: transfer or reduction in grade in the sense of a demotion; suspension of job or deprivation of the right to work; political frame-up; suspension of pay; physical ravage. Alongside them are discrimination and harassment in job transfers and promotion, residence registration and employment of family members, housing assignment, and so forth.[22]

In sum, "unhealthy practices" exemplify what Max Weber called patrimonial rulership. They indicate that official purposes—not only abstract goals such as building communism, but also ordinary, everyday policy directives—are systematically subordinated to individual and local interests. In pursuit of these particularistic interests, official rules and policy directives are ignored, official treasuries are plundered, organizational resources are deployed to pressure others to make contributions, and the take is distributed among friends and family members to further consolidate an unofficial alternate power structure. Finally, the full resources of the alternate network are

20. Beijing Domestic Service, 11 Oct. 1983, trans. in FBIS-CHI-83-199, 13 Oct. 1983, p. K18. For example, in Shaanxi, a 224-member education inspection team toured Shangluo prefecture for 29 days, which cost nearly 150,000 yuan, most of which was spent on board, cigarettes, wine, tea, refreshments, fruits, and theater tickets. See Shaanxi Provincial Service, 14 Aug. 1986, in FBIS-CHI-86-159, 18 Aug. 1986, p. T1.

21. "Strengthen CPC Committees' Leadership Over the Work of Handling People's Letters and Visits," *Renmin Ribao*, 3 Oct. 1983, p. 1, trans. in FBIS-CHI-83-196, pp. K1–3.

22. Liu, "Let Me Tell You Some Secret." In a typical instance, a cadre from a prefectural United Front Work Department with a long history of graft and embezzlement wrote to a "whistle-blower" threatening physical reprisals. Thirty-eight requests from the Prefectural Discipline and Inspection Committee to the United Front Work Department to take disciplinary action against the embezzler failed. See "Leader of Work Team of Central Discipline Inspection Commission Answers Questions" (n. 11 above).

employed to conceal its doings from the public and public-minded higher officials.

What are the implications of patrimonial rulership? First, the Party's organizational capacity and technical efficiency are diminished. Second, authority is decentralized. At each level down the hierarchy, policies are diluted to accord with local priorities, resulting in a gap between announced official policy and actual conditions. Finally, unhealthy practices are particularly relevant for reformers. The theory of reform is that decentralization will create efficient market incentives. However, if the winners in decentralization are cadres who block access to markets, distribute subsidies, extort the profits of others, and so forth, the result will be increased looting of the state treasury, not increased efficiency.[23] For those who favor reform, it is essential that decentralization be accompanied by strengthened laws and procedures. Party rectification was intended to do just this.

RATIONAL-LEGAL RECTIFICATION

Despite entrenched patrimonial networks at lower levels of the state bureaucracy, higher levels retained the autonomy to implement a massive campaign to eliminate unhealthy practices. Like the campaigns discussed in the preceding two chapters, the scope of this campaign pales in comparison with Cultural Revolution campaigns, but nonetheless it involved millions of people across the width and breadth of China and at all levels of the Party hierarchy. In as much as rectification was intended to restore the Party's flagging prestige, it was at least in part a response to pressures from society, but it was designed and implemented from above and imposed on those below. Society had very little opportunity to influence the conduct of rectification.

Both the goals and the formal procedures of this round of rectification were deeply influenced by rational-legal rulership. The goals of Party rectification were to facilitate the "modernizing" of economic reforms and to strengthen Party discipline. Rectification was organized and executed within the Party along hierarchical lines, was conducted according to rules without slander or libel, and was not to disrupt normal economic activity.[24]

23. Jean C. Oi has written about this problem in the countryside, in "Peasant Households Between Plan and Market."
24. Harry Harding calls this strategy of organization "rationalization." See *Organizing China: The Problem of Bureaucracy,* 29–30 and passim.

GOALS

The goals of Party rectification—at least from the reformers' perspective—were to promote the general program of reform and to
strengthen rational-legal procedures within the Party. These were proclaimed in the "four tasks for Party rectification": (1) the achievement of ideological unity, or promoting general agreement with the
reform line; (2) the rectification of the Party's style of work, or putting an end to unhealthy practices; (3) the strengthening of discipline;
and (4) the purification of Party organization, or getting rid of those
who by current standards had committed particularly egregious
crimes in the past. These were announced in the Decision at the outset of rectification and were used to assess the results of rectification
upon its completion.[25] Party members were required to read more
about these goals in an anthology pointedly titled *Required Reading
for Party Members*.[26]

Broadly conceived, the purpose of reform was to reorient the Party
to the new tasks of the new era. Three of the documents in *Required
Reading for Party Members* outlined the reformers' policies and interpretation of the past. These included speeches by Deng Xiaoping and
Hu Yaobang at the Twelfth Party Congress and "On Questions of
Party History." Subsequent documents and statements frequently and
consistently proclaimed that rectification should help economic work.
For example, the Decision stated: "The production and work of all
units should not be disrupted by the work of Party consolidation.
While doing a good job in the Party consolidation, all units should
strive to promote production work."[27]

Another three documents included in *Required Reading for Party
Members* encouraged legality and attention to correct procedures.
These were the then most recent Party and state constitutions, both of
which subordinated the Party to state law. The third, "Some Principles for Inner-Party Political Life," which has been a staple of Party
building since 1980, sets forth twelve principles, such as maintaining
collective leadership, following Party regulations, opposing factionalism, correctly handling variant opinions, protecting the legitimate

25. See "Decision," Xinhua Service, 12 Oct. 1983, trans. in FBIS-CHI-83-199,
13 Oct. 1983, pp. K2–17, and "National Party Rectification Work Basically Completed" (Quanguo zhengdang gongzuo jiben jieshu), *Renmin Ribao*, 28 May 1987. That
Party rectification could formally stick to the same slogan from start to finish is an
important measure of stability.
26. *Dangyuan Bi Du* (Beijing: Renmin Ribao Chubanshe, 1983).
27. "Decision," p. K11.

rights of Party members, having elections that truly reflect the opinions of the electors, and accepting supervision from higher levels and from the masses.

These and many subsequent documents and speeches called for the elimination of factionalism—often defined as protecting the corrupt from the just authority of the official Party. In one example, a prefectural Party committee sought to discipline a district first secretary. He was eventually charged and found guilty of "corruption, taking bribes, embezzling collective funds, dallying with women, and bullying innocent people," but was long protected by his immediate superior, the county Party secretary.[28] Factionalism was also defined as a leftover from the Cultural Revolution, in which an individual or a group covertly resisted reform, for the sake of Cultural Revolution policies, or maintained factional ties to prevent individuals from being brought to justice for crimes committed during that period.[29]

In sum, rectification was intended to unify the Party around the reformers' program and to strengthen rules and procedures in the conduct of Party business. This was not just a change in procedure and policy, but was also an attempt to redistribute power. It pitted those who favored more economic reform against those who favored less, and those who favored rationalization against those who sought to protect some forms of charismatic legitimacy and particularistic privileges. Accordingly, Party rectification was controversial, and as it progressed down the ranks it was expected that high-level and lower-level cadres would attempt to redefine rectification to suit their own purposes.

ORGANIZATION AND EXECUTION

The organization and execution of Party rectification were, in theory, also directed by rational-legal norms. The procedures and timing were publicly presented in the Decision of the Second Plenum of the Twelfth Party Congress in October 1983.[30] To supervise the overall

28. Xinhua Service, 20 Sept. 1984, in FBIS-CHI-84-186, 24 Sept. 1984, pp. K11–12.

29. Keith Forster has written an excellent article on this aspect of rectification. See "Repudiation of the Cultural Revolution in China: The Case of Zhejiang," *Pacific Affairs* 1 (1986): 5–27. See also Mao Lei, " 'People of Three Categories' and the 'Protective Umbrella,' " *Renmin Ribao*, 17 Nov. 1984, in FBIS-CHI-84-226, 21 Nov. 1984, pp. K14–15.

30. "Decision."

process, the Decision announced the formation of a Central Commission for Guiding Party Rectification (CCGPR) under the leadership of the Central Committee. The Decision declared that the CCGPR would not use work teams in any but exceptional circumstances, but recommended the use of "liaison men or inspectors" to aid in monitoring and guiding the process. The Decision declared that rectification would "proceed from the central level to the grass-roots organizations, from the top downward by stages and in groups."[31] Rectification was to begin with central- and provincial-level units that winter and be completed within three years. It is a tribute to the administrative ability and the political staying power of the reformers that rectification was completed within three and a half years, and that the procedures followed were more or less those outlined in the Decision.

The CCGPR promptly turned its attention to organization. It began by mobilizing liaison personnel to guide and monitor the first stage of rectification, which involved central- and provincial-level units.[32] Leaders of the CCGPR spoke at a forum for the first batch of liaison personnel on November 26, and these personnel were dispatched shortly thereafter.[33] Eventually, the CCGPR sent out forty-nine teams with 449 members to supervise the first stage of rectification.[34] Provinces also established leading groups to guide Party rectification, and these offices also dispatched liaison teams. The CCGPR also required all units being rectified to reorganize for rectification. They were to establish two leading groups: one to manage rectification work and the other to manage professional work. In addition, the first or second secretary of each unit being rectified was to devote "full strength" to the rectification effort. A CCGPR circular argued that this division of labor was to insure the simultaneous development of rectification and economic work.[35]

At the same time, Party organizations in the first batch of units to take part in the first stage of rectification, including seventy central state organs, began the first of four phases of rectification. This phase

31. "Decision," p. K9.
32. "Circular Number Four," *One Year of Party Rectification*, 7–9.
33. Xinhua Service, 20 Dec. 1983, trans. in FBIS-CHI-83-247, 22 Dec. 1983.
34. Bo Yibo, speaking to a work conference on rectification, appearing in Xinhua Service, 12 Mar. 1985, trans. in FBIS-CHI-85-050, 14 Mar. 1985, p. K7.
35. "Circular Number Five," *One Year of Party Rectification*, 9–11. The circular repeated that "the purpose of Party rectification, in the final analysis, is to guarantee the victorious development of the four modernizations" (my translation).

consisted of studying the documents in *Required Reading for Party Members*. Some units established training classes for Party members, which met in the afternoon three or four times a week for three weeks. One required members to study rectification documents for 150 hours prior to Spring Festival.[36] Guided by liaison personnel, subsequent batches soon followed suit.

In early March the CCGPR issued a seventh circular, calling on those units that had successfully completed the first phase of study to begin the second phase of comparison and examination.[37] By late May many provincial committees were announcing that their first batches of units were also ready to enter the second phase. Party members were first to study rectification documents further and then to compare local conditions with the official guidelines. Examination, the key component of this phase, was to be a round of criticism and self-criticism. This, too, was to be conducted from the top down. Provincial-level comparison and examination often began with a public self-criticism by the province's first secretary on behalf of the province's leading group. While central authorities cautioned against "perfunctory" criticism and self-criticism, they also emphasized that Cultural Revolution style of "struggle sessions" were prohibited. In each unit the process of comparison and examination was to last about three months.[38]

In late June the CCGPR issued a ninth circular, which announced that some units were ready to begin the third phase of rectification and correction.[39] This stage, unlike the others, was not foreseen in the Decision. Instead, it was first introduced in the CCGPR's Circular Number 6, issued on January 1, 1984, which called for all units to rectify and correct defects throughout the course of Party rectification—emphasizing that problems uncovered in the course of rectification should be dealt with promptly. The ninth circular now called on first-stage rectification units to spend about three months resolving those defects uncovered during comparison and examination. Specifically, units were to correct the guiding ideology of their professional work, to eliminate factionalism and improve Party spirit, to eliminate corruption and bureaucratism, which were causing seri-

36. Xinhua Service, 29 Nov. 1983, trans. in FBIS-CHI-83-234, 5 Dec. 1983, pp. K1–3.
37. This circular was translated in FBIS-CHI-84-044, 5 Mar. 1984, pp. K1–5.
38. See "Provincial CPC Committee Convenes Mobilization Meeting," *Hebei Ribao*, 16 Mar. 1984, trans. in JPRS-CPS-84-064, 1 Oct. 1984, pp. 68–72.
39. *One Year of Party Rectification*, 22–26.

ous political or economic losses, and finally, to eliminate major problems in leading groups. As an example of the kind of activity this entailed, the CCGPR praised the Sichuan provincial committee for sending inspectors to the homes of leading cadres to seek out improper housing arrangements.[40] While urging high-minded adherence to principle, instructions from the center called for an orderly and reasoned process.

A few weeks later than might have been expected, the CCGPR announced that the leading units had spent the requisite three months on rectification and correction and should now move on to the fourth and final phase of organizational measures and reregistration.[41] During this phase, which was to last about a month, all Party members were to apply for reregistration as Party members, those who had violated Party rules were to be disciplined, and the small percentage who were guilty of the most serious mistakes would be refused reregistration. The circular stressed that formal legal principles were to be applied in all such matters:

> It is imperative to keep to the Party's principles, persist in the approach of seeking truth from facts, and act seriously according to the policies related to the Decision of the CPC Central Committee on Party Rectification. The procedures for organizational measures toward Party members as prescribed in the Party constitution must be strictly followed. The organizational conclusion on a Party member and the decision on his treatment should be made known to the Party member himself. He should be allowed to defend himself, make appeals, and have reservations. Other comrades should also be allowed to defend him.[42]

In late December, Bo Yibo, speaking on behalf of the CCGPR, confidently predicted that the first stage of rectification (central- and provincial-level units) would be basically completed by the Spring Festival and that the Party could begin the second stage, which would involve prefectural- and county-level units.[43] Prefectural-level rectification began in late 1984, and county-level rectification began later

40. Xinhua Service, trans. in FBIS-CHI-84-189, 27 Sept. 1984, pp. K6–9.
41. This circular was broadcast by Xinhua Service, 24 Nov. 1984, and reprinted in FBIS-CHI-84-228, 26 Nov. 1984, pp. K1–3.
42. Ibid., p. K2.
43. Xinhua Service, 22 Dec. 1984, trans. in FBIS-CHI-84-248, 24 Dec. 1984, pp. K2–8. The Central Commission for Guiding Party Rectification's Circular Number 11 was still more optimistic, declaring the first stage to be basically completed on January 7. See *One Year of Party Rectification*, 29–33.

that winter.[44] This involved a tremendous expansion in the scale of operations and a shift in the locus of control from the center toward the provinces. Whereas the first stage had involved 338,000 Party members, the second stage would involve 13.5 million.[45] From this point onward, different paces and formats in different provinces strongly suggests that provincial authorities exercised operational control. Jiangxi, for example, announced that second-stage rectification would be "adjusted" into the three phases, including two and a half months of study, three and a half months of comparison and examination and rectification and correction, and one month of "straightening out Party members."[46] However, the center kept watch with roving teams of inspectors, continued to issue statements of general policy, and held forums, which lower-level officials attended.[47]

The final stage of rectification, for township-, district-, and grass-roots-level units, began in late 1985 or early 1986, depending on the province, and was declared fully under way in May 1986.[48] Village-level rectification began in the winter of 1986 and was concluded in the spring of 1987.[49] The still more distant Party center attempted to set policies and guide the course of rectification at these lowest levels through strategies similar to those used during the second stage of rectification. For example, in late 1985 the center released a book of *Guidance Materials for Rural Rectification*,[50] and a national forum on rectification at the grass-roots level was organized by the Organi-

44. *Liaowang* 3 (14 Jan. 1985): 5, trans. in FBIS-CHI-85-015, 23 Jan. 1985, pp. K2–4.

45. Ibid., and Xinhua Service, 26 Nov. 1984, trans. in FBIS-CHI-84-229, 27 Nov. 1984, pp. K1–6.

46. Jiangxi Service, 15 Dec. 1984, trans. in FBIS-CHI-84-244, 17 Dec. 1984, pp. O1–2.

47. Bo Yibo, speaking to a work conference on rectification, discussed these "roving teams," appearing in Xinhua Service, 12 Mar. 1985, trans. in FBIS-CHI-85-050, 14 Mar. 1985, p. K8; an example of central-level statement of policy is the Central Commission for Guiding Party Rectification's Circular Number 12, which appears in Xinhua Service, 12 Apr. 1985, and is translated in FBIS-CHI-85-072, 15 Apr. 1985; and an example of a central-level forum for prefectural-level cadres appears in Xinhua Service, 30 Sept. 1985, trans. in FBIS-CHI-85-189, 30 Sept. 1985, pp. K5–9.

48. Xinhua Service, 17 May 1986, trans. in FBIS-CHI-86-096, 19 May 1986, pp. K1–4.

49. See, for example, Hebei Provincial Service, 13 Jan. 1986, trans. in FBIS-CHI-86-022, 3 Feb. 1986, p. R2. Beijing, which announced that village-level rectification would begin in October, was an early province. See *Beijing Ribao*, 13 Aug. 1986, trans. in FBIS-CHI-86-161, pp. R1–2.

50. Xinhua Service, 12 Dec. 1985, trans. in FBIS-CHI-85-240, 13 Dec. 1985, pp. K3–5. This book had a preface by Du Runsheng, director of the Rural Policy Research Center of the Secretariat of the CPC Central Committee.

zation Department of the Central Committee.[51] Also, in May and June 1986, the CCGPR held a series of four regional forums attended by prefectural-level Party secretaries. These forums were followed in July by meetings in most provinces and prefectures to make concrete preparations. And again the CCGPR observed the whole process with teams of roving inspectors.[52] Nontheless, the tremendous scale of township- and village-level rectification—over a million Party organizations and over 20 million Party members[53]—required provinces to mobilize their own very large rectification organizations. These included provincial rectification committees as well as tremendous corps of liaison and inspection personnel. Shandong alone dispatched over 15,000 liaison and inspection workers for township rectification. Village-level rectification involved as many as half a million inspectors and liaison personnel.[54] Leaders urged county secretaries to exercise direct supervision of village-level rectification, in tones that suggested that they feared that the actual level of control was still lower.[55] Nonetheless, in April 1987 rectification was "by and large" complete.[56]

In its formal, superficial appearance, Party rectification was broadly rational-legal. Taken at face value, rectification exemplified Franz Schurmann's version of Leninism.[57] Ideology was carefully delineated at the outset and linked with organization to build a new society according to the designs of the post-Mao leadership. The new purpose of the Party, its new policies, and its internal procedures were

51. Xinhua Service, 3 Dec. 1985, trans. in FBIS-CHI-85-235, 6 Dec. 1985, pp. K20–22.

52. Xinhua Service, 17 Oct. 1986, trans. in FBIS-CHI-86-202, 20 Oct. 1986, pp. K5–6.

53. Xinhua Service, 30 July 1986, trans. in FBIS-CHI-86-147, 31 July 1986, p. K1; Xinhua Service, 17 May 1986, trans. in FBIS-CHI-86-096, 19 May 1986, pp. K1–4; and Xinhua Service, 31 May 1986, trans. in FBIS-CHI-86-106, 3 June 1986, pp. K10–12.

54. In September, at about the time village-level rectification was officially launched, *Xinhua* reported that Party committees and rectification offices from township to village levels had already dispatched 360,000 cadres to help with rectification, with a goal of one cadre per village to three cadres per two villages (Xinhua Service, 26 Sept. 1986, trans. in FBIS-CHI-86-189, 30 Sept. 1986, pp. K18–19). In December the figure had increased to 550,000, perhaps reflecting more complete statistics at a later stage of the mobilization effort (Xinhua Service, 1 Dec. 1986, trans. in FBIS-CHI-86-235, 8 Dec. 1986, pp. K18–19).

55. See, for example, Fujian Provincial Service, 14 Oct. 1986, trans. in FBIS-CHI-86-208, 28 Oct. 1986, pp. O1–2.

56. Beijing Xinhua Domestic Service, 17 Apr. 1987, trans. in FBIS-CHI-87-075, 20 Apr. 1987, pp. K2–3.

57. Schurmann, *Ideology and Organization in Communist China.*

carefully spelled out in a group of documents that became required reading for all Party members, beginning with those at the top of the hierarchy. There followed a series of specified procedures to insure that these leaders understood these documents, and others to insure that they were implemented. When higher levels were judged to be on the right track, they were in turn mobilized to initiate the same process at lower levels. A network of organizations, including committees to guide rectification at all levels, and very large numbers of liaison personnel and inspectors were mobilized to see that rectification conformed with official specifications. At all times, progress from step to step was supervised by higher levels. Moreover, despite initial controversy, boundaries were carefully established to insure that rectification did not become a wider movement.

RECTIFICATION AS A CHARISMATIC REVIVAL

Party rectification was intended not only to strengthen rational-legal rulership but also to reclaim charismatic legitimacy. The Party claims exclusive rights in Chinese politics. Society will only accept the legitimacy of these claims if it believes that the Party has unique qualities or talents that entitle it to those rights. Weber calls this charismatic rulership, which he defines as rulership based on the belief that the ruler is "endowed with supernatural, superhuman, or at least specifically exceptional powers or qualities."[58] Currently, the Party's attempt to claim this sort of legitimacy places it in a difficult dilemma. Given the ambiguous record of the previous three and a half decades, society's response to the Party's claims to virtue is problematic. Moreover, given the desire to reorient the Party from politics to economics, which virtues the Party could or should claim is a difficult issue.

The Party has an exclusive and privileged leading role in the Chinese state that can only be legitimated by charismatic claims, that is, by reference to unique special abilities. The Party reserves for itself

58. In his discussion of charismatic rulership Max Weber argues that in its pure form it legitimates revolution, transcending the traditional or legal bounds of everyday authority. Members of a charismatic movement are chosen because they are virtuous, not because of their technical competence. Charismatic movements are not bound by ordinary economic considerations and charismatic organization is improvised and impromptu. The central problem charismatic movements face is to routinize their charisma, or in other words, transform it from a revolutionary force to a system of everyday rulership. See Weber, *Economy and Society*, 241–54, 266–70, 1111–57.

the rights to set the limits of public debate, determine policy, and choose leading personnel at all levels of Chinese society. Its choices and its representatives have a profound impact on the daily lives of all Chinese. In theory, the Party's unique ability to effect the transition to socialism and communism justifies these privileges. Namely, the Party claims that it can succeed in the quest for communism because it possesses historical foresight, represents all historically progressive forces, has no selfish aims, and has an unmatched ability for political struggle. The revolution was a test of the Party's special qualities, and victory in 1949 constitutes its most certain demonstration of its charisma, as the oft-repeated slogan "Without the Party, there would be no new China" reminds all who will listen. Indeed, the Party claims that eventual success in the quest for communism is preordained. If one accepts these premises, then the Party would be remiss not to take a leading role upon itself, and whatever costs it may impose on society are outweighed by the importance of its historical mission.

Reformers have shown a willingness to redefine the leading role of the Party, but insist on maintaining the Party's leading role in some form. Since the death of Mao the Party has conceded an increasing measure of autonomy to various spheres of civil society and consults with a wider range of political actors. Nonetheless, the Party still effectively suppresses any serious challenge to its preeminent position and still claims that this is an ethical obligation. For example, while the state constitution no longer explicitly mandates the Party's leading role, its preamble repeatedly refers to the continuing leadership of the Party. The constitution also states that the state is led by the working class, and given that the Party constitution begins by declaring that the Party is the "vanguard of the working class," the Party's leading role is still "legal."[59] The Four Cardinal Principles—"keeping to the socialist road," "upholding the dictatorship of the proletariat," "upholding the leadership of the Communist Party," and "upholding Marxism-Leninism and Mao Zedong Thought"—make the same point and seem an entrenched feature of political rhetoric in post-Mao China.[60] In accord with these slogans and declarations, Party

---

59. "Constitution of the People's Republic of China." See, respectively, pp. 5–9 and p. 9, and "Constitution of the Communist Party of China," p. 8.

60. These four maxims first appeared in a speech delivered by Deng Xiaoping in March 1979, in which he castigated Democracy Wall activists. They were still an important part of the rhetoric of the Thirteenth Party Congress in the fall of 1987. See Deng, "Uphold the Four Cardinal Principles."

rectification was supposed, not to weaken the Party, but to strengthen both its legitimacy and its ability to lead. In Deng Xiaoping's words, "The purpose of reforming the system of Party and state leadership is precisely to adhere to and strengthen, rather than weaken, Party leadership and discipline."[61]

In the wake of the Cultural Revolution, however, it is more difficult for society to accept any claim that the Party really has virtues that justify its privileged position. Traditionally, the Party's virtues were political and ethical, as befits an organization with utopian goals. The Cultural Revolution not only cast doubt on whether the Party had these virtues, but also discredited the utopian quest that they supposedly facilitated. Consequently, the dramatic claims of former times had to be abandoned and suppressed. For example, Mao is regarded no longer as "the greatest genius in ten thousand years" but merely as 70 percent good and 30 percent bad. Inasmuch as the former type of charismatic claims had been thoroughly discredited, banning their use by cadres improved the Party's credibility, but left a worrisome vacuum. The Party has attempted to fill this vacuum by claiming new virtues appropriate to the new task of modernization. The appropriate virtues for this task are technical and managerial excellence, and indeed the Party has made great efforts to demonstrate that it is recruiting younger and better-educated cadres. Both the Party's history of scorn for these virtues and comparisons with far more economically successful capitalist regimes—not to mention the daily experience of millions of Chinese—makes this claim difficult to establish. Moreover, the Party remains far more political than economic. Consequently, the Party is impelled to claim less-dramatic political virtues as well as potential economic virtues, but has little chance that either will be unconditionally accepted.

To meet this need, rectification was intended to strengthen not just laws and procedures but also the Party's claim to charismatic legitimacy. This can be seen in the charismatic character of the terminology of Party rectification. As Tony Saich has argued, the focus of "party building" since the death of Mao has been "work-style."[62] "Work-style" is not a technical procedure and is therefore difficult to capture in a legalistic definition. Despite reams of carefully enumer-

61. "On the Reform of the System of Party and State Leadership," *Beijing Review* 26, nos. 40 and 41 (3 and 10 Oct. 1983): 14–22 and 18–22.

62. Saich, "Party Building since Mao—A Question of Style?" Frederick C. Teiwes states that this term was a consistent feature of rectification movements prior to Mao's death. See his *Politics and Purges in China*.

ated instructions and untold hours of oral instruction, the criteria for what is good "work-style" always seem to boil down to vague terms, such as "fully implementing" Party policy, "thoroughly grasping" Party line, or "completely negating" the Cultural Revolution. This is because "work-style" is a quality or virtue to be fostered, not a skill that can be taught or measured. Similarly, appeals to end factionalism, corruption, and the disregard of official directives are often made in the name of improving "Party spirit," which is also a virtue and difficult to measure by technical means.

Rectification was addressed to two audiences, the Party and society, and means of rectification had to be found that would be persuasive to both groups. All of Max Weber's ideal types define three-way relationships between ruler, staff, and ruled. Social recognition of the Party's charisma makes the Party's leadership legitimate and defines the nature of that leadership. Party members' recognition of the Party's charisma defines the Party's internal organization and members' obligations. Leaders of charismatic movements will always be tempted to focus their attention on gaining social recognition of their claim to virtue rather than on testing the commitment of their membership, as this may lead to painful scrutiny of their organization. Leaders with state power will also be tempted to use coercive means to induce recognition of their supposed virtue. As Cultural Revolution activists learned, in the long run, using coercive means to induce social recognition of virtues that do not really exist does not work. Nonetheless, this "shortcut" is not only superficially expedient, it is also ethically justified in the eyes of true believers.

In China any attempt to revive virtue risks becoming a coercive campaign to induce social recognition of the Party's political and ethical virtues. Such a campaign began to gather momentum at the outset of the Party rectification. Space does not permit a full treatment of the near-campaign to combat "spiritual pollution," but a few important points must be mentioned. As Thomas Gold has pointed out, the first calls to eliminate "spiritual pollution" were in the speeches and documents of the Second Plenum of the Twelfth Party Central Committee, indeed, in the very Decision that outlined the nature of the coming rectification and in a speech by Deng Xiaoping.[63] Leaders such as Deng Lichun and Wang Zhen subsequently invoked these authoritative sources to increase the scope and scale of "eliminating

63. Gold, " 'Just in Time': China Battles Spiritual Pollution on the Eve of 1984."

spiritual pollution" to attack such diverse targets as intellectuals, fashionable dress, pornography, contacts with Westerners, and laxity among cadres. This strident and threatening message was clearly contradictory to the more rational tone of the Decision, and any prolonged mass campaign against "spiritual pollution" not only would have negated the rational-legal goals of Party rectification, but would have constituted a threat to the entire reform program.[64] Cooler heads eventually prevailed, and subsequently, even leaders not associated with the reform faction, such as Bo Yibo, would repeatedly claim that one of the great successes of this round of rectification was the avoidance of the excesses of previous rectifications.[65] Others noted that "some cadres" were dissatisfied precisely because rectification remained within these bounds,[66] and that despite instructions to the contrary, some units "expanded the scope of investigation and adopted oversimplified methods."[67] In other words, any attempt to improve Party discipline or to revitalize the Party members' sense of mission could easily become a new charismatic crusade for ideological purity quite alien to the official intent of Party rectification.

64. The distinction between the two was illustrated at a forum of non-Party personages convened in October. In post-Mao China this sort of forum has served as a venue for communication and consultation between the Party leadership and distinguished non-Party personages. Usually, Party spokespersons adopt a relatively humble and open-minded attitude at such forums, as in the case of Peng Zhen, who told the assembled that "we should guard against 'left tendencies' " and that "Party rectification is solely aimed at rectifying the CPC." And yet this was simultaneously the occasion for one more in a series of speeches from Deng Lichun that adopted a rather high-handed and threatening tone. See Xinhua Service, trans. in FBIS, 24 Oct. 1983, pp. K2–6.

65. For example, summing up the results of the first year of rectification, Bo Yibo stated: "People are generally satisfied with two aspects of the current Party rectification. On the one hand, there is the good relationship between politics and economics. . . . On the other hand, during Party rectification we have not repeated the 'leftist' mistakes of previous political movements and we have not launched mass criticism, thereby creating a tense atmosphere with everyone having the feeling of being endangered." See Xinhua Service, 22 Dec. 1984, trans. in FBIS-CHI-84-248, 24 Dec. 1984, pp. K1–8.

66. For example, speaking at an enlarged plenary session of the CPC Committee of Sichuan Military District, Yang Rudai, secretary of the provincial CPC Committee and first political commissar of the Military District, stated: "At present, a few people feel dissatisfied with the first phase of Party rectification. They hold that as not many people have been punished and removed, the work has been done in a comfortable, easy and superficial way, and there are no experiences worth mentioning. This erroneous idea is a leftover from the pernicious influence of the Great Cultural Revolution and of leftist ideology. It is a major ideological obstacle in the current Party rectification." See Sichuan Provincial Service, 13 Dec. 1984, trans. in FBIS-CHI-84-246, 20 Dec. 1984, pp. Q2–3.

67. "Do Not Ask Everyone to Make Self-Examination in Correcting Unhealthy Trends," *Renmin Ribao*, 24 Mar. 1986, p. 1, trans. in FBIS-CHI-86-059, 27 Mar. 1986, pp. K9–10.

Although society was not coerced into professing recognition of the
Party's virtues, Party rectification was nonetheless intended to revive
the Party's sense of its own virtue. From an individual Party member's vantage, Party rectification was supposed to be more than technical training. In the first stages of rectification, Party members are to
master a certain amount of technical information, that is, the substantive content of the documents. Even this has an element of charisma
inasmuch as the new line is presented not just as statements of policy
but as true guides to a communist future. But the heart of rectification lies in the stage of comparison and examination. The main focus
of this stage is criticism and self-criticism, and this inevitably revives
charismatic terminology such as "revolutionary consciousness." As
was argued above, the Party center has attempted to "rationalize"
this round of criticism and self-criticism by ordering all concerned to
refrain from violence and to "seek truth from facts." But the process
is still supposed to have deep spiritual implications, as is indicated by
references to "heart-to-heart talks." This round of criticism and self-
criticism may lack the fervor of the Cultural Revolution, but it would
be a mistake to regard criticism and self-criticism as an anomalous
aspect of rectification. Instead, it was supposed to provide the catalyst
that would make rectification a reality. Chen argues that if criticism
and self-criticism do not follow the period of study, "it will be difficult for the Party rectification to avoid becoming perfunctory."[68]

In sum, Party rectification contains profound ambivalences and
deep dilemmas. On the one hand, it is concerned with instituting
rules and procedures with the goal of making the Party work in a
machine-like manner and consistently impose its organizational purposes on individual members. On the other hand, Party rectification
is meant to be a spiritual revival, a reawakening to a rediscovered and
redefined historical calling that generates a zealous commitment to
building a communist future. Because of the unfortunate recent past,
the revival is difficult to engineer. Not only has the Party's claim to
special abilities been discredited, but any attempt at a revival creates
the potential for a mass campaign that would disrupt both the attempt to strengthen laws and procedures and the reform project as a
whole. Finally, without such a campaign, Party rectification ran the
risk of "becoming perfunctory." Nor can these dilemmas be avoided.
The revolution cannot last forever, and the Party's charisma must be

68. Ibid.

routinized. The world market demands the shift from "utopia" to "modernization." Neither in China nor in any other Leninist state have these proven to be easy tasks. Ideology and Party policy are not simply matters to be determined by the discretion of powerful leaders; they are shaped and limited by the structures of state power.

RECTIFICATION AND ECONOMIC REFORM

Party rectification was also to propagate the ideology of economic reform and to facilitate its implementation. In theory, economic reform gave substance to rectification. The Party's charisma would be reconfirmed if the Party led the way to prosperity. Rationalization and legalization of state and Party organization were integral aspects of both economic reform and rectification. Unfortunately, reality proved more complex. Party leaders who wished to limit the scope of reform linked economic reform to "new unhealthy trends." While "new unhealthy trends" were not really new, this led to considerable confusion. From a legal perspective, it was unclear whether rectification meant pioneering economic reform, even when that meant breaking through the restraint of existing regulations, or strict enforcement of the same regulations to combat unhealthy trends. From a charismatic perspective, it was difficult to distinguish the principled pursuit of economic results from the selfish pursuit of economic benefits. The result of this confusion is that the nature of the Party's virtue in the new period and the nature of its leading role remain unclear.

From the outset, Party rectification adopted a solicitous attitude toward economic reform, and this commitment deepened over time. As was noted earlier, the documents included in *Required Reading for Party Members* voiced this commitment. For example, Hu Yaobang's speech to the Twelfth Party Congress supported diverse forms of ownership, market regulation, and increasing contact with foreigners.[69] The Central Commission for Guiding Party Rectification's Circular Number Eight of June 7, 1984, called on Party members undergoing rectification to study and implement Zhao Ziyang's then recent report to the Second Session of the Sixth National People's Congress, in which he called for structural reform of the economic system.[70]

69. Hu Yaobang, "Create a New Situation in All Fields of Socialist Modernization."
70. *One Year of Party Rectification*, 20–22.

Thereafter, in some units and localities, economic work "served as a criterion for judging rectification."[71] The "Decision on Reform of the Economic Structure" released by the Third Plenum of the Twelfth Central Committee that fall became additional required reading in some areas.[72] In April 1985 the Twelfth Circular of the Central Commission for Guiding Party Rectification listed the original four tasks for Party rectification as "fundamental tasks," but stated that reform required "special stress."[73] In July 1985 Hu Qili exceeded even this standard, stating: "The most fundamental guideline for Party rectification at this stage is that it must ensure and expedite reform."[74]

Not long after the Third Plenum of the Twelfth Central Committee, the Party secretariat linked economic reform to the emergence of "new unhealthy trends" and stated: "Efforts to prevent and correct some new unhealthy tendencies emerging under the new situation of reform are not good enough."[75] The new term was soon widely used. Bo Yibo defined it as "trying to make personal gains by taking advantage of reform" and gave the following examples:

> After several months of observance and efforts to understand the problem, it has been found that among the unhealthy practices which have appeared under the new circumstances, the following are the most striking and destructive: (1) Party and government organs and cadres engage in businesses and run enterprises (or not in their own names but in the name of their family members, relatives, or friends). (2) Imported machinery and electric equipment and materials urgently needed by the state and in short supply are purchased and resold for profit. (3) State foreign exchange is purchased and sold illegally. (4) Commodity prices are hiked, loans extended, and lottery tickets, raffle sale tickets, and raffle commemorative tickets issued in an arbitrary way. (5) Cash or materials are distributed arbitrarily under one pretext or another. (6) Public funds and property are used extravagantly for hosting banquets and sending gifts. (7) There is crash promotion of positions and grades, thus interfering with the reform of the wage system. (8) Efforts are made to practice formalism, engage in boasting, and resort to deception for making personal gains.[76]

71. *Xinhua* praised the Ministry of Coal Industry for adopting this yardstick. See Xinhua Service, 24 June 1984, trans. in FBIS-CHI-84-124, 26 June 1984, pp. K1–5. For another example, see Anhui Provincial Service, 24 Aug. 1984, trans. in FBIS-CHI-84-170, 30 Aug. 1984, pp. O1–2.

72. *Renmin Ribao*, 16 Dec. 1984, in FBIS-CHI-84-245, pp. O1–2.

73. "Circular No. 12," in FBIS-CHI-85-072, 15 Apr. 1985, pp. K15–19.

74. Xinhua Service, 14 July 1985, trans. in FBIS-CHI-85-135, 15 July 1985, pp. K1–6.

75. *Xinhua*, 26 Nov. 1984, trans. in FBIS-CHI-84-229, 27 Nov. 1984, pp. K1–6.

76. Xinhua Service, 12 Mar. 1985, trans. in FBIS-CHI-85-050, 14 Mar. 1985, pp. K1–9.

Although the new term had minimal empirical content, it served important political purposes. On the one hand, economic reform does create new opportunities for corruption by legitimating profit seeking, removing hierarchical controls, and increasing the level of economic activity and the number of channels for circulating commodities. Taking advantage of official position for private gain is nothing new, however. Attempts to distinguish traditional unhealthy practices from new unhealthy practices were strained.[77] A provincial rectification spokesman stated: "The emphasis should be on checking new unhealthy trends. Nevertheless, we should also solve the problems of abusing one's power to seek personal gains and of bureaucratism because the two are identical."[78] On the other hand, castigating "new unhealthy trends" served distinct political purposes. First, talk of reform led to an unsustainable high rate of economic growth, and criticism of "new unhealthy trends" was one of various measures adopted to slow the economy. Second, and far more important, the term "new unhealthy practices" linked a real problem to economic reform and thereby cast aspersions on reform.

The problem was that while Party rectification and economic reform were supposed to be means of recapturing charismatic legitimacy, many cadres feared that the mundane and materialistic virtues required by economic reform would negate the Party's traditional political and ethical virtues. For example, a Hebei commentator argued that the growth of the commodity economy led to beliefs such as "communism is [at best] a distant hope," goals like seeking "practical benefit," and strategies like "all futures and plans should be aimed at making money."[79] In practice, it was extremely difficult for those in favor of economic reform to explain the difference between high-minded pursuit of reform and the selfish pursuit of worldly goods. Summing up the lessons of the Hainan scandal, participants at a Hainan regional Party meeting tried to draw a series of fine distinctions:

> First, we must draw a distinction between looking for money in everything and improving the socialist enterprises' economic results. These are two

77. Some leaders claimed that "unhealthy practices" had been checked by rectification but that "new unhealthy practices" had then emerged after the Third Plenum of the Twelfth Party Congress. See *Xinhua*, 26 Nov. 1984, trans. in FBIS-CHI-84-229, 27 Nov. 1984, pp. K1–6.

78. Jilin Provincial Service, 10 Mar. 1985, trans. in FBIS-CHI-85-050, 14 Mar. 1985, p. S1.

79. See "Earnestly Remove the Inner Party Erroneous Thought of 'Distant Hope' and 'Practical Benefit,'" *Hebei Ribao*, 28 Jan. 1986, trans. in FBIS-CHI-86-031, 14 Feb. 1986, pp. R1–3.

entirely different things and must not be confused. Second, we must distinguish between looking for money in everything and getting rich through hard work. We oppose the former but we certainly do not oppose the latter, nor do we oppose proper income allowed within the scope of the policies. On the contrary, we advocate that some people should get rich ahead of others by relying on their own labor. Third, we must distinguish between looking for money everywhere and distribution according to work. We oppose looking for money in everything and indiscriminate payment of bonuses and goods in kind, but we must uphold the principle of distribution according to work. Moreover, we must continually improve living standards on the basis of developing production. Fourth, we must distinguish between looking for money in everything and organizing proper accumulation. We oppose the practice of some enterprises in arbitrarily hiking prices for the sake of making money, thus harming the interests of the state and the people. However, we advocate that enterprises should accumulate capital for expanded reproduction on the basis of developing production, improving economic results, and fulfilling the tax and profit payment quotas. It is wrong not to organize proper accumulation on account of opposition to looking for money everywhere.[80]

Guangdong provincial leader Lin Ruo added that it was proper to get rich and to promote "trade aimed at enlivening circulation, serving production, and the people's livelihood," but that "getting rich by relying on trade" was not acceptable.[81]

These fine distinctions were incapable, however, of either ending unhealthy trends or restoring virtue. The point was that according to the reform leaders, Party members were to live in the material world, but were not to be of that world or for that world. They were to work long and hard at creating wealth and prosperity, and were to use efficient techniques, but this wealth was for the greater good of the people, not for Party members personally. That style of virtue— similar to the Protestant work ethic—requires a stern discipline, which few could master and fewer could welcome.

Economic reform presented an equal challenge to the rational-legal aspects of rectification. Whereas in theory the strengthening of laws and regulations was an integral aspect of economic reform, in practice reformers found their efforts blocked by existing rules and proce-

80. Hainan Island Service, 1 Sept. 1985, trans. in FBIS-CHI-85-172, 5 Sept. 1985, pp. P1–10.

81. Lin also criticized attitudes like these: "As long as I do not put the money into my pocket, I can do anything I like" and "I am working for the interests of the local people. [So] I am not afraid of making mistakes." Lin Ruo, "We Must Win Complete Victory in Party Rectification," *Nanfang Ribao*, 26 July 1985, pp. 1, 2, trans. in FBIS-CHI-85-149, 2 Aug. 1985, pp. P3–11.

dures. Some reformers invoked the charismatic qualities of economic reformers as heroic pioneers to legitimate breaking rules. A reformer quoted in *Renmin Ribao* said:

> Reform is a new undertaking which was never done by our forefathers. Doing it will certainly violate some old rules and regulations. If we are sticks-in-the-mud, act overcautiously, and have no courage, how can we carry out reform? In the execution of the reform, we will certainly encounter some difficulties and commit some mistakes and errors.[82]

Again, resolving the dilemma called for drawing a series of fine distinctions, like those drawn by Chen Guangyi, governor of Gansu:

> It is necessary to draw a demarcation line between the people who conduct explorations and experiments corresponding to reforms and those who violate the interests of the state and collectives by taking advantage of the reforms and changing their means. It is necessary to summarize, perfect, and improve explorations and experiments corresponding with the reforms and carry them out selectively. Those who take advantage of the reform and violate laws and discipline should be dealt with severely.[83]

Others evidently believed that reform would be blocked by any form of discipline.[84]

In conclusion, squaring Party rectification with economic reform has proven a difficult task. The Party cannot and has not given up its claim to charismatic legitimacy. It must retain some element of charisma to legitimate its exclusive leading role in society. But it has had trouble in routinizing any type of charisma compatible with the ev-

---

82. Xiao Di, "Han Tianshi Addresses Tianjin Forum of Factory Directors and Party Committee Secretaries," *Renmin Ribao*, 1 Aug. 1986, p. 1, trans. in FBIS-CHI-86-150, 5 Aug. 1986, pp. K14–15.

83. Gansu Provincial Service, 15 Apr. 1985, trans. in FBIS-CHI-85-076, 19 Apr. 1985, pp. T1–2.

84. The Central Commission for Guiding Party Rectification replied to cadres with that attitude while commenting on the Coal Ministry, which it had earlier praised for linking economic work with rectification. It stated: "Once Party style is on the correct track, it will encourage people to carry out reform more boldly. . . . It is wrong to think that correcting unhealthy style will frustrate reform," (Xinhua Service, 15 July 1985, trans. in FBIS-CHI-85-136, 16 July 1985, pp. K1–4). Guangdong leader Lin Ruo made similar distinctions a year later when he identified and criticized "leading group members" for having the following attitudes: (1) believing that material civilization and professional work are more important than spiritual civilization and ideological and political work; (2) believing that enforcing discipline will do harm to enlivening the economy; (3) believing that punishing cadres who violate law and discipline would dampen cadres' enthusiasm; (4) believing that they can do anything except pocket money. See Lin Ruo, "Excerpts," in *Nanfang Ribao*, 8 June 1986, pp. 1, 2, trans. in FBIS-CHI-86-114, 13 June 1986, pp. P1–5.

eryday world of socialist modernization. Few people believe that the revolutionary charisma of the Cultural Revolution period is compatible with socialist modernization, but it is nonetheless substantially more appealing to many Party members than any available alternative. The reform version of charisma not only lacks appeal but is poorly defined. Neither has proven capable of controlling "unhealthy trends" or "new unhealthy trends." And this is not surprising. Even Weber argues that the greatest impetus to rational efficiency in the West was not religious charisma but the "illegitimate" market.[85] In China at present, despite economic reforms, few Party members are forced to accept the discipline of market pressures. To the contrary, the charisma of the Party's historic mission is easily invoked to deny the legitimacy of market outcomes and to protect personal and particularistic prerogatives, however inefficient. And when charismatic inspiration fails, discipline is to be invoked from above—as the Legalists traditionally invoked law in China. It seems doubtful that any system of rules so enforced can become practically workable. The real solution to this dilemma is more likely to be more patrimonial rulership and more fine distinctions that are not really observed.

PARTY RECTIFICATION CAPTURED BY PATRIMONIALISM

At one level, Party rectification was a great success. Forty million Party members basically followed the procedures spelled out in the Decision, and the process was completed more or less on time. Speaking at a meeting held in May 1987 to sum up the results, Bo Yibo claimed that each of the four tasks set out in the Decision had been accomplished. Moreover, rectification had not become a destructive mass movement, and the economy had not been disrupted. Bo allowed that some units had avoided real rectification, and that Party building would have to be an ongoing process.[86] Even these qualifications pointed to a deeper success, as they illustrated the rational-minded objective work-style that rectification was supposed to foster.

85. Weber calls "exchange through the market" the "archetype of all rational social action." See *Economy and Society*, 635–40. He also refers to market-based cities as examples of "non-legitimate domination," perhaps referring to the coercive interest-based character of market domination rather than the authority-based character of legitimate rulership (1212, 731, 943).
86. "National Party Rectification Work Basically Completed," p. 1.

Success could be demonstrated with a wealth of statistics. Many provinces reported impressive results in clearing up "new unhealthy practices." Hebei reported that 1,926 enterprises led by government and Party cadres had been shut down and that 6,896 cases of arbitrary price hikes had been ferreted out, returning 4.51 million yuan in confiscated money and fines.[87] Heilongjiang reported recovery of 4.98 million yuan in illegal bonuses distributed to 48,000 cadres, and 549,000 yuan in bribes returned by 6,700 cadres.[88] Guangdong provincial authorities checked 4,210 types of fees and penalties in 60 cities, prefectures, and counties and canceled 1,025 and lowered 1,015.[89] During rural rectification, one county in Shaanxi found 3,100 rural cadres illegally buying, selling, or occupying land.[90]

Patrimonial rulership has a tremendous ability, however, to cloak itself in the outward forms of bureaucracy and rational-legal rulership. Despite many warnings against "perfunctoriness," rectification was not always what it seemed, as in the case of too many meetings in Hubei:

> As upper levels have had too many meetings, the unfolding of Party rectification work at grass-roots levels and industrial and agricultural production have been affected. . . . In the 55 days from 15 January when Party rectification began in Huanggang prefecture to 10 March, prefectural subordinate units at and above the bureau level attended 173 meetings on a total of 1,148 days. Of them, 57 units went to the capital of the province to attend meetings and 6 units went to Beijing to attend meetings. Each of 80 meetings lasted over 5 days; each of 14 meetings lasted over 10 days; 5 meetings each lasted over 15 days; and 4 meetings lasted over 1 month. A total of 315 people attended these meetings, of whom 104 were cadres of departments, offices and committees who were at and above the bureau level.[91]

Nor do reported results necessarily indicate what they seem to indicate:

> However, the comrades of some other units are not [making achievements]. They even do superficial things and play tricks in the name of

---

87. Hebei Provincial Service, 1 Apr. 1985, trans. in FBIS-CHI-85-070, 11 Apr. 1985, p. R1.

88. Heilongjiang Provincial Service, 2 July 1986, trans. in FBIS-CHI-86-130, 8 July 1986, pp. S1–2.

89. Guangdong Provincial Service, 30 Nov. 1985, trans. in FBIS-CHI-85-234, 5 Dec. 1985, p. P1.

90. Shaanxi Provincial Service, 11 Sept. 1986, trans. in FBIS-CHI-86-176, 11 Sept. 1986, p. T1.

91. Hubei Provincial Service, 31 Mar. 1985, trans. in FBIS-CHI-85-064, 3 Apr. 1985, pp. P1–2.

reform. Some units put efforts only into things that others can see. They have not done anything to solve practical problems that should be solved without delay. Other units, stealthily substituting one thing for another, recount achievements made several years ago as they present reform achievements. Still others are exaggerating small changes in working methods or rules and regulations as major breakthroughs. . . . A reform carried out in this way exists more in name than in reality and is very likely to defame our reform drive.[92]

The official remedies for perfunctoriness were traditional Leninist administrative strategies: leading cadres were to take an active role in rectification, and higher levels were to supervise lower levels. As was noted above, however, leading cadres were capable of ignoring instructions or putting local factional interests before official Party concerns, and inspection tours conducted by upper levels to supervise lower levels were themselves opportunities for "unhealthy practices."[93]

These problems were discussed at a meeting on the Party style of the central organs attended by 8,000 cadres of those organs in January 1986. This was a tacit admission that Party rectification had not succeeded, as these units had been rectified a year earlier. Speaker after speaker affirmed the persistence of serious problems. Further, although there were already two central-level offices concerned with improving Party style, the Central Discipline and Inspection Commission and the Central Commission for Guiding Party Rectification, this meeting founded another, the Leading Group for the Rectification of

92. Beijing Domestic Service, 26 Dec. 1984, citing "We Should Not Do Superficial Things, Especially in the Course of Reform," *Jiefang Jun Bao*, 26 Dec. 1984, trans. in FBIS-CHI-84-250, 27 Dec. 1984, p. K1.

93. Bo Yibo described problems with local leading groups as follows: "In some localities and units, the phenomena of leading bodies and Party-member cadres disregarding Party spirit and discipline is very serious. The striking thing about them is that they have forgotten the Communist Party members' lofty ideal of waging lifelong struggle for the socialist and communist cause, the principle of subordinating partial interests to overall interests and of fulfilling and enhancing personal and small-group interests only after safeguarding the overall interests of the state and society at large. They have completely ignored the instructions and circulars issued by the Party Central Committee and the State Council, or have decided to comply or not to comply with them depending on their personal or small-group interests. Those instructions that are in their favor are implemented, while those that are not in their favor are not implemented. Some of them even openly claim that 'the higher authorities have policies, the lower authorities have countermeasures.' They spare no efforts in adopting every improper means to counteract the Party and the state and undermine the national interest." See Bo Yibo, speech at work meeting, February 22, 1985, on second-stage Party rectification, Xinhua Service, 12 Mar. 1985, trans. in FBIS-CHI-85-050, 14 Mar. 1985, pp. K1–8.

the Central Organ's Party Style. Although the leading groups of the different Party-style organizations had some overlap, the Central Discipline and Inspection Committee was dominated by Chen Yun, the Central Commission for Guiding Party Rectification by Bo Yibo, and the Leading Group for the Rectification of the Central Organ's Party Style by Hu Yaobang, each representing one of the three then most important factions in Chinese politics.[94] Rectification, which was to end factionalism, was plagued by factionalism.

In sum, many of the problems that rectification was to solve were part of rectification. A substantial portion of what passed as rectification was a sort of ritual activity in which Party committees at various levels received instructions, held meetings, formed committees, listened to speeches, studied documents, adopted resolutions, transmitted further instructions, made investigations, compiled statistics, and dispatched reports, but were nonetheless unable to come to grips with the underlying problems. Bo Yibo, who has led Party rectification movements since the early 1950s, portrayed resistance to rectification as a systemic problem:

> Since the fifties we have mainly been engaged in carrying out movements, and the repeated movements have enabled some people to learn a set of methods to deal with "movements." When a movement is launched, they maintain their composure and lie concealed by every means, and think that the movement can only last for a time and everything will be all right when it goes past. In carrying out Party rectification this time, we have repeatedly stressed that we will carry out no movement, but some people have still adopted the old "method," which they used to deal with movements, to deal with this Party rectification. Are there not some people who say that "you have your measures and I have my countermeasures"? They have methods to deal with any method that we can think out.[95]

This round of rectification was not something completely new, but was another round in a series with origins older than the People's Republic.

CONCLUSION

States, especially Leninist states, have a certain autonomy and respond to their own interests. Leninist states are not dependent on so-

94. My thanks to Edward Friedman for pointing this out to me.
95. Bo Yibo, "Do a Good Job in Party Rectification in One Vigorous Effort," *Liaowang* 26 (30 June 1986): 9–11; trans. in FBIS-CHI-86-133, 11 July 1986, pp. K1–4.

cial classes but are the revolutionary creations of parties and armies. They eliminate traditional elites and sources of autonomous power and wealth, such as private ownership of the means of production and independent political parties. Their comprehensive organization and control of the means of communication inhibit the organization and articulation of any effective opposition. Consequently, Leninist states are relatively free to respond to their own interests.

Leninist states are presently faced with a dilemma. What was intended to be a means of creating a prosperous, democratic, egalitarian, and stateless society first resulted instead in "a desperate attempt to adapt the whole of living society into the crystalline structure of the state,"[96] and later led to economic stagnation, a suffocating network of patrimonial rulership, and a gradual loss of ideological legitimacy. Their relative autonomy allowed them to postpone dealing with these problems for decades. At last reformers are anxious to come to grips with these problems before more damage is done. Nonetheless, they seek to strengthen and revitalize the existing state, not to make another revolution. They are trying to redefine the Party as the agent of "modernization" instead of "utopia," and to recapture the charismatic commitment of the population and Party members alike in a new quest for socialist prosperity, and they hope to improve the Party's ability to govern itself and society by creating a new legal structure.The reformers have no intention, however, of giving up the Party's privileged position in politics.

Party rectification was a large-scale, comprehensive, and in the sense in which the term has been used in this book, rational plan to transform China's most important political institution to meet these new goals. The hierarchical nature of this campaign, its massive scale, and the tenor of the language used all indicate that China's central authorities still have considerable autonomy. Society was only able to respond in a passive manner.

Nonetheless, Party rectification encountered obstacles that severely limited its ability to transform organization or ideology. Most Party organs properly went through the motions of rectification, but networks of personal relationships—from the top of the Party hierarchy to the bottom—so diffused and diverted official intentions that the degree of real change was marginal. The sources of this opposition, ironically, are the institutions of state power. The same vertical hier-

96. Rudolf Bahro, *The Alternative in Eastern Europe*, 38.

archies that stifle society and give state power holders the autonomy to implement political campaigns also form the foundation for the patrimonial networks that inhibit rectification. In the 1980s China's Leninist state institutions have proven their ability to withstand pressures for change from above and below. The unwelcome stability of institutions may well prove a more important and lasting form of autonomy than the ability of leaders to define and implement policies.

The results of reform in general, like rectification, have been mixed. At least until the crackdown began in June 1989, reform yielded a wide range of benefits. Economic growth came as a welcome relief to a society that had endured two decades with only miniscule improvements in the standard of living, even if the growth was accompanied by inflation and other dislocations. China's cadres are now younger and better educated. For a time the Party's official ideology was more reasonable. Government was more predictable and allowed for a wider range of opinions, a more lively culture, and more intercourse with the wider world. These were all very significant accomplishments.

But fundamental problems were not solved. Patrimonial networks remain a pervasive aspect of social, political, and economic life. They will continue to impede the efficiency of markets and corrode the Party's claim to legitimacy, as well as its ability to govern. Nor has the Party been able to determine what unique attributes it has that give it the right to its privileged position in the era of modernization. The failure to formulate a convincing definition of the Party's role in the new period both reinforces the need for patronage and patrimonial rulership and breeds frustration in society and within the Party, which contributes to both civil opposition and the current campaign of repression. More political movements organized and orchestrated from above are unlikely to solve these problems. Moreover, in Leninist states this is common knowledge. In a public opinion survey taken in China, over half the respondents were dissatisfied with the results of Party rectification.[97]

The success of reform has been limited by the staying power or autonomy of Leninist state institutions. As long as the fundamental

97. This poll was supervised by Fei Yuan and Zhang Lun of the Beijing Economic and Social Sciences Research Institute. They distributed 5,000 questionnaires and received 3,000 in return. Of these, 52.35% expressed dissatisfaction with the results of the rectification campaign against unhealthy tendencies within the Communist Party. See Zhu Yuchao, "Opinion Polls and Democratization," *China Reconstructs* 4 (1988): 33.

structures of state power remain intact, there will be some problems that cannot be solved. Capitalist states also face a range of chronic problems. Reforms like building bureaucracies to provide social welfare and institutions to regulate economic cycles can ameliorate these problems and improve the lives of millions, but the underlying problems remain. Similarly, Leninist states can make real progress, but still not solve fundamental problems. The differences are that in the prosperous liberal democracies the conflict between state and society is much milder than in Leninist states, and that liberal democracies do not need to redefine their basic purposes.

Conclusion

Contemporary Chinese political thought is divided. On the one hand, there is broad support for rationalizing state and Party administrative structures, empowering economic and social organizations to make the best use of their own resources, and granting citizens political and civil liberties. There is considerable ambiguity about how far reforms in these directions could or should go. Some intellectuals appear to favor something like a Western-style democracy, even including competition between multiple political parties. But even the most reform-minded leaders do not want a Western-style democracy, and some reformers would prefer to rationalize state and Party organizations while minimizing the autonomy of society. Although the official Party position has wavered, from the beginning of the reforms to at least the spring of 1989, on the whole the Party moved toward a progressively deeper commitment to both rationalizing administration and creating a more autonomous civil society. Public discussion was more about what measures are required to realize these goals and what standards should be used to assess success than over the merits of the goals themselves.

On the other hand, China remains officially committed to the Four Cardinal Principles: keeping to the socialist road, upholding the dictatorship of the proletariat, upholding the leadership of the Communist Party, and upholding Marxism-Leninism and Mao Zedong Thought. These are inscribed in the constitution and are one of the most pervasive political symbols of post-Mao China. They represent a commitment to maintain the essential institutional structures of China's Leninist state, especially the leading role of the Party. They also imply that all political speech and action should maintain continuity with the Party's official ideology. There is deep confusion about exactly what Marxism-Leninism Mao Zedong Thought is in the new era, and at times the Party has looked the other way and allowed penetrating "explorations" beyond the frontiers of official ideology. At the very least, "socialism" still entails the Party-state leading the way toward the creation of a virtuous society.

Both of these trends are deeply embedded in the ideology of reform. The intellectual foundations of post-Mao reforms were first publicly proclaimed in an article by Hu Fuming, "Practice Is the Only Standard of Truth," which was published in *Guangming Ribao* on May 11, 1978. Professor Hu cited the second of Marx's "Theses on Fuerbach" and Mao's "On New Democracy" to argue that the truth of theory can only be demonstrated in practical action. He argued that Marxism is a science and, like science, is open to rational argument, should consider new evidence, and is open to change and development. Hu gathered together concepts like "Marxism," "materialism," and "science" and correlated them with their alleged opposites, "dogma," "idealism," and "superstition," thus providing a foundation for rejecting the shibboleths of the Cultural Revolution and asserting that progress, truth, and justice depend on autonomous critical reflection, free discussion, and dissent. Consequently, the "practice" argument is of considerable comfort to those who want a rational efficient bureaucracy, more autonomy for civil society, and individual rights.

Nonetheless, the "practice" argument is neither liberal nor pragmatic and is not at odds with the Four Cardinal Principles. "Practice" means, not that theory can be abandoned or ignored, only that it must be tested in practice; it is not a license to try anything that "works," but is supposed to be a disciplined quest for a moral and material truth based on Marxist principles. Just as science has permanent ground rules, and just as scientists ignore nonscientists who reject those rules, practice can emphasize alleged continuities in Marxism, such as the Four Cardinal Principles, and can exclude those who reject those principles from taking part in "legitimate" discussion. Even while the practice argument admits that the truth that can be perceived at the present is a partial truth subject to later revision, it still insists that the purpose of political discussion is to locate truth and that the purpose of the state is to implement truth. Most important of all, this truth is not just a technical or factual truth, it is also a moral and ethical truth.

Main currents in Western thought argue that individual autonomy and efficiency stand in contradiction to the quest for a virtuous state. Liberalism argues that politics cannot be a quest for a moral and material truth and also respect the freedom of each individual to decide autonomously what that truth is. Instead, liberalism confines itself to asserting institutional and procedural "truths" and maintains at least the pretense of relativism with regard to substantive truths. Science, the core of the ethic of technical efficiency, similarly asserts a hollow set of procedural values. A technically efficient bureaucracy is not a value-free tool, but few Westerners would follow Marx or the practice argument in asserting that science can determine the nature of virtue. Instead, from Christian fundamentalists to the Greens, substantial sectors of Western society are increasingly skeptical of the value of science.

Liberal values and technical efficiency are complementary. We are used to the argument that markets are a more efficient means of coordinating economic activity than hierarchically organized command planning. At a microeconomic level of analysis, efficient organization also requires the stimulation of individual initiative and, within limits prescribed by official organizational purposes, individual autonomy. Those who fear bureaucratic domination tend to focus on its hierarchical structure. But hierarchy is only one aspect of rational-legal organization. Experts are effective only when they have the autonomy to search continually for technically better means of accomplishing organizational goals, to criticize existing procedures, and to experiment with new ideas. Consequently, rational-legal organization is characterized by formally specified spheres of competence that guarantee an appropriate sphere of autonomy to protect technical experts from the arbitrary abuse of organizational authority. Rational-legal organization lacks moral or ethical goodness, but it is nonetheless derived from the European Enlightenment and requires an autonomous and skeptical staff.[1]

In the historical development of Western society, markets have been the main force promoting efficiency and autonomy, as Max Weber, Adam Smith, and Karl Marx would all agree. Markets are not the

---

1. A. J. Polan develops this theme throughout his excellent book *Lenin and the End of Politics.*

natural human condition but were created by states in a series of brutal interventions that destroyed the "moral economy" of traditional society.[2] Peasants were sundered from common lands and communal ties and left weak and isolated to compete against each other and concentrations of capital and wealth. It is little compensation for those who suffered this fate that their descendants came to enjoy material prosperity and civil and political liberties beyond their wildest imagination.

Marx, Lenin, and Mao are but three of many who rejected this bargain. As the world market developed, the gap between the center and the periphery increased and the costs of entering the market mounted. Nations like China that were first exposed to Western civilization through commercial exploitation and wars of aggression were naturally skeptical of the virtue of this form of society. And yet, as the practice argument tells us, it is not enough to reject the Western version of modernity philosophically, politically, or even militarily. Instead, a solution to the problem of modernity must be found. Nations that fail to create efficient institutions and competitive economies are trapped in poverty and denied freedom.[3]

As I argued in the introduction, Lenin had little understanding of modern organization or how to control it. In *State and Revolution* he argued that modernization reduced administrative complexity and diminished the division of labor. He argued that bureaucracy could be controlled if the salary of bureaucrats was limited and they were subject to immediate recall. He argued that legislators could only be really effective if they both represented their constituents and did the executive work formerly assigned to bureaucrats. His concept of "democratic-centralism" left no room for an organized autonomous opposition. Although reducing bureaucratic salaries diminishes the attractiveness of a career in the bureaucracy, this hardly seems an effective way to control the use of bureaucratic power. And it is obvious that subjecting bureaucrats to immediate recall would eliminate the benefits of modern civil service systems and increase the likelihood of corruption and the arbitrary intervention of political leaders. Nor could a combined legislature-bureaucracy with no organized opposi-

---

2. This is the masterful argument of Karl Polanyi in *The Great Transformation*. The concept of a traditional "moral economy" is ably developed in James C. Scott, *The Moral Economy of the Peasant: Rebellion and Subsistence in Southeast Asia*.

3. Colin Leys argues that one of the biggest problems with dependency theory is that it creates the illusion that there is an alternative to participation in the world market. See "African Economic Development in Theory and Practice."

tion effectively investigate its own transgressions. In sum, Lenin understood neither the sources of technical efficiency nor the importance of organizational or individual autonomy. States based on Leninist principles were handicapped from the beginning.

In contrast, Lenin did understand the politics of charisma. A Leninist party was able to use its members' deep commitment to the party's historical mission, as well as the party's ability to gain broader social acceptance of its claim to virtue, to build effective "political combat organizations."[4] Leninist parties not only managed to establish militarily strong states in competitive international settings but, within the state, were able to dismantle and demobilize virtually all organized opposition. The result was a new form of state, which, though not technically efficient, was nonetheless highly autonomous and at least temporarily capable of mobilizing popular energies.

In these states individual leaders had the ability to attempt to impose their personal vision of the revolution on the whole of society. Like Pol Pot, Mao imagined that it would be possible to build a modern prosperous nation without training an autonomous corps of technical experts. As I argued in chapter 1, Mao attempted to use revolutionary charisma, not least his personal charisma, to centrally direct a revolution from above. This quest led first to the catastrophic Great Leap Forward and then to the murderous Cultural Revolution. By the time Mao died, the Chinese people's standard of living had stagnated for twenty years and the nation was farther than ever from democracy. The state itself was in urgent need of repair, and the new leadership had little choice but to initiate comprehensive reform.

While no less murderous, Stalin had a somewhat better grasp of the nature of modern organization and the importance of technical experts. Because of this, he left his successors not just a more developed economy but a state with a much stronger administrative capacity. This had its drawbacks, as it created the potential for the long period of stagnation that followed Khrushchev. More than three decades passed between Stalin's death and the rise of Gorbachev, whereas less than three years after Mao's death China's leadership had endorsed sweeping reforms.

The "easy" alternative to Stalinism or Maoism is a form of despotism with a human face—patrimonial bureaucracy. Without a com-

4. This concept is developed in Jeremy T. Paltiel, "The Cult of Personality: Some Comparative Reflections on Political Culture in Leninist Regimes."

petitive market and without an environment conducive to individual autonomy, the comprehensive organization of a Leninist state is governed by a compromise between official rules and purposes and the personal interests of officials. Patrimonial rulership has a human face inasmuch as it depends on personal relationships and allows for exceptions and special deals. For officials who have the resources to negotiate in earnest, it allows freedom with the law, not just freedom under law.[5] Moreover, patrimonial bureaucracy can reduce the autonomy of individual leaders and diminish the chances that another Mao or Stalin will arise. But patrimonial bureaucracy does not liberate society from the state. Instead, the autonomy of individual leaders is replaced by the autonomy of stifling institutions. Patrimonial bureaucracy is inevitably arbitrary and unpredictable. It entangles everyday human endeavors in a web of restraint and resistance. A nation wrapped in this form of organization is condemned to inefficiency, poverty, and weakness.

Patrimonial bureaucracy is a risky form of rulership for contemporary Leninist states. First, in a competitive world economy, inefficient organization is a dreadful handicap. Second, in traditional states, traditional norms sanctioned features of patrimonial bureaucracy like special privileges for officials and, within limits, tolerated what would now be labeled corruption. But Leninist parties and Leninist states are legitimated and organized according to claims of a very high standard of virtue that allows for little corruption. As Leninist states decay they find their own ideological heritage to be a source of trenchant criticism.

So China's reformers reached the conclusion that the Party's virtuous leadership was not enough but had to be supplemented by markets and social autonomy. There is a strong tendency among Western politicians, journalists, and ideologues to indulge in self-congratulation and proclaim that reformers in both the Soviet Union and China have abandoned socialism for capitalism, but this is clearly not the case. In the first place, whatever the real results of Marxism as a social movement may have been, Marx as a social theorist surely did not intend that socialism would be anything like Stalinism, Maoism, or patrimonial bureaucracy. Reformers can rightfully reject these

5. In Liu Xinwu's novella "The Overpass" the character Ge Youhan is an archetypical portrait of the kind of wheeler-dealer that prospers in a Leninist state. See Liu Xinwu, "Overpass," in *Mao's Harvest*, 29–90.

interpretations and institutions as not living up to the true standards of socialism. Second, the reformers have every intention of maintaining substantial portions of the existing state, not least the Four Cardinal Principles and the leading role of the Party.

We come at last to the central question—what will reform lead to? I will evaluate three possible scenarios: a long period of repression and retrenchment; the gradual transformation of China's Leninist state into a non-Leninist state; and the collapse of China's Leninist state as a result of a confrontation with society. No one can confidently predict the future, so I will not estimate which of these scenarios is most likely. My intention is to estimate only the obstacles China's leaders and the Chinese people face, not the outcomes that will occur.

The first scenario calls for a long period of repression and retrenchment. The current leaders have chosen to utilize what they perceive to be the strengths of Leninist state institutions in an attempt to enforce conformity and to resist autonomy. They are desperately seeking to reaffirm the Party's traditional virtues and reestablish its charismatic right to rule. For now, they are enjoying a measure of success. The brutal violence used to end the demonstrations, and the subsequent wave of arrests, manifest the power of the state. The pace of reform has been slowed and some reforms have been rolled back. They have isolated social activists and suppressed open manifestations of social discontent. These strategies might enjoy success for a long period: in Czechoslovakia the repression and retrenchment instituted upon the fall of Dubcek lasted more than twenty years.

There are good reasons to think that China will not suffer that fate. First, Chinese society and Chinese state institutions have the capacity to passively resist the political campaigns initiated by conservatives and reformers alike. Patrimonial bureaucracy will diffuse current and future campaigns just as it has diffused past campaigns. Second, forceful political campaigns will intensify the problems that necessitated reform in the first place. China's leaders are likely to discover, as did Poland's leaders before them, that violence and repression and resistance to necessary reforms will further diminish their legitimacy and weaken the state. Finally, while conservative leaders may mobilize social support from those adversely affected by the negative aspects of economic reform, they still lack an economic alternative to continued reform. In sum, repression and retrenchment might succeed, but only at a very high price to both the state and the economy, and China's leaders will face continuous pressure to reinvigorate the process of reform.

The second scenario imagines the gradual transformation or decay of a Leninist state. In 1986, with considerable foresight, Szelenyi raised the possibility of a "Spanish road" for Hungary, in which, as in Franco's Spain, the ruling apparatus first promotes the growth of the private economy to a point where it overwhelms the state-owned economy, and then accepts the status and economic autonomy of a bourgeoisie. Szelenyi argued that in this scenario Communist parties would "abandon their ideology and become pragmatist organizations whose main aim is to preserve the political monopoly of their organization."[6] At that time, Szelenyi quite reasonably found this an unlikely scenario for Hungary because of likely Soviet opposition. He can hardly be faulted for failing to foresee the extent of change that Gorbachev would allow.

There are reasons besides Soviet opposition to discount the likelihood of this outcome in Chinese politics. Currently, China's leadership is vigilantly guarding against just such a course. But even if reformers should return to power, they would have great difficulty in effecting a gradual transition to the type of state Szelenyi envisages. First, in China it is far too early to speak of the development of a significant bourgeoisie. While there are frequent complaints from ordinary citizens that private entrepreneurs make too much money, there are only 225,000 private firms, averaging sixteen employees, and they typically have only limited capital.[7] Private firms are also limited to less strategic economic sectors and, as the recent crackdown has demonstrated, remain highly vulnerable to arbitrary interference from state and Party officials.

Second, as things turned out, the Hungarian party was not able to retain its monopoly of political power. Szelenyi rightfully argues that "embourgeoisement" does not lead immediately to democratization, but it does lead to a significant redistribution of power, which a Leninist state is unlikely to survive. If the private sector did gain control of a major portion of China's capital resources and employed a major portion of the work force, and if the market became the dominant mechanism for exchange, then the Party's partrimonial rulership

6. Ivan Szelenyi, "The Prospects and Limits of the East European New Class Project."

7. "New Rules for Private Firms," *Beijing Review* 31, no. 9 (18 July 1988), pp. 10–11.

would be imperiled. The Party would be unable to prevent the emergence of relatively autonomous interest groups and would lose its political monopoly.

Third, it matters that Leninist states originate with utopian ideologies that proclaim chiliastic and charismatic purposes. Even if society ceases to believe in it, ideology is still politically useful to the Party, even as an empty shell, as long as it impedes the articulation of potentially threatening alternate points of view.[8] Moreover, because the Party originally justified its political monopoly and the privileges of its members in terms of revolutionary purposes, any admission that the goals of the revolution cannot be achieved threatens to unravel the Party's claim to charisma and the justification of its privileges. Hence the Party would be hard pressed to justify or maintain its monopoly on power without its charismatic ideology.

In sum, if China's leaders chose to respond to the continuing pressures for reform by setting off in the direction of a Spanish model, they would begin to descend a slippery slope. Nowhere in the world have Leninist reformers managed to establish a stable, long-term, reformed socialist system. Consequently, any future return to extensive reform is likely to be punctuated by periods of repression. One of China's most likely futures is a cycle of reform and retrenchment.

The third scenario is another confrontation between state and society, which could lead to a rapid collapse of China's Leninist state. First, as I argued in chapter 1, since the founding of the People's Republic there have been many confrontations between the state and various sectors of Chinese society. The confrontation that lasted from April until June of 1989 is unlikely to be the last. Harry Harding states: "Thus a veneer of unity, which masks a cauldron of conflict underneath, often characterizes Chinese politics. In short, Chinese politics is usually less stable than it appears."[9] This is because of the structure of China's Leninist state. Comprehensive state organization and state domination of the means of communication create the illusion of unity and minimize opportunities to organize and articulate meaningful opposition. At the same time, the high relative autonomy

---

8. Michael Szokolny writes: "It is generally assumed that a contradiction ... between propaganda and belief represents an ideological dysfunction. This opinion derives from the tacit assumption that the function of propaganda is to convince the recipient of its truth. Such an assumption is, however, *a priori*, unjustified. If the ideology of the ruling class serves to protect the existing order, then the only necessary function of the propaganda is to induce a set of beliefs in the ruled which in no way threatens that order. Propaganda does not have to be believed to be effective." Cited in Starski, *Class Struggle in Classless Poland*, 23–24.

9. Harding, *China's Second Revolution*, 289.

of the state means that it is poorly rooted in society and that there is a very high potential for conflict between state and society. The possibility for confrontation increases as the Party's claim to virtue is diminished and as reforms marginally increase the autonomy of civil society. To the extent that unity in the Party's higher levels depends on personal relationships, there is a strong prospect for division and conflict among personal cliques and factions, which could at least immobilize the Party during periods of crisis and at worst lead to grave internal conflicts.

The recent dramatic changes in Eastern Europe give testimony to the potential for society to triumph over a Leninist state. Of course, Eastern Europe is different from China. Socialism in Eastern Europe did not grow from native roots, and enforced alliances with the Soviet Union have eroded the legitimacy of Eastern Europe's Leninist states. Eastern Europe is also affected by the cultural and geographic proximity of Western Europe. In Poland, the church retained a measure of autonomy, which facilitated the growth of broader social autonomy. Moreover, Eastern Europe's generally more developed economies facilitate the dissemination of all kinds of information. These important differences can be overemphasized. The pattern of rulership in China and in Eastern Europe and the political problems faced by the state are similar.

It is difficult to predict the outcome or timing of confrontations between the state and society. Since timing and resolution of such confrontations are subject to a myriad of individual actions and random events, we can neither predict when such events might occur or how they would be resolved. Despite the results of citizen movements in the fall of 1989, confrontations in Eastern Europe have led to repression more often than democracy. Leninist states have enormous resources for demobilizing society.[10] In sum, we can guess that there

10. Referring to Eastern Europe, Gyorgy Markus writes that "there are deep structural tendencies in these societies due to which a dichotomous opposition of interests is constantly reproduced between the corporate ruling group and the unorganized and amorphous grouping of direct producers, which is the source not only of incessant skirmishes between the two, but also of a possible open conflict. . . . There is no modern society where rebellious masses could so certainly count on such overwhelming support or at least sympathy from the whole population—with the exception of the members of the apparatus itself—as those of Eastern Europe. . . . But if these moments of sudden political collapse are seen as revealing the truth, the deep hidden structure of these societies, then the ease with which the whole apparatus of dominance is reconstituted after what seemed to be its complete disintegration, perhaps no less belongs to their essence." See Feher, Heller, and Markus, *Dictatorship Over Needs*, 127.

will be further confrontations, but the outcome is uncertain. However, we cannot dismiss the possibility that China's Leninist state, like so many Eastern European states, could experience a sudden and dramatic collapse.

Reform has meant significant change in China, and it is most likely that the current wave of repression will not wipe out all the gains of the previous decade. The Chinese people have escaped from the Cultural Revolution. The economy as a whole has made remarkable gains. There are more channels for communication, carrying a wider range of messages. In political, economic, and cultural spheres there is more room for individual autonomy. The state intervenes less often and less arbitrarily. These are enormously positive steps. While at present these gains are imperiled, there are strong pressures to resume the course of reform.

But this remains progress within limits. The Leninist state still holds a commanding position in the economy, and in a broader sense, politics still dominates economics. Patrimonial bureaucracy and the Four Cardinal Principles continue to limit organizational and individual efficiency and autonomy. The conflict between state and society has not been resolved, and China is enmeshed in the competitive world economy. China's leaders are unwilling to abandon their position of authority to make way for the brutal market forces that led to the rationalization of Western society, and they are unwilling to abandon the Four Cardinal Principles. Neither are Chinese leaders or citizens willing to accept a future of weakness and poverty. In sum, the contradiction between the autonomous efficiency of liberal markets and the Four Cardinal Principles is more than an artifact of liberal ideology: it is a real contradiction that will remain at the center of Chinese politics for some time to come.

Select Bibliography

Almond, Gabriel A. "Communism and Political Culture Theory." *Comparative Politics* 15, no. 2 (1983): 127–38.

Almond, Gabriel A., and Sidney Verba. *The Civic Culture*. Princeton: Princeton University Press, 1963.

Althusser, Louis. "Ideology and Ideological State Apparatuses." In *Lenin and Philosophy*, 127–86. New York: Monthly Review Press, 1971.

Amnesty International. "China: Torture and Ill-Treatment of Prisoners." London: Amnesty International Publications, 1987.

———. "China: Violations of Human Rights." London: Amnesty International Publications, 1984.

Anderson, Perry. "The Antinomies of Antonio Gramsci." *New Left Review* 100 (November 1976–January 1977): 5–77.

Andors, Steven. *China's Industrial Revolution*. New York: Pantheon, 1977.

Antonov-Ovseyenko, Anton. *The Time of Stalin: Portrait of a Tyranny*. New York: Harper & Row, 1983.

Arendt, Hannah. *On the Human Condition*. Chicago: University of Chicago Press, 1978.

———. *The Origins of Totalitarianism*. New York: World, 1971.

Bahro, Rudolf. *The Alternative in Eastern Europe*. London: New Left Books, 1978.

Bannister, Judith, and Samuel H. Preston. "Mortality in China." *Population and Development Review* 7, no. 1 (March 1981): 98–110.

Bao Ruo-Wang. *Prisoner of Mao*. New York: Penguin, 1976.

Barnet, Richard J. *Roots of War*. Baltimore: Penguin, 1972.

Barnett, A. Doak. *Communist China in the Early Years, 1945–55*. New York: Praeger, 1964.

Baum, Richard. "Modernization and Legal Reform in Post-Mao China: The

Rebirth of Socialist Legality." *Studies in Comparative Communism* 29, no. 2 (Summer 1986): 69–103.

Bennett, Gordon A., and Ronald Montaperto. *Red Guard.* New York: Anchor Books, 1972.

Bernstein, Thomas P. "Stalinism, Famine, and Chinese Peasants." *Theory and Society* 13 (1984): 339–77.

Besançon, Alain. *The Rise of the Gulag: Intellectual Origins of Leninism.* New York: Continuum, 1981.

Bettelheim, Charles. "The Great Leap Backward." In Neil G. Burton and Charles Bettelheim, *China Since Mao,* 37–130. New York: Monthly Review Press, 1978.

Billeter, Jean-François. "The System of 'Class Status.' " In *The Scope of State Power in China,* ed. Stuart Schram, 127–70. Hong Kong: Chinese University Press, 1985.

Blecher, Marc. "Peasant Labour for Urban Industry: Temporary Contract Labour, Urban-Rural Balance, and Class Relations in a Chinese County." *World Development* 8 (1983): 731–45.

Bloodworth, Dennis, and Chang Ping. *Heirs Apparent.* London: Secker and Warburg, 1973.

Bodde, Derk, and Clarence Morris. *Law in Imperial China.* Philadelphia: University of Pennsylvania Press, 1967.

Brady, James. *Justice and Politics in People's China.* New York: Academic Press, 1982.

Brown, Archie. "Political Power and the Soviet State." In *The State in Socialist Society,* ed. Neil Harding, 51–103. Albany: State University of New York Press.

Broyelle, Claudie and Jacques, and Evelyne Tschirhart. *China: A Second Look.* Atlantic Highlands, N.J.: Humanities Press, 1980.

Brugger, Bill. *China: Radicalism to Revisionism 1962–79.* Totowa, N.J.: Barnes and Noble, 1981.

Brus, Wlodzimierz. *Socialist Ownership and Political Systems.* Boston: Routledge and Kegan Paul, 1975.

Burke, Edmund. *Reflections on the Revolution in France.* Indianapolis: Bobbs-Merrill, 1955.

Burton, Barry. "The Cultural Revolution's Ultraleft Conspiracy: The 'May 16' Group." *Asian Survey* 11, no. 11 (November 1971): 1029–53.

Cao Zudan. "On the Relationship Between Crime and Class Struggle." *Zhengfa Yanjiu* 1 (1964). Translated in *Chinese Law and Government* 1, no. 3 (Fall 1968).

Cardoso, Fernando Enrique. "The Characterization of Authoritarian Regimes." In *The New Authoritarianism in Latin America,* ed. David Collier, 33–57. Princeton: Princeton University Press, 1979.

Carnoy, Martin. *The State and Political Theory.* Princeton: Princeton University Press, 1984.

"The CCP Central Committee's Instructions Concerning the Improvement of Political and Judicial Work." *Issues and Studies* 20, no. 4 (October 1984).

Chen, Theodore Hsi-en, and Wen-hui Chen. "The 'Three-Anti and Five-Anti' Movements in Communist China." *Pacific Affairs* 26, no. 1 (March 1953): 3–23.

Chen Chuchang, Qu Wanshan, and Xia Weiyang. *Questions and Answers on the Socialist Legal System* (Shehuizhuyi fazhi wenda). Xian: Shaanxi Renmin Chubanshe, 1979.

Chen Chunlong, et al. *Questions and Answers on Legal Knowledge* (Falu zhishi wenda). Beijing: Beijing Chubanshe, 1979.

Chen Erjian. *Crossroads Socialism*. London: Verso, 1984.

Chen Liang. "Freedom of Speech and Law that Guarantees Freedom of Speech" (Yanlun ziyou yu baozhang yanlun ziyou de falu). *Minzhu yu Fazhi* (Democracy and legal system) 4 (1979).

Chen, Philip. *Law and Justice: The Legal System in China 2400 B.C. to 1960 A.D.* New York: Dunellen, 1973.

Chen Ruoxi. *Democracy Wall and the Unofficial Journals*. Berkeley: Center for Chinese Studies, 1982.

——— (Chen Jo-hsi). *The Execution of Mayor Yin*. Bloomington: Indiana University Press, 1978.

Chi Hsin. *The Case of the Gang of Four*. Hong Kong: Cosmos Books, 1978.

———. *Teng Hsiao-Ping*. Hong Kong: Cosmos Books, 1978.

Chien Yu-shen. *China's Fading Revolution*. Hong Kong: Centre for Contemporary Chinese Studies, 1969.

Chiu Hungdah. *Socialist Legalism: Reform and Continuity in Post-Mao People's Republic of China*. Occasional Papers/Reprint Series in Contemporary Asian Studies. Baltimore: School of Law, University of Maryland, 1982.

Cleaves, Peter S. "Implementation Amidst Scarcity and Apathy." In *Politics and Policy*, ed. Merilee S. Grindle, 281–303. Princeton: Princeton University Press, 1980.

Coale, Ansley J. "Population Trends, Population Policy, and Population Studies in China." *Population and Development Review* 7, no. 1 (March 1981): 85–97.

Cohen, Jerome A. *The Criminal Process in the People's Republic of China 1949–1963*. Cambridge: Harvard University Press, 1963.

Connor, Walter. *Socialism, Politics, and Equality*. New York: Columbia University Press, 1979.

Conquest, Robert. *The Harvest of Sorrow: Soviet Collectivization and the Terror-Famine*. New York: Oxford University Press, 1986.

"Constitution of the Communist Party of China." *Beijing Review* 25, no. 38 (20 Sept. 1982).

Dahl, Robert. *Pluralist Democracy in the United States*. Chicago: Rand McNally, 1967.

Daubier, Jean. *A History of the Chinese Cultural Revolution*. New York: Vintage Books, 1974.

Deng Xiaoping. "Uphold the Four Cardinal Principles." In *Selected Works of Deng Xiaoping*, 166–91. Beijing: Foreign Languages Press, 1984.

Di Franceisco, Wayne, and Zvi Gitelman. "Soviet Political Culture and 'Covert Participation' in Policy Implementation." *American Political Science Review* 78, no. 3 (September 1984): 603–21.

Djilas, Milovan. *The New Class.* New York: Praeger, 1946.

Dunayevskaya, Raya. *Marxism and Freedom.* Atlantic Highlands, N.J.: Humanities Press, 1982.

Eastman, Lloyd. *The Abortive Revolution: China Under Nationalist Rule, 1927–37.* Cambridge: Harvard University Press, 1974.

Eisenstadt S. N., and Louis Roniger. "Patron-Client Relations as a Model of Structuring Social Exchange." *Comparative Study of Society and History* 22, no. 1 (1980): 42–77.

——— . *Patrons, Clients, and Friends: Interpersonal Relations and the Structure of Trust in Society.* Cambridge: Cambridge University Press, 1984.

Esmein, Jean. *The Chinese Cultural Revolution.* Garden City, N.Y.: Anchor Press, 1973.

Falkenheim, Victor C. "Citizen and Group Politics in China: An Introduction." In *Citizens and Groups in Contemporary China,* ed. Victor C. Falkenheim, 1–16. Ann Arbor: Center for Chinese Studies, 1987.

——— . "Political Participation in China." *Problems of Communism* 27 (May–June 1978): 18–32.

Feher, Ferenc, Agnes Heller, and Gyorgy Markus. *Dictatorship Over Needs.* New York: St. Martin's, 1983.

Ferdinand, Peter. "Interest Groups and Chinese Politics." In *Groups and Politics in the People's Republic of China,* ed. David S. G. Goodman, 10–25. New York: M. E. Sharpe, 1984.

Forster, Keith. "The 1976 Ch'ing-ming Incident in Hangchow." *Issues and Studies* 4 (1986): 13–33.

Fraser, John. *The Chinese: Portrait of a People.* New York: Summit Books, 1980.

Friedman, Edward. "The Innovator." In *Mao Tse-tung in the Scales of History,* ed. Dick Wilson. New York: Cambridge University Press, 1977.

——— . "Three Leninist Paths Within a Socialist Conundrum." In *Three Visions of Chinese Socialism,* ed. D. J. Solinger, 11–45. Boulder: Westview, 1984.

Gao Xiaosheng. "Li Shunda Builds a House." In *New Realism,* ed. Lee Yee, 31–55. New York: Hippocrene Books, 1983.

Gelatt, Timothy A. "The People's Republic of China and the Presumption of Innocence." *Journal of Criminal Law and Criminology* 73, no. 1 (1982): 259–316.

Gilison, Jerome M. "Soviet Elections As a Measure of Dissent: The Missing One Percent." *American Political Science Review* 62 (September 1968): 814–26.

Ginneken, Jaap Van. *Lin Piao.* New York: Avon, 1972.

Gold, Thomas B. " 'Just In Time': China Battles Spiritual Pollution on the Eve of 1984." *Asian Survey* 24, no. 9 (September 1984): 947–74.

Gouldner, Alvin W. "Stalinism: A Study of Internal Colonialism." *Telos* 33 (Fall 1977): 5–48.

────. *The Two Marxisms*. New York: Oxford University Press, 1988.

Gramsci, Antonio. *Prison Notebooks*. Translated and edited by Quintin Hoare and Geoffrey Nowell Smith. New York: International Publishers, 1971.

Grindle, Merilee. "Policy Content and Context in Implementation." In *Politics and Policy Implementation in the Third World,* ed. Merilee Grindle, 3–34. Princeton: Princeton University Press, 1980.

Grossman, Gregory. "The Solidary Society." In *Socialism and Planning in Honour of Carl Landauer,* ed. G. Grossman, 184–211. Englewood Cliffs, N.J.: Prentice-Hall, 1970.

Gu Hua. *Hibiscus*. Beijing: Panda Books, 1983.

Hamilton, Nora. *The Limits of State Autonomy: Post-Revolutionary Mexico*. Princeton: Princeton University Press, 1982.

Harding, Harry. *China's Second Revolution*. Washington, D.C.: Brookings, 1987.

────. *Organizing China: The Problem of Bureaucracy*. Stanford: Stanford University Press, 1981.

────. "Political Development in Post-Mao China." In *Modernizing China: Post-Mao Reform and Development,* ed. A. Doak Barnett and Ralph N. Clough, 13–37. Boulder: Westview, 1986.

Harper, Paul. "Trade Union Cultivation of Workers." In *The City in Communist China,* ed. J. W. Lewis, 23–52. Stanford: Stanford University Press, 1971.

Harsanyi, J. C. "Rational-Choice Models of Political Behavior vs. Functionalist and Conformist Theories." *World Politics* 21, no. 1 (July 1969): 513–38.

Hartz, Louis. *The Liberal Tradition in America*. New York: Harcourt, Brace and World, 1955.

Hinton, William. *Shenfan*. New York: Vintage Books, 1983.

Hirszowicz, Maria. *The Bureaucratic Leviathan*. Oxford: Martin Robertson, 1980.

────. *Coercion and Control in Communist Society: The Visible Hand in a Command Economy*. New York: St. Martin's, 1986.

Hodges, Donald. *The Bureaucratization of Socialism*. Amherst: University of Massachusetts Press, 1981.

Hough, Jerry, and Merle Fainsod. *How the Soviet Union Is Governed*. Cambridge: Harvard University Press, 1979.

Hsia Tao-tai. "Legal Developments in the PRC since the Purge of the Gang of Four." *Review of Socialist Law* 2 (1979): 109–30.

Hu Ping. "On Freedom of Speech." *SPEAHRhead* 12 and 13 (Winter and Spring 1982): 35–57.

Hu Qiaomu. "Observe Economic Laws, Speed Up the Four Modernizations." *Beijing Review* 45 (10 Nov. 1978): 7–12.

Hu Yaobang. "Create a New Situation in All Fields of Socialist Modernization." *Beijing Review* 25, no. 37 (13 Sept. 1982).

Huang Huoqing. "Report on the Work of the Supreme People's Procuratorate." In *Main Documents of the Third Session of the Fifth National*

People's Congress of the People's Republic of China. Beijing: Foreign Languages Press, 1980.

Hunter, Neale. *Shanghai Journal.* Boston: Beacon, 1969.

Huntington, Samuel P. *Political Order in Changing Societies.* New Haven: Yale University Press, 1968.

Ionescu, Ghita. "Patronage Under Communism." In *Patrons and Clients in Mediterranean Societies,* ed. Ernest Gellner and John Waterbury. London: Gerald Duckworth, 1977.

Jackson, Robert, and Carl G. Rosberg. "Personal Rule: Theory and Practice in Africa." In *Comparative Politics* 16, no. 4 (July 1984): 421–42.

Jacobs, Everett M. "Norms of Representation and the Composition of Local Soviets." In *Soviet Local Politics and Government,* ed. Everett M. Jacobs, 78–94. Boston: George, Allen and Unwin, 1985.

Janos, Andrew. "Group Politics in Communist Society." In *Authoritarian Politics in Modern Society,* ed. Samuel Huntington and Clement Moore, 437–50. New York: Basic Books, 1970.

Jessop, Bob. *The Capitalist State.* New York: New York University Press, 1982.

Jiang Zilong. *All the Colors of the Rainbow.* Translated by Wang Mingjie. Beijing: Chinese Literature, 1983.

Johnson, Chalmers. *MITI and the Japanese Economic Miracle.* Stanford: Stanford University Press, 1982.

———. "What's Wrong With Chinese Political Studies?" *Asian Survey* 22, no. 10 (October 1982): 919–33.

Jowitt, Kenneth. *The Leninist Response to National Dependency.* Berkeley: University of California Institute of International Studies, 1978.

———. "An Organizational Approach to the Study of Political Culture in Marxist-Leninist Systems." *American Political Science Review* 68, no. 3 (September 1974): 1171–88.

———. "Soviet Neo-Traditionalism: The Political Corruption of a Leninist Regime." *Soviet Studies* 35, no. 3 (July 1983): 275–97.

Kalgren, Joyce. "Social Welfare and China's Industrial Workers." In *Chinese Communist Politics in Action,* ed. A. Doak Barnett, 540–73. Seattle: University of Washington Press, 1969.

Kau, Michael Y. M. *The Lin Piao Affair.* White Plains, N.Y.: International Arts and Sciences Press, 1975.

Ke Pu and Chen Yi-ko. "Origin and Development of Unrest at Nanjing University." *Bai Hsing* 79 (1 Sept. 1984). Translated as "Hong Kong Journal on Unrest at Nanjing University." FBIS-CHI-084-175 (7 Sept. 1984): W3–6.

Kenedi, Janos. *Do It Yourself.* London: Pluto Press, 1981.

Kiernan, Ben. *How Pol Pot Came to Power.* London: Verso, 1985.

Kilker, Ernest. "Max Weber and the Possibilities for Socialism." In *Bureaucracy Against Democracy and Socialism,* ed. Ronald M. Glassman, William Swatos, Jr., and Paul L. Rosen. New York: Greenwood, 1987.

Kolakowski, Leszek. *Main Currents of Marxism.* Vols. 1–3. Oxford: Clarendon Press, 1978.

Konrad, George, and Ivan Szelenyi. *The Intellectuals on the Road to Class Power.* Brighton, Sussex: Harvester Press, 1979.

Krasner, Stephen D. *Defending the National Interest.* Princeton: Princeton University Press, 1978.

Kuron, Jacek, and Karol Modzelewski. *Open Letter to Party Members.* New York: Merit, 1968.

Lampton, David. "Xu Shi-You: A Soldier's Soldier." In David Lampton, "Paths to Power: Elite Mobility in Contemporary China," 203–46. *Michigan Monographs in Chinese Studies 55.* Ann Arbor: Center for Chinese Studies, 1986.

Lan Ling. "Getting to the Bottom of 'What One Person Says Goes' " (Yi yan tang zhuigen). *San Wen* 11 (1980); also *Xinhua Yuebao* 2 (1981): 141.

Lande, Carl H. "Networks and Groups in Southeast Asia." In *Friends, Followers, and Factions,* ed. Steffen Schmidt et al., 75–99. Berkeley and Los Angeles: University of California Press, 1977.

Lardy, Nicholas R. *Agriculture in China's Modern Economic Development.* New York: Cambridge University Press, 1983.

Lee, Hong Yung. "The Implications of Reform for Ideology, State, and Society in China." *Journal of International Affairs* 39, no. 2 (Winter 1986): 77–90.

Leff, Nathaniel H. "Economic Development Through Bureaucratic Corruption." In *Political Corruption,* ed. Arnold J. Heidenheimer, 510–20. New York: Holt, Rinehart, and Winston, 1970.

Legal Studies Dictionary (Faxue cidian). Edited by Legal Studies Dictionary Editing Committee. Shanghai: Shanghai Dictionary Press, 1979.

Leng Shao-Chuan, and Hungdah Chiu. *Criminal Justice in Post-Mao China.* Albany: State University of New York Press, 1985.

Lenin, V. I. *State and Revolution.* New York: International Publishers, 1969.

Leys, Colin. "African Economic Development in Theory and Practice." *Daedalus* 111, no. 2 (Spring 1982): 99–124.

Li Genhe, and Lin Qun. "A Preliminary Study of the Struggle Against Feudal Remnants During the Period of Socialist Construction in Our Country" (Shi lun wo guo jianshe shehuizhuyi de shiqi fan fengjian canyu de douzheng). *Lishi Yanjiu* 9 (1979); also *Xinhua Yuebao* 11 (1979): 74–79.

Li Honglin. *Socialism and Freedom* (Shehuizhuyi yu ziyou). Shanghai: Shanghai Renmin Chubanshe, 1980.

Li Kan. "The Nature of the Feudal Diehard Faction and the Characteristics of Its Thought" (Fengjian wangu pai de xingqing jiqi sixing tezheng). *Lishi Yanjiu* 11 (1978); also *Xinhua Yuebao* 1 (1979).

Li Shu. "Destroying the Influence of Feudal Remnants Is an Important Requirement for China's Modernization" (Xiaomie fengjian canyu yingxiang shi zhongguo xiandaihua de zhuyao tiaojian). *Lishi Yanjiu* 1 (1979); also *Xinhua Yuebao* 2 (1979): 54–65.

Li, Victor H. "The Evolution and Development of the Chinese Legal System." In *China: Management of a Revolutionary Society,* ed. John M. Lindbeck, 221–55. Seattle: University of Washington Press, 1971.

———. *Law Without Lawyers: A Comparative View of Law in China and the United States.* Boulder: Westview, 1978.

Lieberthal, Kenneth G. *Revolution and Tradition in Tientsin.* Stanford: Stanford University Press, 1980.

Linz, Juan. "Non-Competitive Elections in Europe." In *Elections Without Choice,* ed. Guy Hermet, Richard Rose, and Alain Rouquie. New York: Wiley, 1978.

Liu, Alan P. *Political Culture and Group Conflict in China.* Santa Barbara: Clio Books, 1976.

Liu Binyan. *Because I Love* (Yinwei wo ai). Beijing: Gongren Chubanshe, 1984.

———. "Let Me Tell You Some Secret." *Baogao Wenxue* (Reportage Literature) 6 (June 1984). Translated in JPRS-CPS-84-064 (1 Oct. 1985): 31–54.

———. "People or Monsters." In *People or Monsters,* ed. Perry Link. Bloomington: University of Indiana Press, 1984.

———. "A Second Kind of Loyalty" (Di er zhong zhongcheng). *China Spring* 34 (April 1986): 43–56.

Liu Binyan and Li Guosheng. "An Invisible Machine—A Negative Example of Perfunctorily Carrying Out Party Rectification." *Renmin Ribao* (8 Feb. 1984). Translated and reprinted in *Policy Conflicts in Post-Mao China,* ed. John P. Burns and Stanley Rosen. Amronk, N.Y.: M. E. Sharpe, 1986.

Liu Xinwu. "Awake, My Brother." In *The Wounded,* 179–204. Hong Kong: Joint Publications, 1979.

———. "The Overpass." In *Mao's Harvest,* ed. Helen Siu and Zelda Stern, 29–89. New York: Oxford University Press, 1983.

Liu Zhuanchen, Pan Bowen, and Cheng Jiyou. *Questions and Answers on Election Law Knowledge* (Xuanju fa zhishi wenda). Shanghai: Shanghai Social Sciences Institute, undated.

Louie, Gennie, and Kam Louie. "Role of Nanjing University in the Nanjing Incident." *China Quarterly* 86 (June 1981): 332–48.

Lowenthal, Richard. "Development vs. Utopia in Communist Policy." In *Change in Communist Systems,* ed. C. Johnson, 33–116. Stanford: Stanford University Press, 1970.

———. "The Postrevolutionary Phase in China and the Soviet Union." In *Perspectives on Development in Mainland China,* ed. K. Y. Chang, 1–15. Boulder: Westview, 1985.

Lu Min. "Democracy or Bureaucracy." *Beijing Spring* (Beijing Zhi Qun) 1 and 2 (January 1979).

Lubman, Stanley. "Mao and Mediation: Politics and Dispute Resolution in Communist China." *California Law Review* 55, no. 5 (November 1967): 1284–359

McAuley, Mary. *Politics and the Soviet Union.* New York: Penguin, 1977.

MacFarquhar, Roderick. *The Origins of the Cultural Revolution.* Vol. 2, *The Great Leap Forward 1958–60.* New York: Columbia University Press, 1983.

Markov, Georgi. *The Truth That Killed*. New York: Ticknor and Fields, 1984.

Marx, Karl. "The Civil War in France." In *Karl Marx on Revolution,* ed. Saul K. Padover. New York: McGraw-Hill, 1971.

———. "Eighteenth Brumaire of Louis Napoleon." In *Karl Marx on Revolution,* ed. Saul K. Padover, 243–328. New York: McGraw-Hill, 1971.

Mathews, Mervyn. *Privilege in the Soviet Union*. London: Allen and Unwin, 1978.

Medvedev, Roy A. *Let History Judge*. New York: Knopf, 1971.

Meisner, Maurice. *Mao's China*. New York: Free Press, 1977.

Meyer, Alfred. "Communist Revolutions and Cultural Change." *Studies in Comparative Communism 5,* no. 4 (Winter 1972).

Miliband, Ralph. "The Capitalist State: Reply to Nicos Poulantzas." *New Left Review 59* (January–February 1970): 53–60.

Milton, David, and Nancy Milton. *The Wind Will Not Subside*. New York: Pantheon, 1976.

Myrdal, Gunnar. *Asian Drama: An Inquiry Into the Poverty of Nations*. New York: Twentieth Century Fund, 1968.

Nathan, Andrew J. *Chinese Democracy: An Investigation into the Nature and Meaning of "Democracy" in China Today*. New York: Knopf, 1985.

———. "A Factional Model for CCP Politics." *China Quarterly 53* (January–March 1973): 34–66.

Naughton, Barry. "False Starts and the Second Wind: Financial Reforms in China's Industrial System." In *The Political Economy of Reform in Post-Mao China,* ed. Elizabeth Perry and Christine Wong, 223–52. Cambridge: Harvard University Press, 1985.

Nee, Victor. "Between Center and Locality: State, Militia, and Village." In *State and Society in Contemporary China,* ed. Victor Nee and David Mozingo, 223–43. Ithaca: Cornell University Press, 1983.

———. "Revolution and Bureaucracy: Shanghai in the Cultural Revolution." In *China's Uninterrupted Revolution,* ed. Victor Nee and James Peck, 322–414. New York: Pantheon, 1975.

Nelson, Harvey W. *The Chinese Military System*. Boulder: Westview, 1977.

———. "Military Forces in the Cultural Revolution." *China Quarterly 51* (July–September 1972).

Nordlinger, Eric. *On the Autonomy of the Democratic State*. Cambridge: Harvard University Press, 1981.

Nove, Alec. *The Soviet Economic System*. London: Allen and Unwin, 1977.

Oakeshott, Michael. "Rationalism in Politics." In Michael Oakeshott, *Rationalism in Politics,* 1–36. London: Methuen, 1962.

O'Donnell, Guillermo. "Corporatism and the Question of the State." In *Authoritarianism and Corporatism in Latin America,* ed. James Malloy, 47–88. Pittsburgh: University of Pittsburgh Press, 1977.

———. "Tensions in the Bureaucratic Authoritarian State." In *The New Authoritarianism in Latin America,* ed. David Collier, 285–318. Princeton: Princeton University Press, 1979.

O'Hearn, Dennis. "The Second Economy in Consumer Goods and Services." *Critique* (Glasgow) 15 (1981): 98–109.

Oi, Jean. "Commercializing China's Rural Cadres." *Problems of Communism* 35, no. 5 (September–October 1986): 1–15.

———. "Communism and Clientelism: Rural Politics in China." *World Politics* 37, no. 2 (January 1985): 238–66.

———. "Peasant Households Between Plan and Market." *Modern China* 2 (April 1986): 230–51.

Oksenberg, Michel, and Richard Bush. "China's Political Evolution: 1972–82." *Problems of Communism* (September–October 1982): 1–19.

"Ordeal of a Deputy's Motion." *Renmin Ribao* (7 May 1981). Translated in *Chinese Law and Government* 15, nos. 3 and 4 (Fall and Winter 1982–83).

Pakulski, Jan. "Bureaucracy and the Soviet System." *Studies in Comparative Communism* 14, no. 1 (Spring 1980): 3–24.

Paltiel, Jeremy T. "The Cult of Personality: Some Comparative Reflections on Political Culture in Leninist Regimes." *Studies in Comparative Communism* 16, nos. 1 and 2 (Spring and Summer 1983): 49–64.

Peng Zhen. "Explanation of the Seven Draft Laws." In *Main Documents of the Second Session of the Fifth National People's Congress of the People's Republic of China*. Beijing: Foreign Languages Press, 1979.

"People's Republic of China Electoral Law for the National People's Congress and Local People's Congresses at All Levels, Article 28." In *Chinese Law and Government* 15, nos. 3 and 4 (Fall and Winter 1982–83).

Polan, A. J. *Lenin and the End of Politics*. Berkeley and Los Angeles: University of California Press, 1984.

Polanyi, Karl. *The Great Transformation*. Boston: Beacon, 1944.

Potter, Pitman B. "Peng Zhen: Evolving Views on Party Organization and Law." In *China's Establishment Intellectuals*, ed. Carol Lee Hamrin and Timothy Cheek, 21–50. Armonk, N.Y.: M. E. Sharpe, 1986.

Poulantzas, Nicos. *Political Power and Social Classes*. London: New Left Books, 1974.

Pye, Lucian. *The Dynamics of Chinese Politics*. Cambridge: Oelgeschlager, Gunn, and Hain, 1981.

———. "On Chinese Pragmatism in the 1980's." *China Quarterly* 86 (June 1986): 207–34.

Pye, Lucian, and Nathan Leites. "Nuances in Chinese Political Culture." *Asian Survey* 22, no. 12 (December 1982): 1147–65.

Racz, Barnabas. "Political Participation and Developed Socialism: The Hungarian Elections of 1985." *Soviet Studies* 39, no. 1 (January 1987): 40–62.

Remmer, Karen L. "Redemocratization and the Impact of Authoritarian Rule in Latin America." *Comparative Politics* 17, no. 3 (April 1985): 253–75.

Rice, Edward. *Mao's Way*. Berkeley and Los Angeles: University of California Press, 1972.

Richman, Barry. *Industrial Society in Communist China*. New York: Random House, 1969.

Rosen, Stanley. "Guangzhou's Democracy Movement in Cultural Revolution Perspective." *China Quarterly* 101 (March 1985): 1–31.

Roth, Guenther. "Personal Rulership, Patrimonialism, and Empire Building." In R. Bendix and G. Roth, *Scholarship and Partisanship*, 156–69. Berkeley and Los Angeles: University of California Press, 1971.

Saich, Tony. "Party Building since Mao—A Question of Style?" *World Development* 11, no. 8 (1983): 747–65.

Schmitter, Philippe C. "Still the Century of Corporatism?" In *Trends Toward Corporatist Intermediation*, ed. Philippe C. Schmitter and Gerhard Lehmbruch, 7–51. Beverly Hills: Sage Press, 1979.

Schram, Stuart, ed. *Chairman Mao Talks to the People*. New York: Pantheon, 1974.

———. *The Political Thought of Mao Tse-Tung*. New York: Praeger, 1963.

Schurmann, Franz. *Ideology and Organization in Communist China*. Berkeley and Los Angeles: University of California Press, 1968.

———. *The Logic of World Power*. New York: Pantheon, 1974.

Schwartz, Benjamin. *Communism and China*. Cambridge: Harvard University Press, 1968.

———. "On Attitudes Toward Law in China." In *Government Under Law and the Individual*, ed. Milton Katz. Washington, D.C., 1957.

———. "The Reign of Virtue: Some Broad Perspectives on Leader and Party in the Cultural Revolution." In *Party Leadership and Revolutionary Power in China*, ed. J. W. Lewis, 149–69. London: Cambridge University Press, 1970.

Scott, James C. *Comparative Political Corruption*. Englewood Cliffs, N.J.: Prentice-Hall, 1972.

———. *The Moral Economy of the Peasant: Rebellion and Subsistence in Southeast Asia*. New Haven: Yale University Press, 1976.

Selden, Mark. "Cooperation and Conflict: Cooperative and Collective Formation in China's Countryside." In *The Transition to Socialism in China*, ed. Mark Selden and Victor Lippit, 32–97. Armonk, N.Y.: M. E. Sharpe, 1982.

———. *The Yenan Way in Revolutionary China*. Cambridge: Harvard University Press, 1971.

Seymour, James D. *The Fifth Modernization: China's Human Rights Movement, 1978–1979*. Stanfordville, N.Y.: Human Rights Publishing Group, 1980.

Sha Yexin, Li Shoucheng, and Yao Mingde. "If I Were For Real." In *New Realism*, ed. Lee Yee, 261–322. New York: Hippocrene Books, 1983.

Shen Rong. "Snakes and Ladders." In Shen Rong, *At Middle Age*, 119–236. Beijing: Panda Books, 1987.

Shue, Vivienne. "The Fate of the Commune." *Modern China* 10, no. 3 (July 1984): 259–83.

Simis, Konstantin. *USSR: The Corrupt Society*. New York: Simon and Schuster, 1982.

Skocpol, Theda. "Social Revolutions and Mass Military Mobilization." *World Politics* 2 (1988): 147–68.

―――. *States and Social Revolution*. New York: Cambridge University Press, 1979.

Smolar, Andrew. "The Rich and the Powerful." In *Poland: Genesis of a Revolution*, ed. Abraham Brumberg. New York: Vintage Books, 1983.

Starski, Stanislaw. *Class Struggle in Classless Poland*. Boston: Southend Press, 1982.

Stepan, Alfred. *The State and Society: Peru in Comparative Perspective*. Princeton: Princeton University Press, 1979.

Stojanovic, Svetozar. *In Search of Democracy in Socialism*. Buffalo: Prometheus, 1981.

Szelenyi, Ivan. "The Prospects and Limits of the East European New Class Project: An Auto-critical Reflection on the Intellectuals on the Road to Class Power." *Politics and Society* 15, no. 2 (1986–87): 103–44.

Talmon, J. L. *The Origins of Totalitarian Democracy*. London: Secker and Warburg, 1952.

Tang Jianzhong, and Li Liangyu. "Unforgettable March 29" (Nan wang de san-er jiu). *Nanjing Daxue Xuebao* 1 (1979).

Teiwes, Frederick C. *Politics and Purges in China*. Armonk, N.Y.: M. E. Sharpe, 1979.

Tilman, Robert O. "Emergence of Black-Market Bureaucracy: Administration, Development, and Corruption in the New States." *Public Administration Review* 28 (1968): 437–44.

Tong Chao. "Criticizing the System of Powerful Families and Feudal Special Privileges" (Ping menfa zhidu yu fengjian tequan). *Guangming Ribao* (26 Sept. 1979); also *Xinhua Yuebao* 11 (1979): 82–84.

Townsend, James R. *Political Participation in Communist China*. Berkeley and Los Angeles: University of California Press, 1968.

Trimberger, Ellen Kay. *Revolution from Above*. New Brunswick: Transaction Books, 1978.

Tsou, Tang. "Back from the Brink of Revolutionary-'Feudal' Totalitarianism." In *State and Society in Contemporary China*, ed. Victor Nee and David Mozingo, 53–88. Ithaca: Cornell University Press, 1983.

―――. "Mao Tse-tung Thought: The Last Struggle for Succession and the Post-Mao Era." *China Quarterly* 71 (September 1977).

Urban, George, ed. *The "Miracles" of Chairman Mao*. Los Angeles: Nash Publishers, 1971.

Urban, Michael E. "Conceptualizing Political Power in the USSR: Patterns of Binding and Bonding." *Studies in Comparative Communism* 18, no. 4 (Winter 1985): 207–26.

Vajda, Mihaly. *The State and Socialism*. London: Allison and Busby, 1981.

Vogel, Ezra. *Canton Under Communism: Programs and Politics in a Provincial Capital, 1949–1968*. Cambridge: Harvard University Press, 1980.

―――. "Preserving Order in the Cities." In *The City in Communist China*, ed. John Wilson Lewis, 75–93. Stanford: Stanford University Press, 1971.

von Senger, Harro. "Recent Developments in the Relations Between State and Party Norms in the People's Republic of China." In *The Scope of State Power in China*, ed. Stuart Schram, 171–207. Hong Kong: Chinese University Press, 1985.

Voslensky, Michael. *Nomenklatura: The Soviet Ruling Class*. Garden City: Doubleday, 1983.

Walder, Andrew. *Chang Ch'un-Chiao and Shanghai's January Revolution*. Ann Arbor: Center for Chinese Studies, 1978.

———. *Communist Neo-Traditionalism: Work and Authority in Chinese Industry*. Berkeley and Los Angeles: University of California Press, 1986.

———. "Dependence and Authority in Chinese Industry." *Journal of Asian Studies* 43, no. 1 (November 1983): 51–76.

Wang Meng. "The Barber's Tale." In Wang Meng, *The Butterfly and Other Stories*, 113–37. Beijing: Panda Books, 1983.

Wang Shiwei. "Wild Lily." *New Left Review* 92 (July–August 1975): 96–102.

Wang Ting. *Chairman Hua*. London: C. Hurst and Co., 1980.

Wang Xizhe. *Mao Zedong and the Cultural Revolution*. Hong Kong: Plough Publications, 1981.

Wang Yaping. "Sacred Duty." In *Prize-Winning Stories from China, 1978–79*, 27–57. Beijing: Foreign Languages Press, 1981.

Wang Zhizhong. "Feudal Obscurantism and the Yihetuan Movement" (Fengjian mengmeizhuyi yu yihetuan yundong). *Lishi Yanjiu* 1 (1980); also *Xinhua Yuebao* 5 (1980): 54–61.

Weber, Max. *Economy and Society*. Edited by Gunther Roth and Claus Wittich. Berkeley and Los Angeles: University of California Press, 1971.

———. *The Protestant Ethic and the Spirit of Capitalism*. Translated by Talcott Parsons. New York: Charles Scribner's Sons, 1958.

Wei Jingsheng. "The Fifth Modernization." In *The Fifth Modernization*, ed. James Seymour. Stanfordville, N.Y.: Human Rights Publishing Group, 1980.

Wei Keming. "The Evil Legacy of the Patriarchal System Cannot Be Neglected" (Jiazhang zhi yidu bu rong hushi). *Wen Hui Bao* (12 Aug. 1980); also *Xinhua Yuebao* 10 (1980): 4–5.

Wertheim, W. F. "Sociological Aspects of Corruption in Southeast Asia." In *State and Society*, ed. Reinhard Bendix, 561–81. Boston: Little, Brown, 1968.

White, Lynn T., III. "Leadership in Shanghai, 1955–69." In *Elites in the PRC*, ed. Robert Scalapino. Seattle: University of Washington Press, 1972.

———. "Workers' Politics in Shanghai." *Journal of Asian Studies* 1 (1976): 98–116.

White, Stephen. "Soviet Political Culture Reassessed." In *Political Culture and Communist Studies*, ed. Archie Brown, 62–99. London: Macmillan, 1984.

Wiarda, Howard J. "Law and Political Development in Latin America." In *Politics and Social Change in Latin America*, ed. Howard J. Wiarda, 199–229. Amherst: University of Massachusetts Press, 1974.

————. "Social Change and Political Development in Latin America." In *Politics and Social Change in Latin America,* ed. Howard J. Wiarda, 269–92. Amherst: University of Massachusetts Press, 1974.

Womack, Brantly. "Modernization and Democratic Reform in China." *Journal of Asian Studies* 43, no. 3 (May 1984): 417–39.

————. "The 1980 County-Level Elections in China: Experiment in Democratic Modernization." *Asian Survey* 22, no. 3 (March 1982): 261–77.

Wright, Erik Olin. "To Control or to Smash Bureaucracy: Weber and Lenin on Politics, the State, and Bureaucracy." *Berkeley Journal of Sociology* 19 (1974–75): 69–108.

Wu Min. "Bureaucratism and the Appointment System" (Guanliaozhuyi yu weirenzhi). *Shanxi Ribao* 14 (November 1980); also *Xinhua Wenzhai* 1 (1980).

Xu Chongde and Pi Chunxie. *Questions and Answers on the Election System* (Xuanju zhidu wenda). Beijing: Qunzhong Publishing Co., 1980.

Xu Sheng. "Are Peasant Wars the Only Direct Impetus of Development in Feudal Society?" (Zhi you nongmin zhanzheng cai shi fengjian shehui fazhan de dongli ma?). *Xinhua Yuebao* 5 (1979): 68–69.

Xue Mudao. "The Systems of Stratification and Special Privileges of Feudal Society" (Fengjian shehui de dengji tequan zhidu). *Guangming Ribao* (7 Oct. 1980); also *Xinhua Yuebao* 7 (1980): 68–69.

Ye Linsheng."On Special Privileges and the Growth of Family Power in Feudal Bureaucracy" (Lun tequan yu fengjian guanliao de menfa hua). *Shehui Kexue* 1 (1980); also *Xinhua Yuebao* 7 (1980): 82–85.

You Chunmei. "Current Administrative Reform in China." *International Review of Administrative Sciences* 52 (1986): 123–44.

Yu Youzhi. "The Evolution of Contract Law in China: Comparisons with the West and the Soviet Union." *Studies in Comparative Communism* (Autumn and Winter 1986): 193–212.

Yuan Shi. "The Ideology of Special Privileges Is the Ideology of Decadent Exploiting Classes" (Tequan sixiang shi fuxiu de boxue jieji sixiang). *Beijing Ribao* (19 June 1979); also *Xinhua Yuebao* 8 (1979): 26–28.

Zafanolli, Wojtek. "China's Second Economy: Second Nature?" *Revue d'Etudes Est-Ouest* 14, no. 3 (September 1983): 103–51.

Zaslavsky, Victor, and Robert J. Brym. "The Structure of Power and the Functions of Soviet Local Elections." In *Soviet Local Politics and Government,* ed. Everett M. Jacobs, 69–77. Boston: George Allen and Unwin, 1985.

Zhang Chunqiao. "On Exercising All-Round Dictatorship Over the Bourgeoisie." Translated in *And Mao Makes Five,* ed. Raymond Lotta, 209–20. Chicago: Banner Press, 1978.

Zhang Pufan. "Patriarchal Leadership Style Is a Pernicious Vestige of Feudalism" (Jiazhang shi de lingdao zuofeng shi fengjian yidu). *Beijing Ribao* (31 Aug. 1979); also *Xinhua Yuebao* 1 (1979): 7.

Zhang Shapo, Zhang Pufan, and Zeng Xuanyi. " 'The Big Official's Will' Cannot Replace Law" (Chang guan yizhi bu neng daiti falu). *Beijing Ribao* (9 Nov. 1979); also *Xinhua Yuebao* 1 (1979): 7.

Zheng Changgan. "Feudal Society's Patriarchal Clan System" (Fengjian she-
    hui de zongfa zhidu). *Hongqi* 20 (1980); also *Xinhua Yuebao* 12 (1980):
    70–71.
Zhou Jizhi. "The Basic Characteristics of the Development of Chinese Feudal
    Society" (Zhongguo fengjian shehui fazhan de jiben tezheng). *Anhui
    Daxue Xuebao* 1 (1980); also *Xinhua Yuebao* 9 (1980): 9–11.
Zhou Xinqiang. "Female Relatives of the Emperor in the Feudal Era and
    Their Disaster" (Fengjian shidai de waiqi jiqi huohai). *Renmin Ribao*
    (1 Sept. 1980); also *Xinhua Yuebao* 10 (1980): 54–55.
Zhou Zheng. "China's System of Community Mediation." *Beijing Review* 47
    (1981): 23–28.
Zhu Yuchao. "Opinion Polls and Democratization." *China Reconstructs* 4
    (1988).
Zweig, David, Kathy Hartford, James Feinerman, and Deng Jianxu. "Law,
    Contracts, and Economic Modernization: Lessons from Recent Chinese
    Rural Reforms." *Stanford Journal of International Law* 23, no. 1 (Spring
    1987): 319–64.

Index

Administrative detention, 120–21, esp. 120n.93
Arendt, Hannah, 12n.30, 30
Autonomy of state, ix, 6–7, 8, 9, 22, 56, 158, 187–90; impact of Cultural Revolution on, 35–36

Bahro, Rudolf, 12
Baixia district, 138–44
Barnett, A. Doak, 74–75
Bo Yibo, 75, 161–62, 168n.34, 170, 171n.47, 177, 180, 186n.93
Bodde, Derk, 97
Bourgeois liberalization, 2, 104, 132
Brady, James, 95n.4, 115–16
Brezhnev, Leonid, 13
Brus, Wlodzimierz, 13–14
Bureaucracy. *See* Rational-legal rulership
Bureaucratic-authoritarian states, 10–12
Burke, Edmund, 10, 98n.14
Bush, Richard, 2

Cambodia, 28
Cao Diqiu, 36–41
Cardoso, Fernando, 11
Central Commission for Guiding Party Rectification (CCGPR), 168–72
Charismatic rulership, 5, 18–19, 43, 44, 158–59, 196–97, 199; defined, 18; Party rectification and, 173–79
Cheng Zihua, 133n.6, 137, 141, 142, 144, 152–53
Civic culture, 10
Civil society. *See* Society

Class struggle, 29–30, 58, 102
Cleaves, Peter, 132
Confession. *See* Law: rewarding confessions and guilty verdicts
Contract workers, 38–41, 44
Corporatism, 11, 16–17
Corruption, 65–70, 77–82, 90, 92–93, 127–28, 132, 147, 160–65. *See also* Patrimonial rulership
Courts, 122–24. *See* Law
Cult of personality, 33, 57, 101–2
Cultural Revolution, 3, 22, 31–35, 57–59, 101–3, 117–18, 134–35, 176, 178, 195
Czechoslovakia, 197

Dahl, Robert, 9, 10
Dai Hsiao-ai, 34
Danwei. See Organized dependency
Decision on Party Rectification, 157, 158
Democracy Wall, 100, 103, 105–6, 107, 134
Deng Xiaoping, 45, 48–49, 53, 105, 134, 175
Di Franceisco, Wayne, 64
Duck transporters, 89
Dunayevskaya, Raya, 28–30

Economic reform, 1–2, 61, 165; and Party rectification, 179–84
Election Law for the National People's Congress and the Local People's Congresses. *See* Election laws